• Bartholomew •
GLASGOW
Streetfinder
ATLAS

KU-247-237

Contents

Copyright © Bartholomew 1993
Bartholomew is a Division of HarperCollins*Publishers*.

Based upon the Ordnance Survey with the permission of the Controller of Her Majesty's Stationery Office, with additions obtained from Local Authorities. © Crown copyright. The Ordnance Survey is not responsible for the accuracy of the National Grid on this production.

Printed by Bartholomew, The Edinburgh Press Limited

ISBN 0 7028 2309 0   F/B 6784 CNM

Bartholomew
A Division of HarperCollins*Publishers*

2

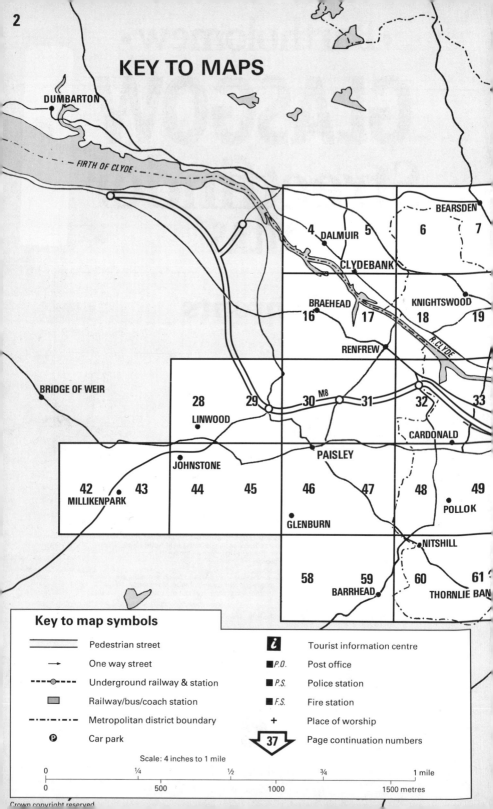

KEY TO MAPS

DUMBARTON

FIRTH OF CLYDE

4 DALMUIR 5 BEARSDEN
6 7

CLYDEBANK

BRAEHEAD KNIGHTSWOOD
16 17 18 19

RENFREW

R CLYDE

BRIDGE OF WEIR

28 29 30 M8 31 32 33

LINWOOD

CARDONALD

JOHNSTONE PAISLEY

42 43 44 45 46 47 48 49
MILLIKENPARK POLLOK

GLENBURN

NITSHILL

58 59 60 61
BARRHEAD THORNLIE BAN

Key to map symbols

——— Pedestrian street	**i** Tourist information centre
→ One way street	■ *P.O.* Post office
----●---- Underground railway & station	■ *P.S.* Police station
▨ Railway/bus/coach station	■ *F.S.* Fire station
–·–·–·– Metropolitan district boundary	+ Place of worship
℗ Car park	⬇37 Page continuation numbers

Scale: 4 inches to 1 mile

0	¼	½	¾	1 mile

0	500	1000	1500 metres

Crown copyright reserved

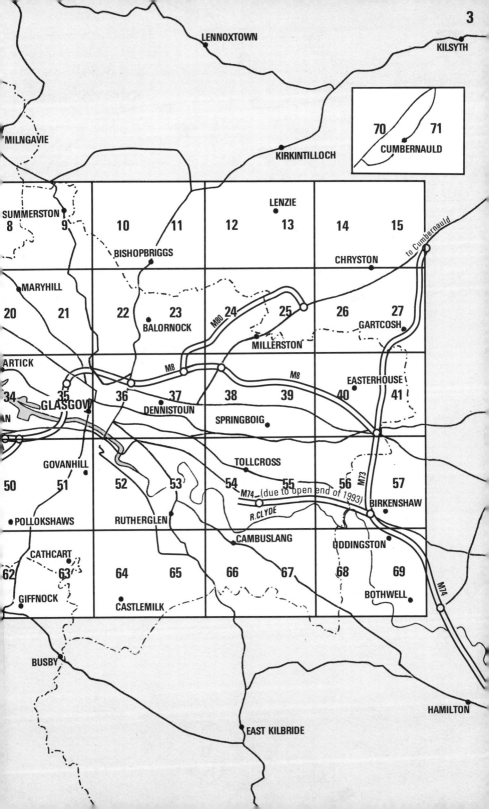

3

LENNOXTOWN

KILSYTH

MILNGAVIE

KIRKINTILLOCH

| 70 | 71 |
CUMBERNAULD

SUMMERSTON
8   9   10   11   12   13   14   15

LENZIE

BISHOPBRIGGS

CHRYSTON

to Cumbernauld

MARYHILL

20   21   22   23   24   25   26   27

BALORNOCK   M80   GARTCOSH

MILLERSTON

ARTICK

34   35   36   37   38   39   40   41

GLASGOW   M8

DENNISTOUN   M8   EASTERHOUSE

SPRINGBOIG

GOVANHILL   TOLLCROSS

50   51   52   53   54   55   56   57

M74 (due to open end of 1993)   M73

POLLOKSHAWS   BIRKENSHAW

RUTHERGLEN   R.CLYDE

CAMBUSLANG   ODDINGSTON

CATHCART

62   63   64   65   66   67   68   69

GIFFNOCK   BOTHWELL

CASTLEMILK   M74

BUSBY

HAMILTON

EAST KILBRIDE

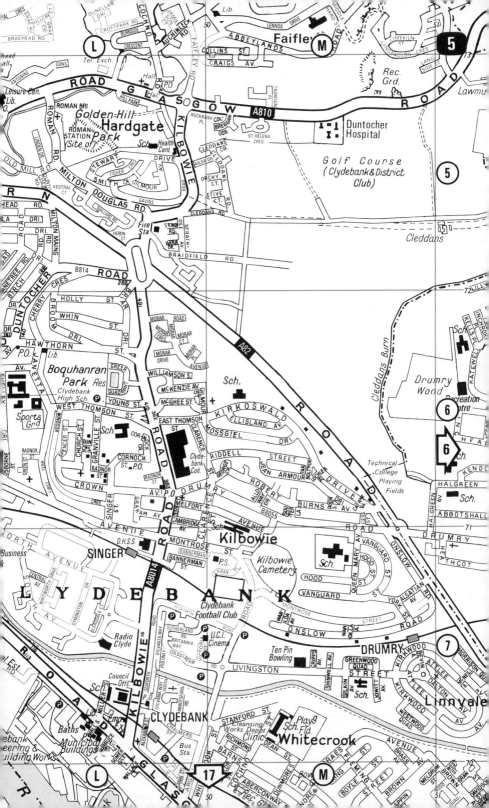

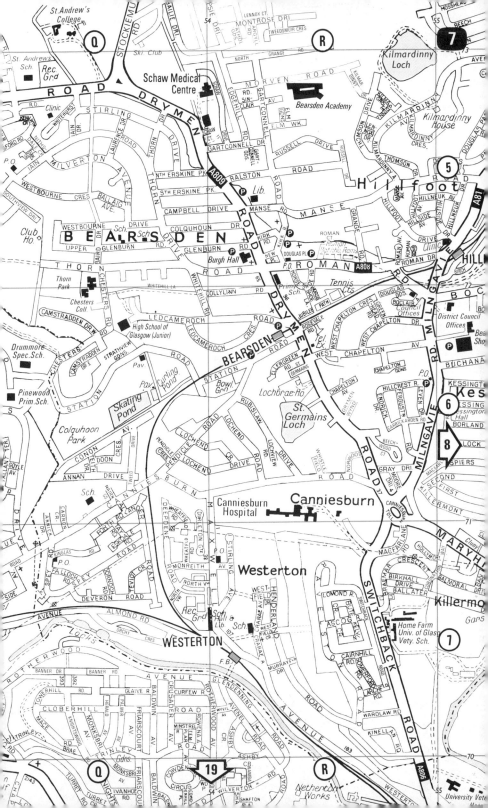

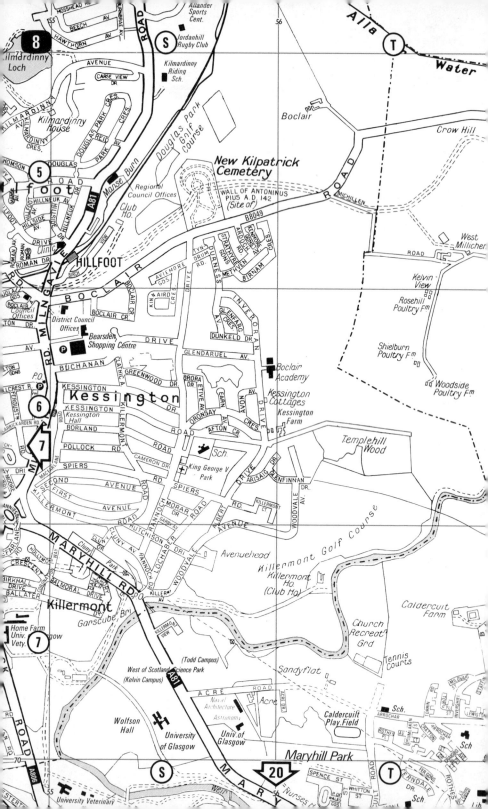

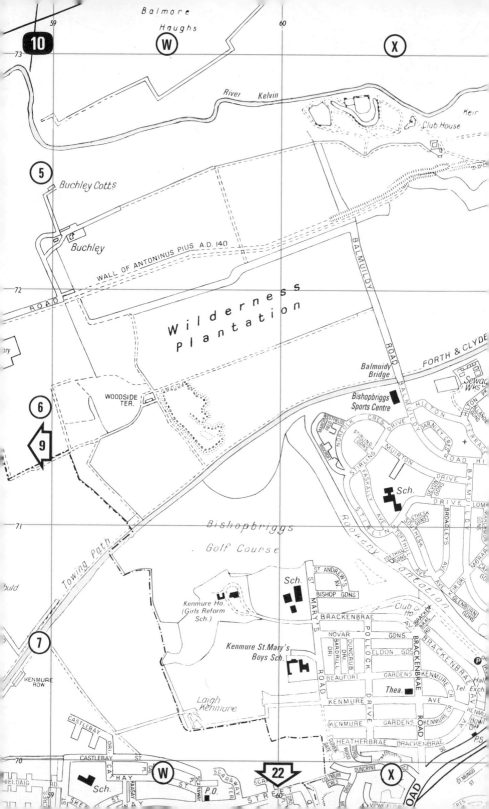

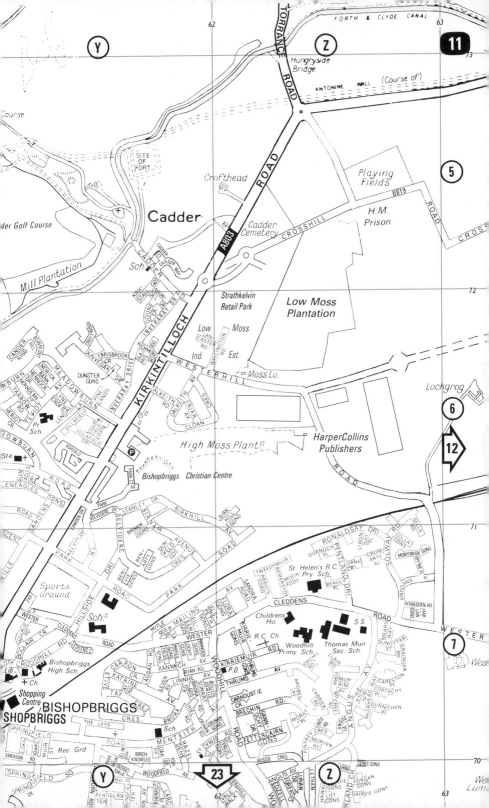

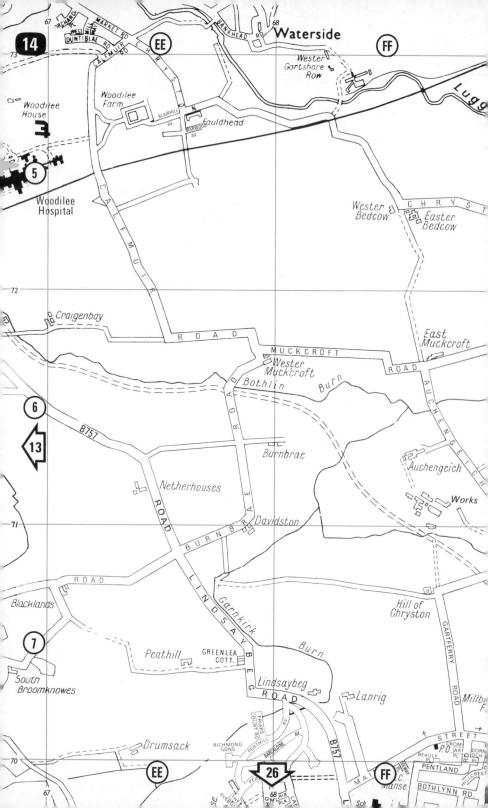

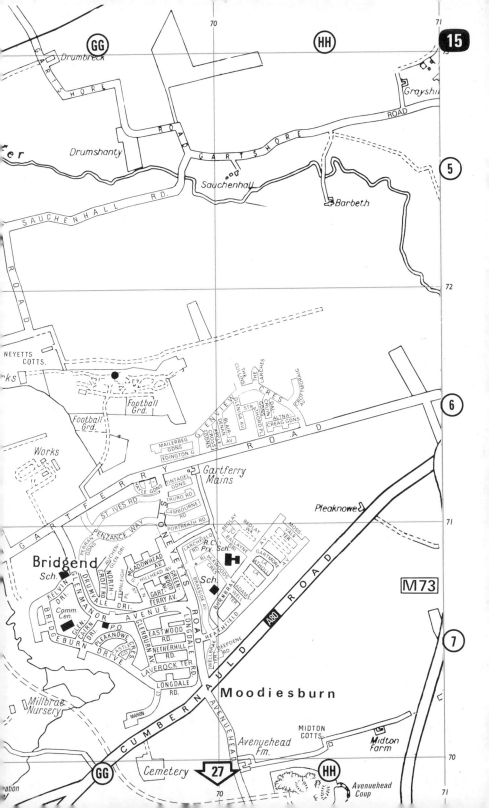

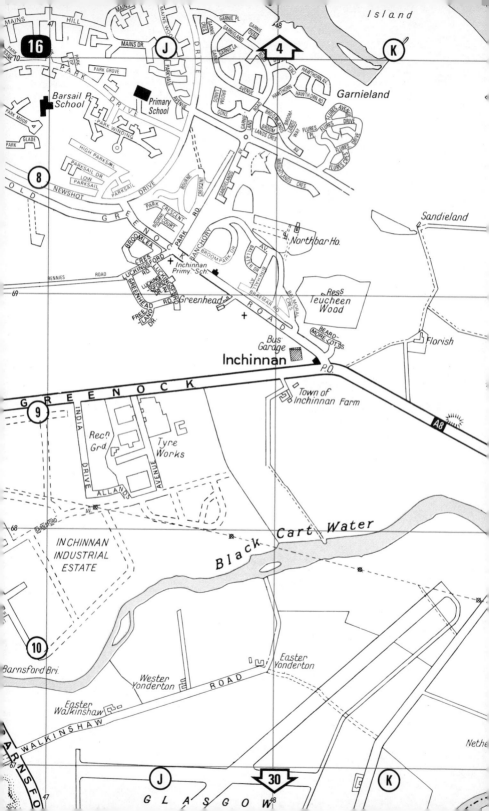

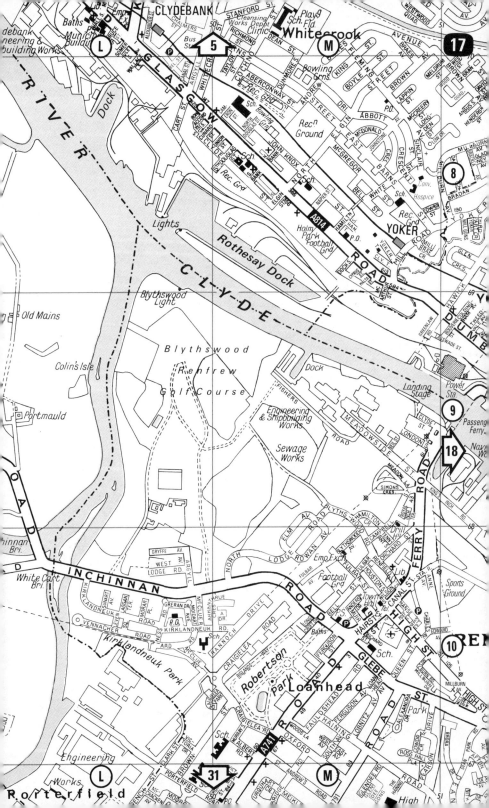

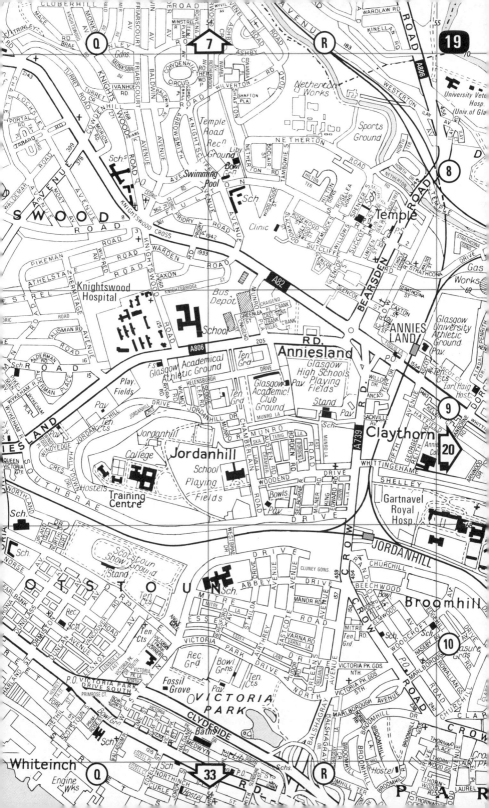

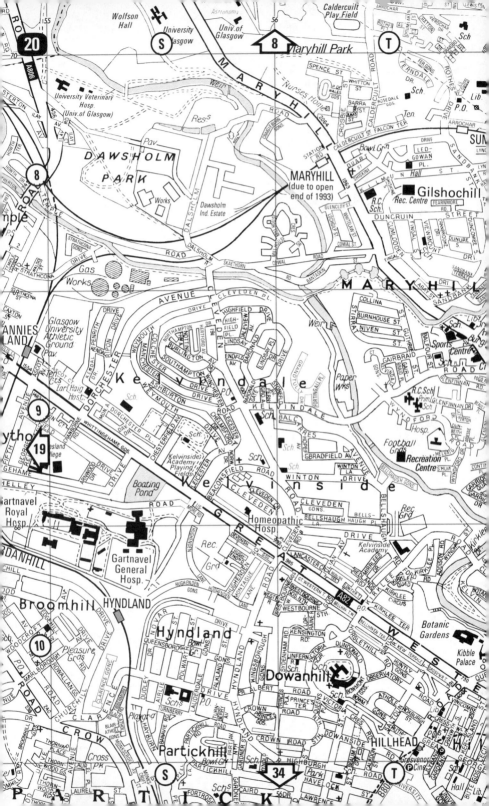

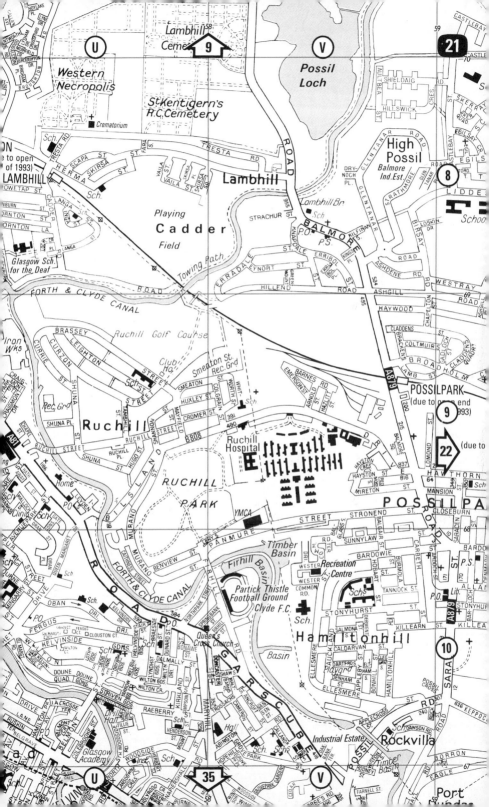

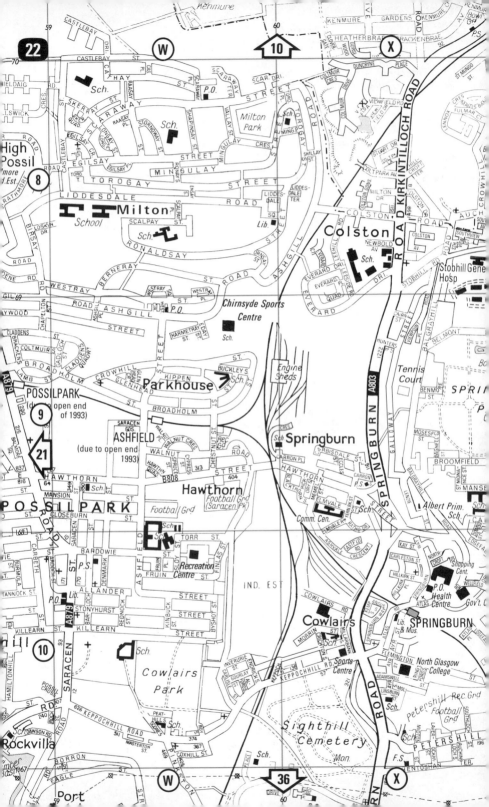

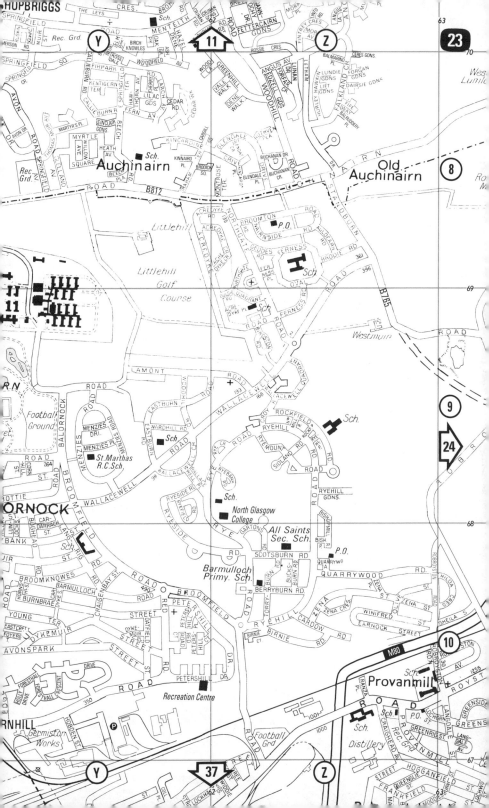

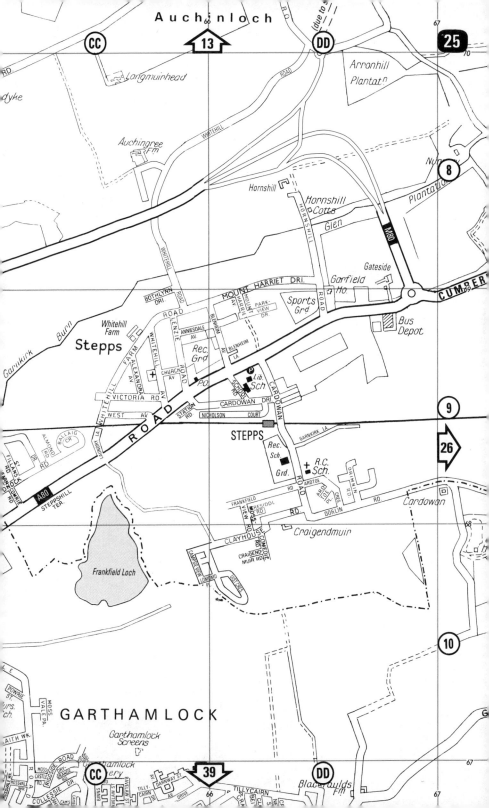

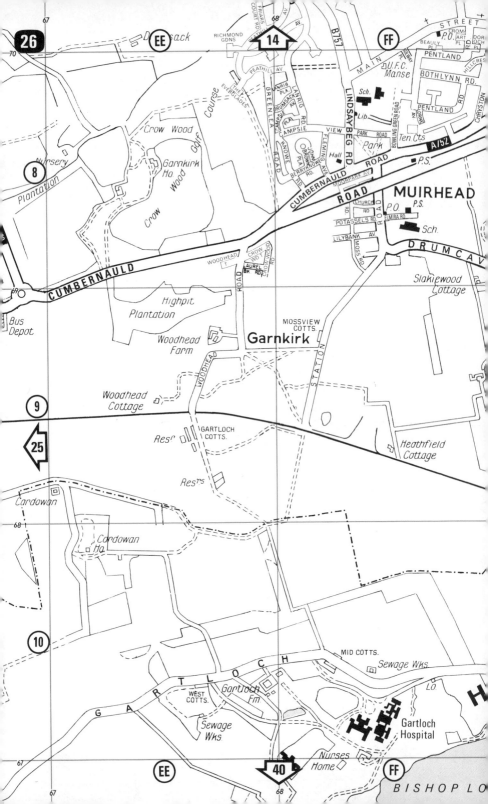

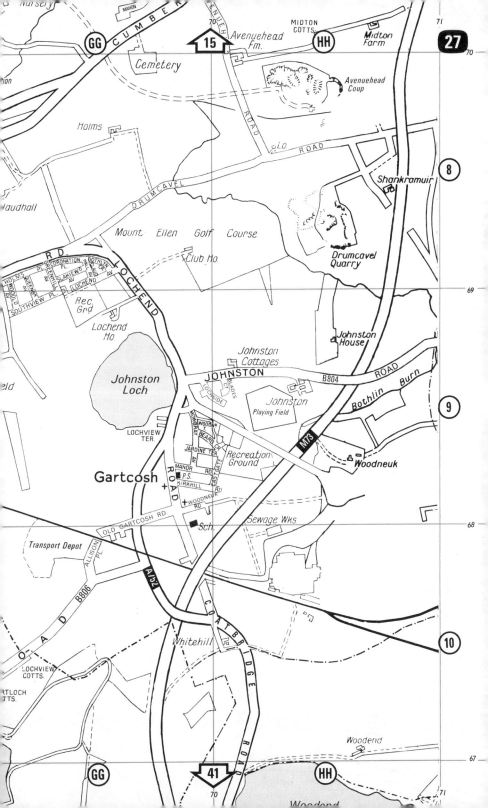

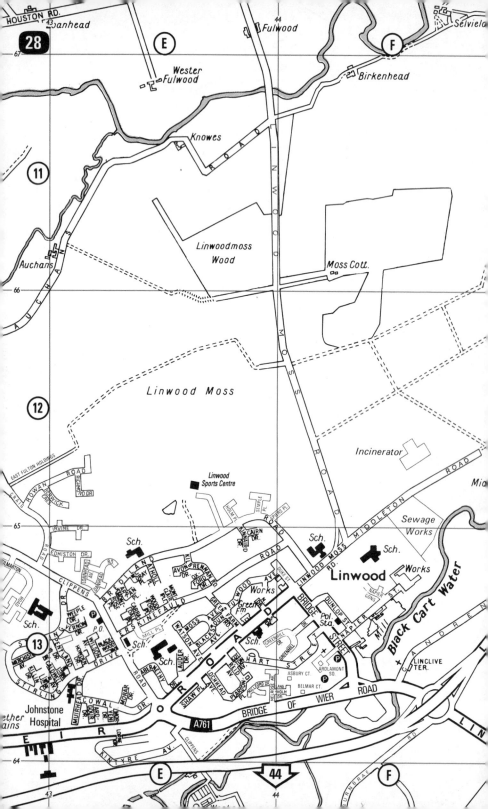

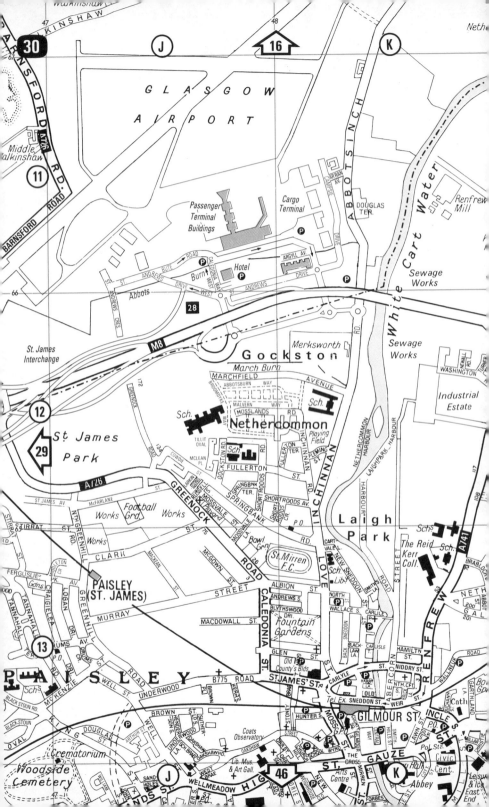

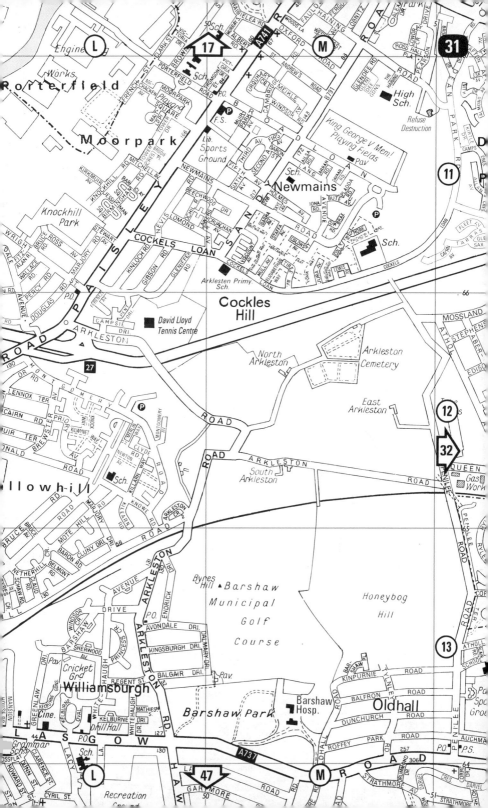

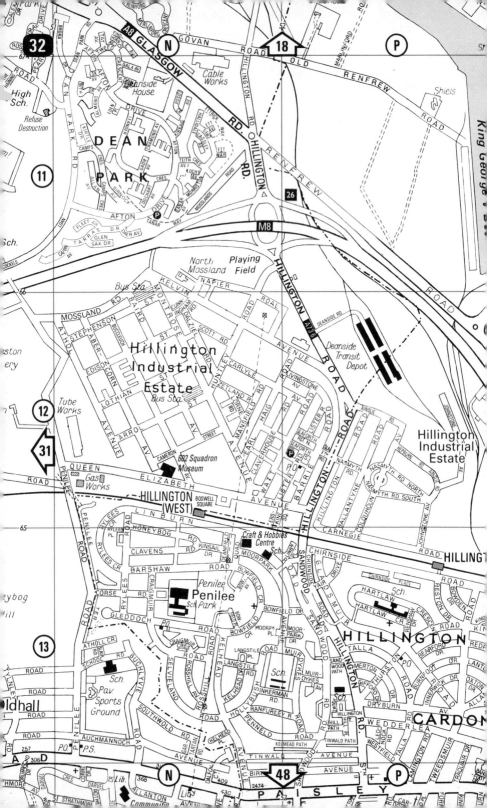

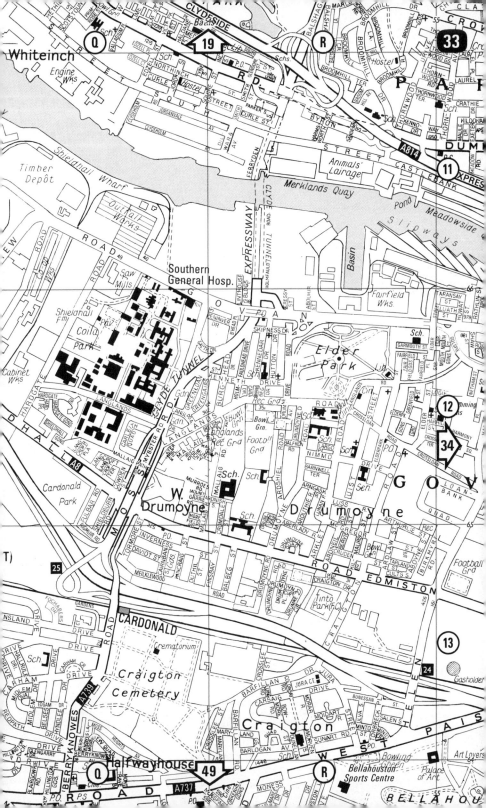

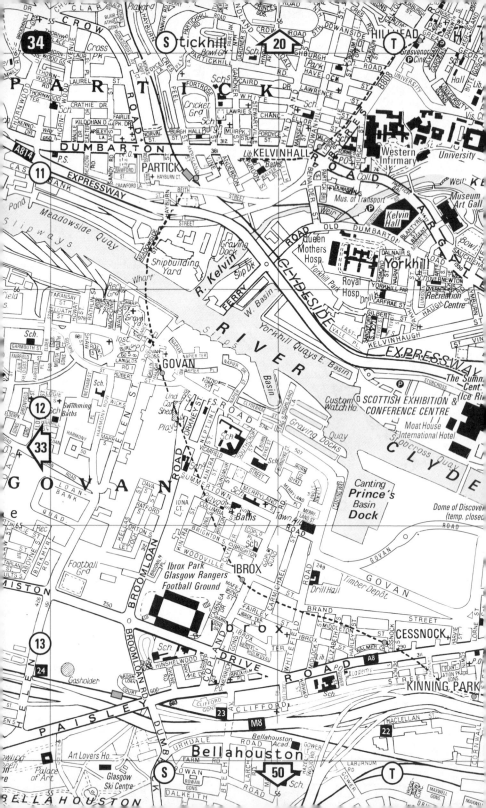

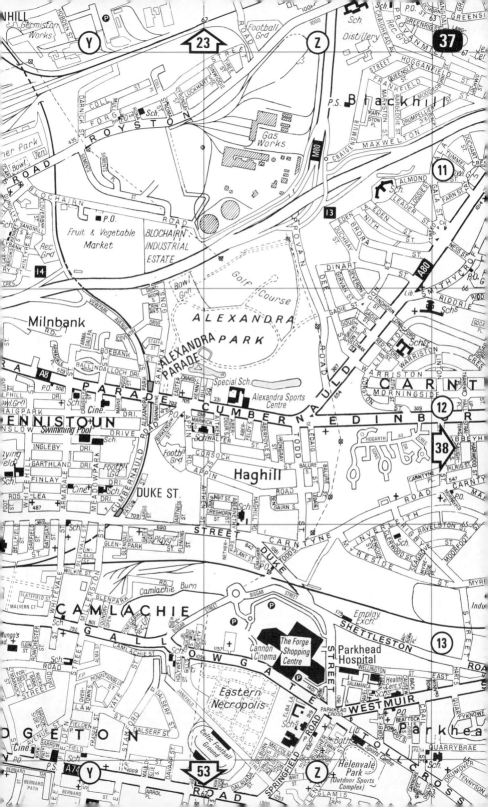

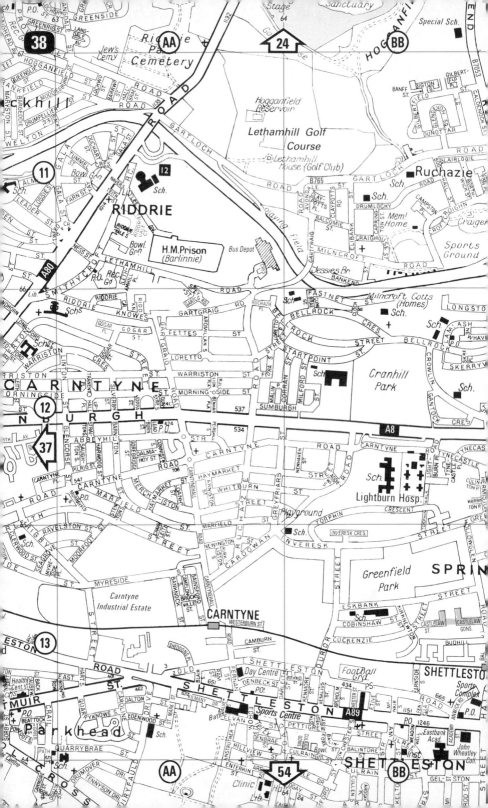

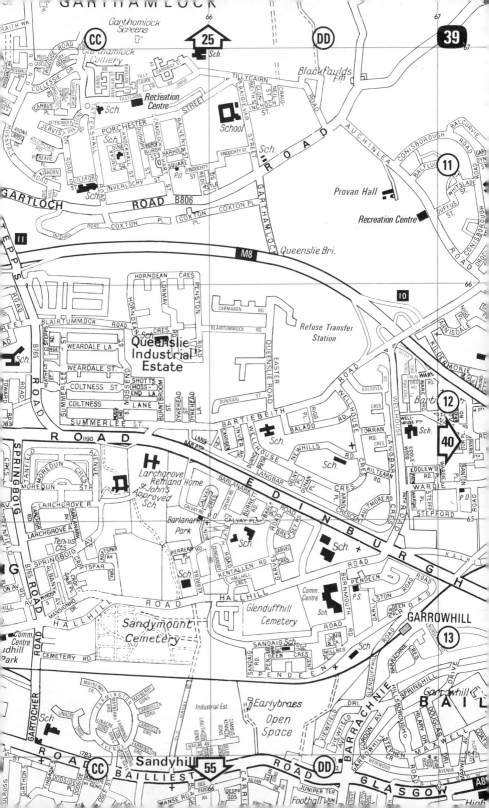

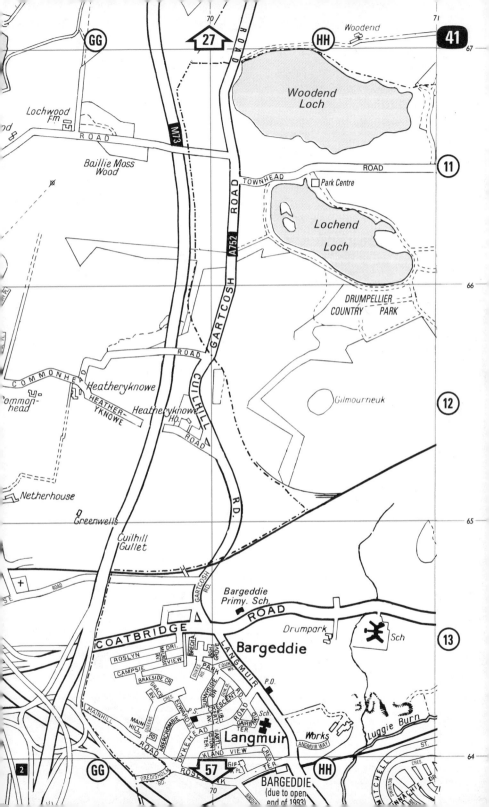

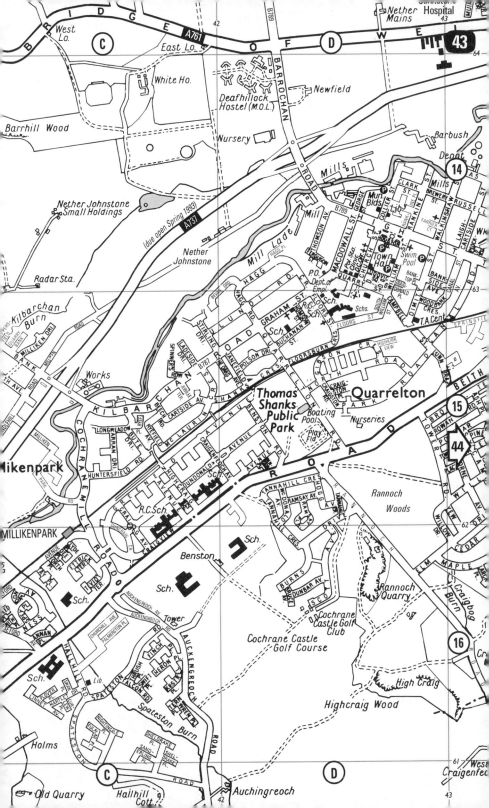

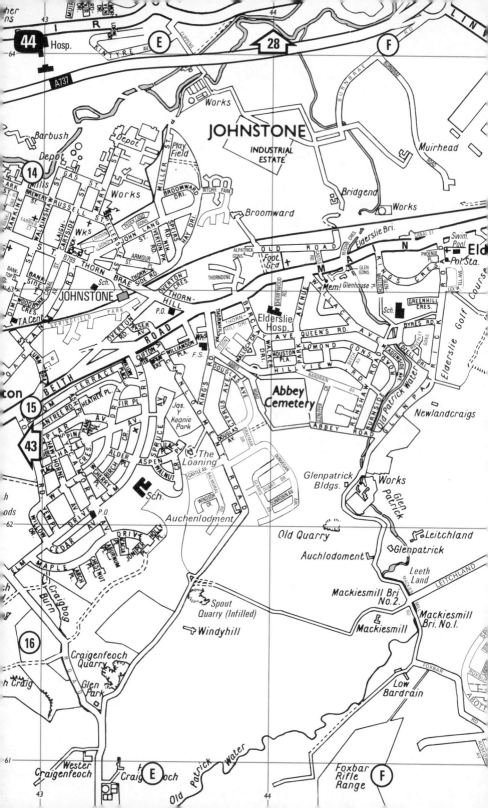

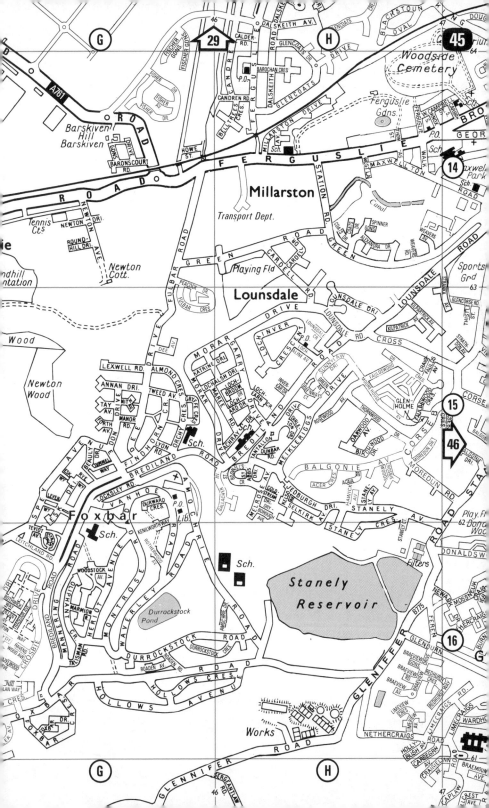

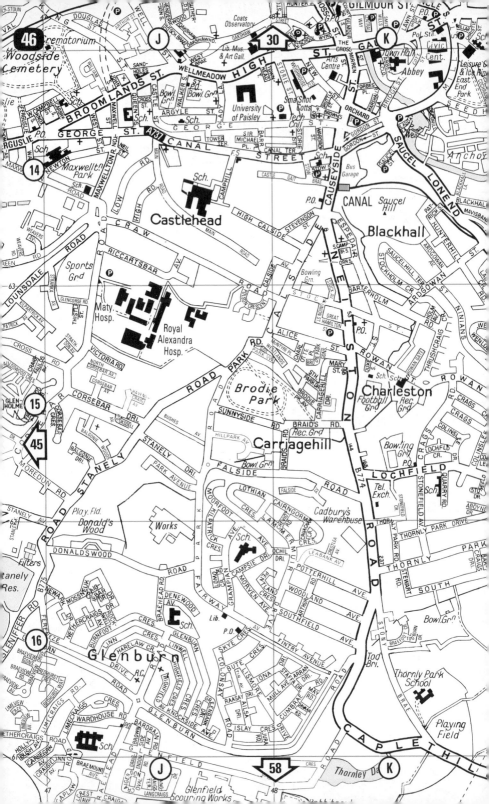

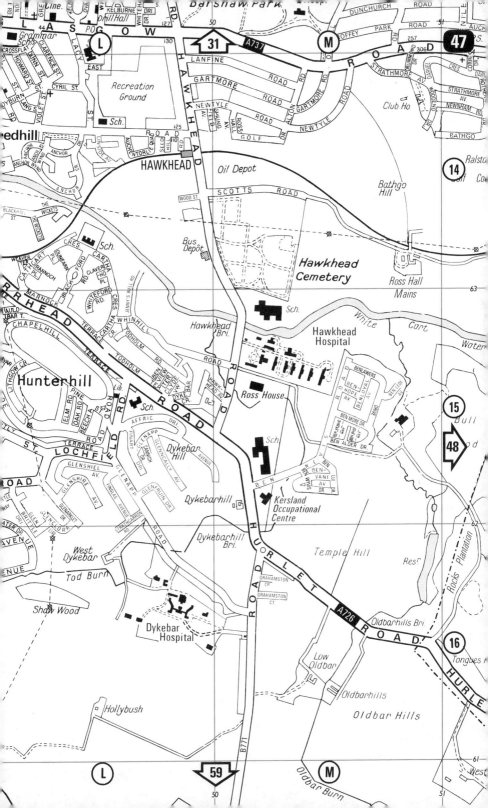

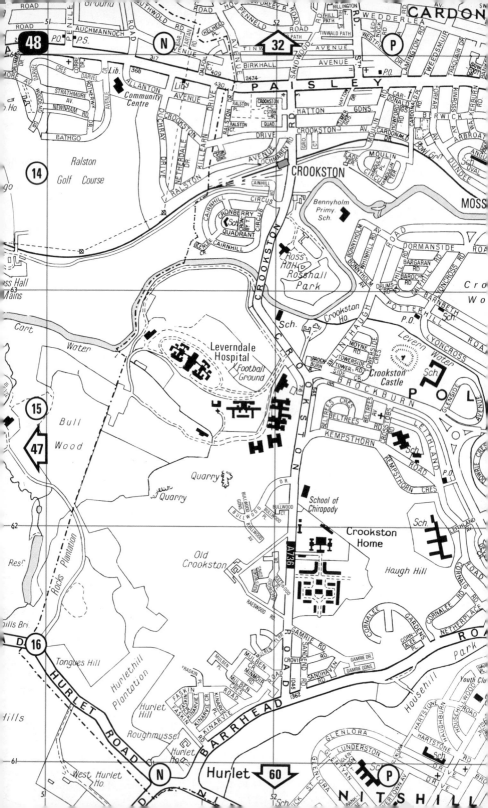

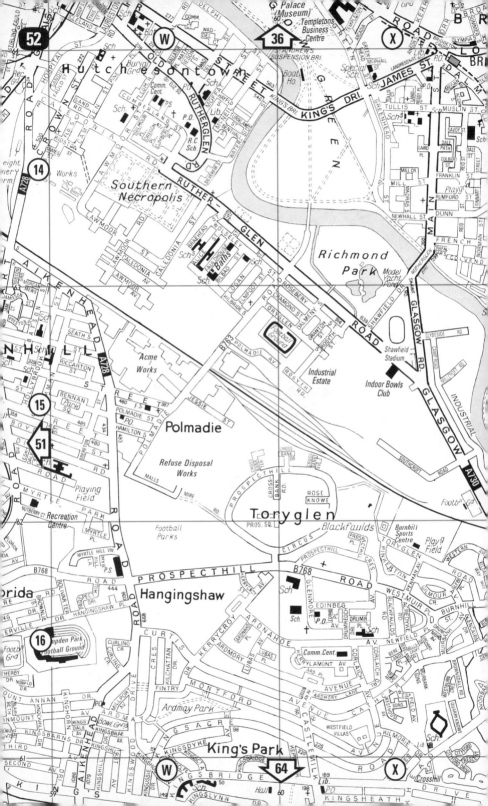

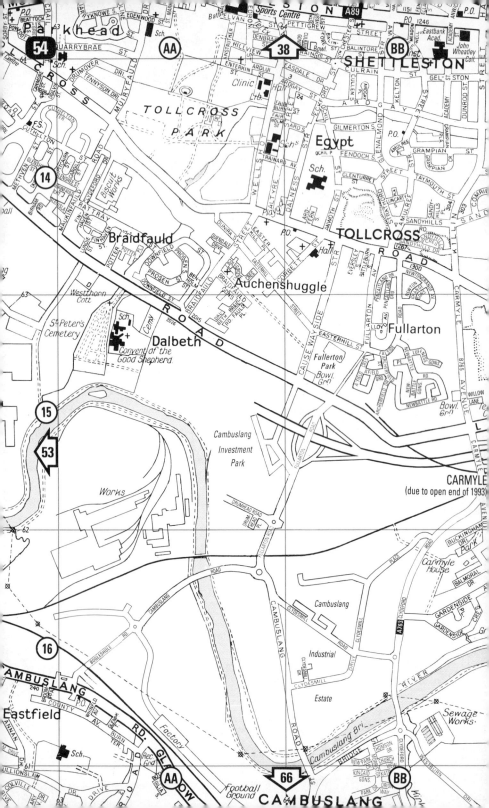

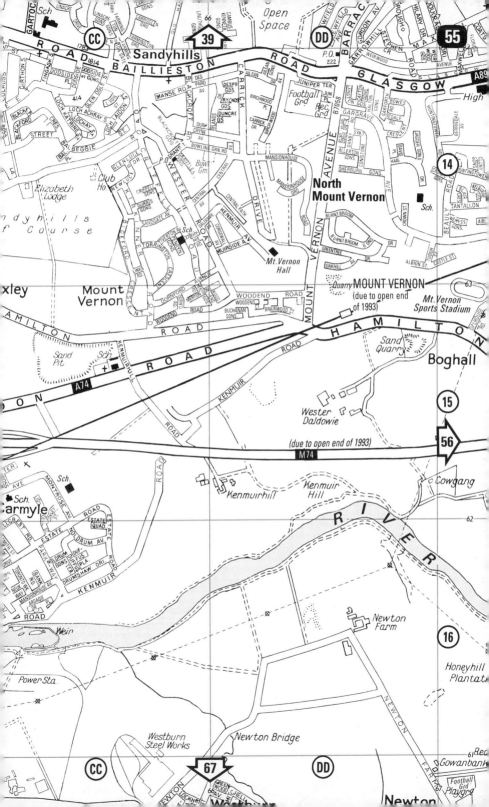

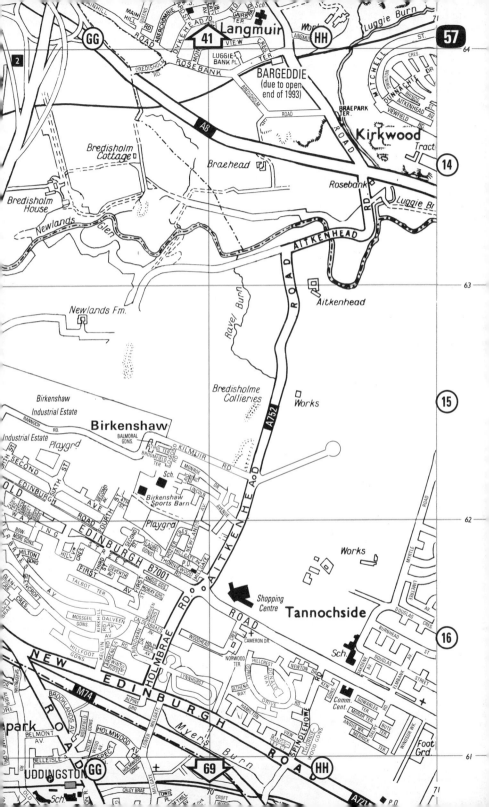

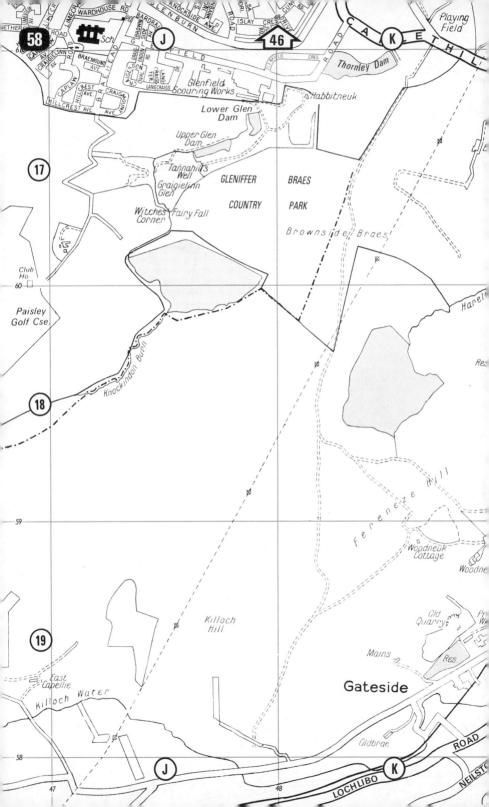

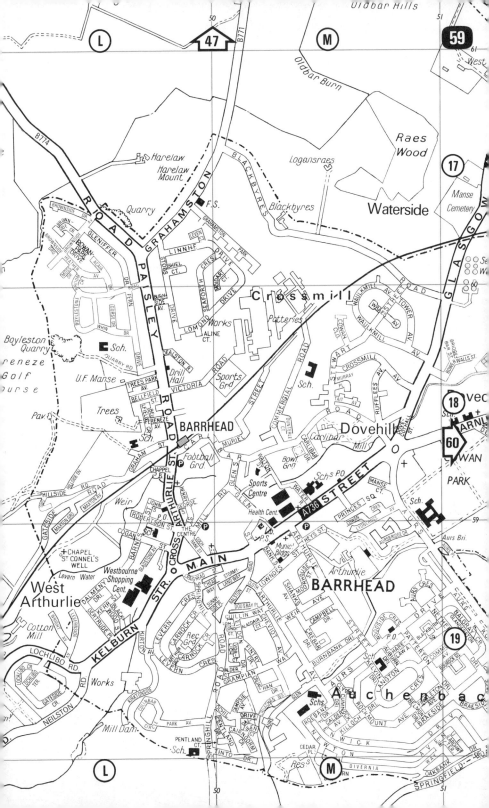

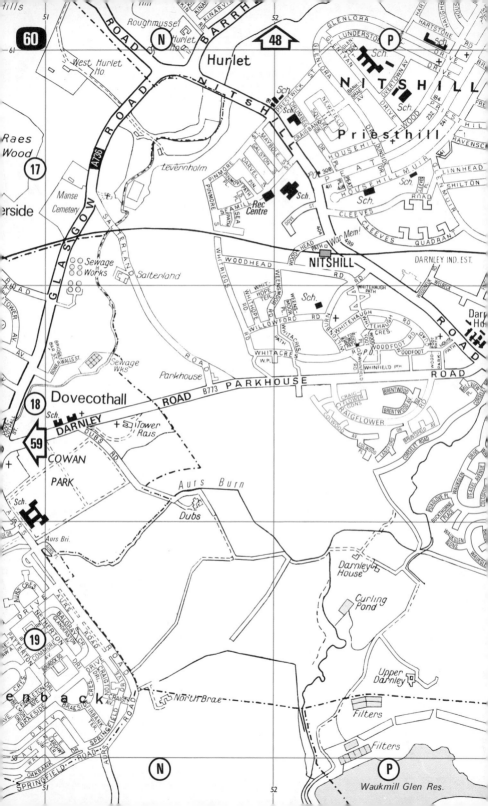

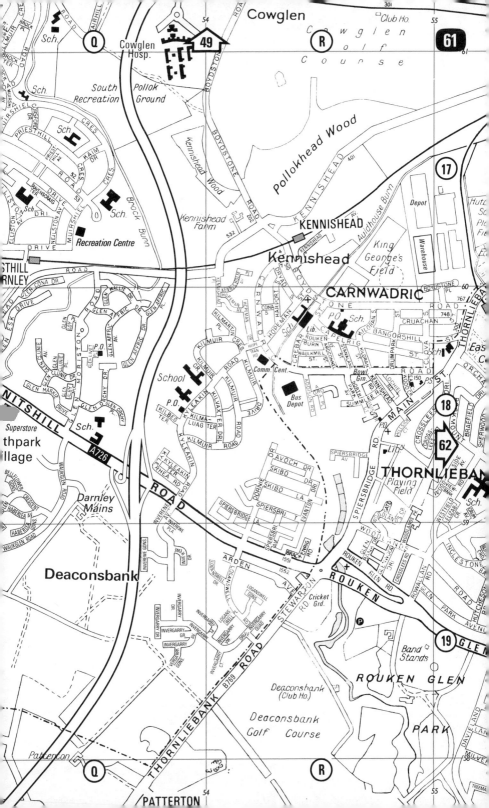

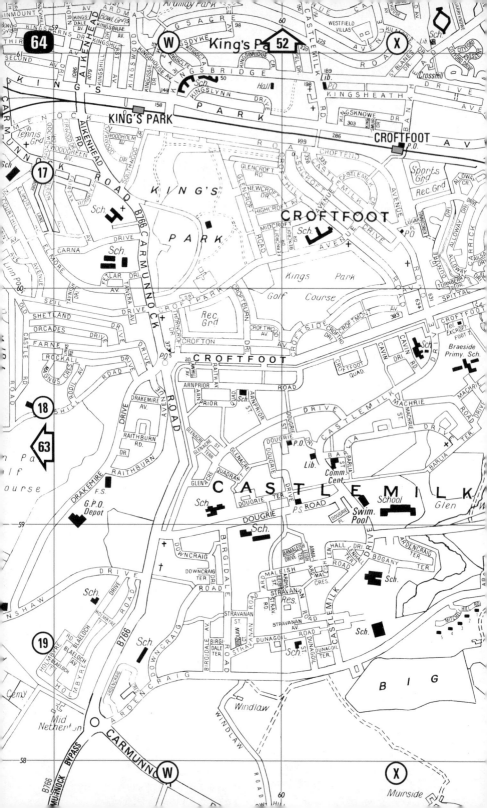

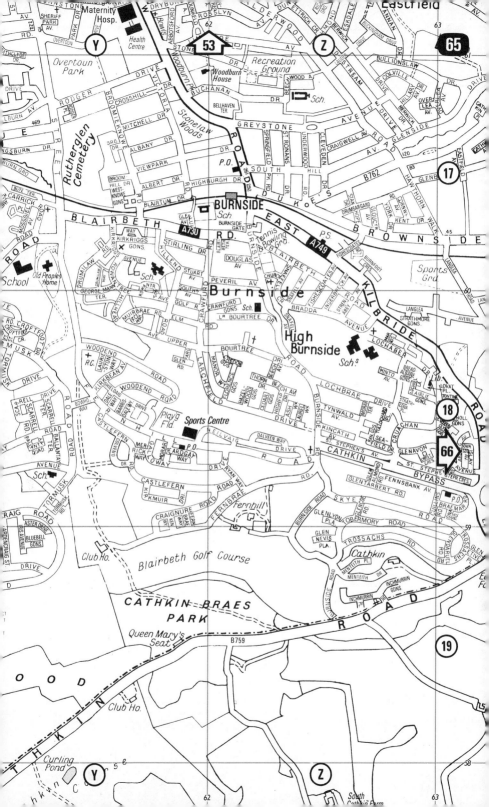

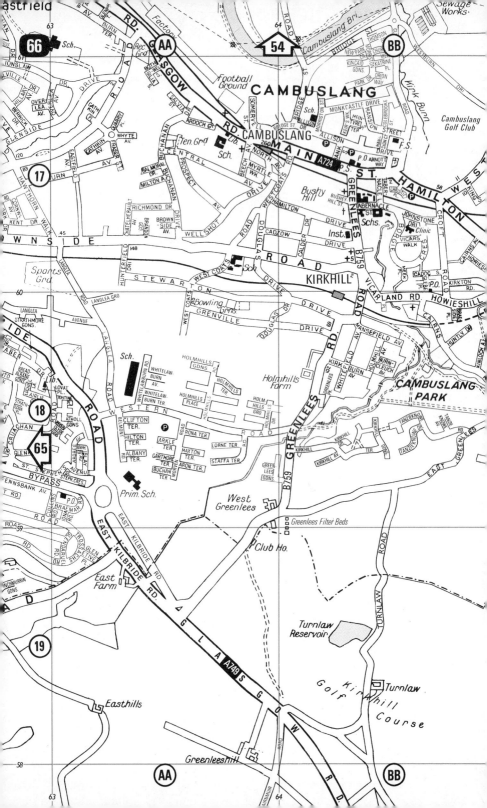

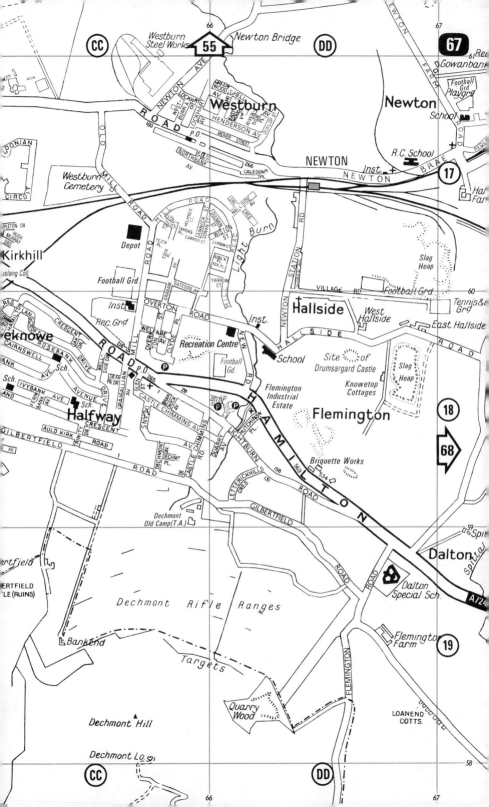

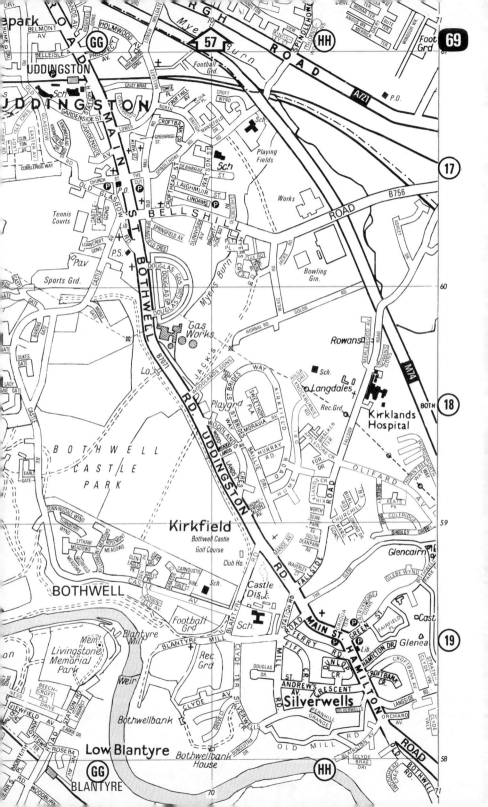

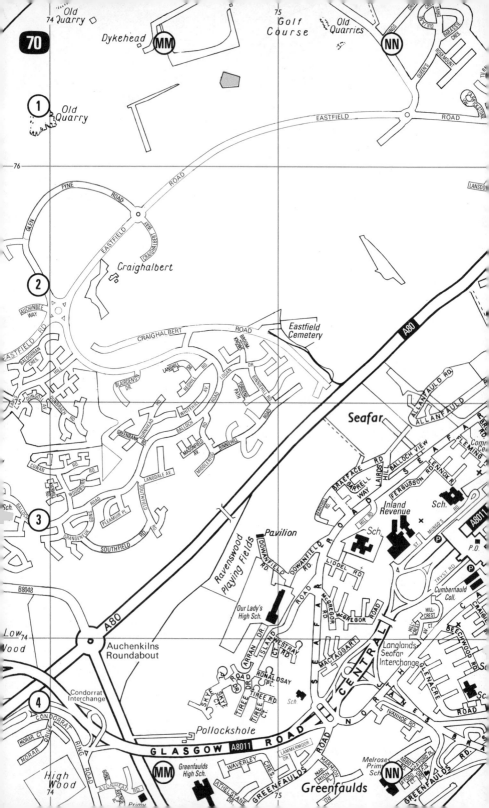

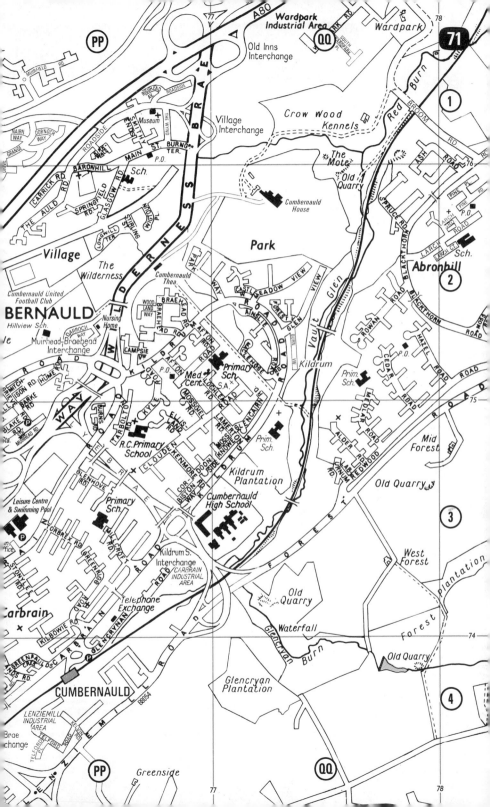

City of Glasgow Local Information Guide

Useful Information

Area of City 79 sq. miles (approx)

Population (Glasgow City)
(1989 estimate) 696,577

Early Closing Days
Tuesday with alternative of Saturday.
Most of the shops in the central area
operate six-day trading.

Electricity 240 volts A.C.

Emergency Services
Police, Fire and Ambulance. Dial 999
on any telephone.

Licensing Hours
Public Houses
Daily (except Sundays) 11 a.m. to 2.30
p.m. and 5 to 11 p.m. (many open
continuously 11 a.m. to 11 p.m.)
Sundays, 12.30 to 2.30 p.m. and 6.30
to 10.30 p.m.
Restaurants, Hotels and Public Houses
with catering facilities, same as above
but can be extended for drinks with
meals.

Information Bureau

Tourist Information Centres:
35 - 39 St. Vincent Place
Glasgow. 041 204 4400
Town Hall, Abbey Close,

Paisley. 041 889 0711

Glasgow Airport 041 848 4440

Strathclyde Transport Travel Centre
St. Enoch Square
Open Monday - Saturday 9.30 a.m. to
5.30 p.m. 041 226 4826 (Monday to
Saturday 7 a.m. to 9 p.m., Sunday 9
a.m. to 7.30 p.m.) for City services,
ferry services, local airlines, train and
express services. Free timetables are
available.

Help & Advice

British Broadcasting Corporation
Queen Margaret Drive, G12 8DQ.
041 339 8844

British Council
6 Belmont Crescent, G12 8ES.
041 339 8651

**British Telecom Scotland
Glasgow Area**
Westergate Chambers, 11 Hope Street,
Glasgow, G2 6AB. All Enquiries 041
220 1234 or dial 100 and ask for
FREEFONE BT GLASGOW.

Chamber of Commerce
30 George Square, G2 1EG.
041 204 2121.

Citizens Advice Bureau
87 Bath Street, Glasgow, G2 4HW
041 331 2345/6/7/8
119 Main Street, Glasgow, G40 1HA
041 554 0336
27 Dougrie Drive, Castlemilk, Glasgow,
G45 9AD 041 634 0338

139 Main Street (Town Hall),
Rutherglen, G73 2JJ 041 647 5100
216 Main Street, Barrhead, G78 1SN
041 881 2032
1145 Maryhill Road, Glasgow, G20 9AZ
041 946 6373/4
46 Township Centre, Easterhouse,
Glasgow, G34 9DS 041 771 2328

Consumer Advice Centre
St. Enoch House, 1 St. Enoch Square,
Glasgow, G1 4BH 041 204 0262

Customs and Excise
21 India Street, G2 4PZ 041 221 3828

H.M. Immigration Office
Admin Block D, Argyll Avenue, Glasgow
Airport 041 887 4115

Housing Aid and Advice
Shelter, 53 St. Vincent Crescent,
Glasgow, G3 8NQ 041 221 8895/6

Legal Aid and Advice
Castlemilk Advice and Law Centre
27 Dougrie Drive, Glasgow, G45 9AD
041 634 0338

Law Centre
30 Dougrie Drive, G45 9AG
041 634 0313

Lost Property
Strathclyde Passenger Transport
Executive
Glasgow Central Station 041 335 4362
(Scotrail Trains)
Glasgow Queen Street Station 041 335
3276 (Scotrail Trains and Underground)
St. Enoch Underground Station
041 248 6950 (City Buses)
Other Buses - Office of bus company.
Trains - Station of arrival.
Elsewhere in City - Strathclyde Police.
Lost Property Department, 173 Pitt
Street, G2 041 204 1468

Passport Office
Northgate 96 Milton Street, Glasgow,
G4 0BT 041 332 0271

**Registrar of Births, Deaths and
Marriages**
1 Martha Street, G1 4PF 041 225 7677
Hours - Monday to Friday 9.15 a.m. to
4.00 p.m.

Births must be registered within twenty-
one days, deaths within eight days and
marriages within three days. The
Registrar should be consulted at least
one month before intended date of
marriage.

**Royal Scottish Society for the
Prevention of Cruelty to Children**
15 Annfield Place, G31 2XE
041 556 1156

**RNID - Royal National Institute for
the Deaf**
9 Clairmont Gardens, Glasgow, G3
7LW 041 332 0343

Samaritans
218 West Regent Street, Glasgow, G2
4DQ 041 248 4488

**Scottish Society for the Mentally
Handicapped**
13 Elmbank Street, Glasgow, G2 4QA
041 226 4541

Scottish Television
Cowcaddens, G2 041 332 9999

**Society for the Prevention of Cruelty
to Animals**
15 Royal Terrace, G3 7NY (Business
Hours) 041 332 0716

Newspapers

Morning Daily
Daily Record
Anderston Quay, G3 8DA.
041 248 7000

Glasgow Herald
195 Albion Street, G1 041 552 6255

Scottish Daily Express
Park Circus Place, G3 041 332 9600

The Scotsman
181 - 195 West George Street, G2 2LB
041 221 6485

Evening Daily
Evening Times
195 Albion Street, G1 041 552 6255

Weekly
Scottish Sunday Express
Park Circus Place, G3 041 332 9600

Sunday Mail
Anderston Quay, G3 8DA
041 248 7000

Sunday Post
144 Port Dundas Road, G4 0HF
041 332 9933

Parking

Car Parking in the central area of Glasgow is controlled. Parking meters are used extensively and signs indicating restrictions are displayed at kerbsides and on entry to the central area. Traffic Wardens are on duty.

British Rail Car Parks
(Open 24 hours)
Central Station
Queen Street Station

Multi-Storey Car Parks
(Open 24 hours)
Anderston Cross: Cambridge Street: George Street: Mitchell Street: Port Dundas Road: Waterloo Street.

(Limited Opening)
Charing Cross: Cowcaddens Road: St. Enoch Centre:Sauchiehall Street Centre

Surface Car Parks
Cathedral Street (Concert Hall):Dunlop Street: High Street: Ingram Street: King Street: McAlpine Street: Oswald Street: Shuttle Street:

Post Offices

Head Post Office
George Square, G2 041 248 2882
Open Monday to Thursday 9 a.m. to 5.30 p.m. Fridays 9.30 a.m. to 5.30 p.m. Saturdays 9 a.m. to 12.30 p.m. Closed Sunday.

Branch Offices
85-91 Bothwell Street, G2
216 Hope Street, G2
533 Sauchiehall Street, G3

Taxis

Glasgow has over 1400 traditional London type taxis, all licensed by the Glasgow District Council and all fitted with meters sealed and approved by the Council. A fare card stating the current tariff is displayed in a prominent position within each taxi. At the time of publishing a three mile journey costs £3.10 and waiting time is charged at 13½p per minute. The total price of each journey is shown on the meter. Fares are normally reviewed annually by the council. Each taxi can carry a maximum of five passengers.

The major taxi companies in the city offer City tours at fixed prices, listing the places of interest to be visited, leaflets are available at all major hotel reception areas. Tours vary from 2 to 3 hours and in price between £20 and £28. A tour "Glasgow by Night" is also available at a cost of £10.00.

Any passenger wishing to travel to a destination outside the Glasgow District Boundary should ascertain from the driver the fare to be charged or the method of calculating the fare PRIOR to making the journey.

Complaints
Any complaints regarding the conduct of a taxi driver should be addressed to the Senior Enforcement Officer, Town Clerk's Office, City Chambers, Glasgow. 041 227 4535

Local Government

Strathclyde Regional Council
Strathclyde House, 20 India Street
Glasgow, G2 4PF
041 204 2900

District Councils:

Argyll & Bute
District Council Headquarters
Kilmory, Lochgilphead PA31 8RT
0546 2127

Bearsden & Milngavie
Municipal Building, Boclair
Bearsden G61 2TQ
041 942 2262

Clydebank
Council Offices, Rosebery Place
Clydebank G81 1TG
041 941 1331

Clydesdale
Clydesdale District Offices
Lanark ML11 7JT
0555 61331

Cumbernauld & Kilsyth
Council Offices, Bron Way
Cumbernauld G67 1DZ
0236 722131

Cummock & Doon Valley
Council Offices, Lugar
Cummock KA18 3JQ
0290 22111

Cunninghame
Cunninghame House
Irvine KA12 8EE
0294 74166

Dumbarton
Crosslet House
Dumbarton G82 3NS
0389 65100

East Kilbride
Civic Centre
East Kilbride G74 1AB
0352 71200

Eastwood
Council Offices
Eastwood Park, Rouken Glen Road
Rouken Glen, Giffnock
Glasgow G46 6UG
041 638 6511
041 638 1101

Glasgow City
City Chambers
Glasgow G2 1DU
041 221 9600

Hamilton
Town House
102 Cadzow Street
Hamilton ML3 6HH
0698 282323

Inverclyde
Municipal Buildings
Greenock PA15 1LY
0475 24400

Kilmarnock & Loudoun
Civic Centre
Kilmarnock KA1 1BY
0563 21140

Kyle & Carrick
Burns House
Burns Statue Square
Ayr KA7 1UT
0292 281511

Monklands
Municipal Buildings
Dunbeth Road
Coatbridge ML5 3LF
0236 441200

Motherwell
P.O. Box 14
Civic Centre
Motherwell ML1 1TW
0698 266166

Renfrew
Municipal Buildings
Cotton Street
Paisley PA1 1BU
041 889 5400

Strathkelvin
Tom Johnston House
Civic Way
Kirkintilloch
Glasgow G66 4TJ
041 776 7171

Parks & Gardens

There are over 70 public parks within the city. The most famous is Glasgow Green. Abutting the north bank of the River Clyde, it was acquired in 1662. Of interest are the Winter Gardens attached to the People's Palace. Kelvingrove Park is an 85-acre park laid out by Sir Joseph Paxton in 1852. On the south side of the city is the 148-acre Queen's Park, Victoria Road, established 1857 - 94. Also of interest: Rouken Glen, Thornliebank, with a spectacular waterfall, walled garden, nature trail and boating facilities; Victoria Park, Victoria Park Drive, with its famous Fossil Grove flower gardens and yachting pond. In Great Western Road are the Botanic Gardens. Founded in 1817, the gardens' 42 acres are crammed with natural attractions, including the celebrated Kibble Palace glasshouse with its fabulous tree ferns, exotic plants and white marble Victorian statues.

The main public parks in Glasgow are:

Alexandra
671 Alexandra Parade, G31.

Bellahouston
Paisley Road West, G52.

Botanic Gardens
730 Gt. Western Road, G12.

Hogganfield Loch
Cumbernauld Road, G33.

Kelvingrove
Sauchiehall Street, G3.

King's
325 Carmunnock Road, G44.

Linn
Clarkston Road at Netherlee Road, G44.

Queen's
Victoria Road, G42.

Rouken Glen
Rouken Glen Road, G46.

Springburn
Broomfield Road, G21.

Tollcross
461 Tollcross Road, G32.

Victoria
Victoria Park Drive North, G14.

Kibble Palace

Entertainment

As Scotland's commercial and industrial capital, Glasgow offers a good choice of leisure activities. The city now has many theatres where productions ranging from serious drama to pantomime, pop and musicals are performed. The Theatre Royal, Hope Street is Scotland's only opera house and has been completely restored to its full Victorian splendour. The Royal Scottish National Orchestra gives concerts at the Glasgow Royal Concert Hall every Saturday night in winter and is the venue for the proms in June. Cinemas are still thriving in Glasgow, as are the many public houses, some of which provide meals and live entertainment. In the city centre and Byres Road, West End, there is a fair number of restaurants where traditional home cooking, as well as international cuisines, can be sampled. More night life can be found at the city's discos and dance halls.

Outdoors, apart from the many parks and nature trails, there is Calderpark Zoological Gardens, situated 6 miles from the centre between Mount Vernon and Uddingston. Here you may see white rhinos, black panthers and iguanas among many species. Departing from Stobcross Quay, you can also cruise down the Clyde in 'P.S. Waverley' - the last sea-going paddle-steamer in the world.

Cinemas

Cannon Cinema, 380 Clarkston Road
041 637 2641
MGM Film Centre
326 Sauchiehall Street 041 332 9513
(Admin Dept), 326 Sauchiehall Street
 041 332 1592
326 Sauchiehall Street
041 332 1593
Caledonian Associated Cinemas Ltd
Regent House, 72 Renfield Street
 041 332 0606
Glasgow Film Theatre
12 Rose Street (Box Off)
041 332 6535
Grosvenor Cinema
Ashton Lane 041 339 4298

Kelburne Cinema
(Manager), Glasgow Road, Paisley. 041 889 3612
Odeon Film Centre
56 Renfield Street 041 332 8701

Halls

City Halls, Candleriggs
Couper Institute
86 Clarkston Road
Dixon Halls, 650 Cathcart Road
Glasgow Royal Concert Hall
2 Sauchiehall Street
Govan Hall, Summertown Road
Kelvin Hall, Argyle Street,
Langside Hall, 5 Langside Avenue
Partick Burgh Hall, 9 Burgh Hall Street,
Pollokshaws Hall
2025 Pollokshaws Road,
Woodside Hall, Glenfarg Street
(More information about the above G.D.C. halls and others from the Director, Halls and Theatres Department, Candleriggs 041 552 1202).

Theatres

Arches Theatre
Midland Street 041 221 9736
Citizens' Theatre
Gorbals Street 041 429 0022
King's Theatre
Bath Street 041 227 5511
Mitchell Theatre and Moir Hall
Granville Street 041 227 5511
New Athenaeum Theatre
Renfrew Street 041 332 5057
Old Athenaeum Theatre
Buchanan Street 041 332 2333
Pavilion Theatre
Renfield Street 041 332 1846
Theatre Royal
Hope Street 041 332 9000
Tramway
Albert Drive 041 227 5511
Tron Theatre
38 Parnie Street. 041 552 4267
The Ticket Centre
Glasgow's Central Box Office for Arches Theatre, Centre for Contemporary Arts, Citizens' Theatre, City Hall at Candleriggs, G1, Kelvin Hall, King's Theatre, Mitchell Theatre, New Athenaeum Theatre, Old Athenaeum Theatre, Theatre Royal, Tron Theatre.
Open Monday to Saturday 10.30 a.m. to 6.30 p.m. 041 227 5511

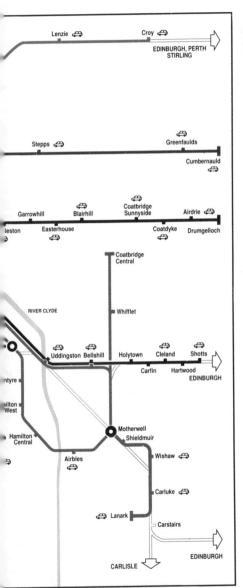

Lenzie

Croy

EDINBURGH, PERTH
STIRLING

Stepps

Greenfaulds

Cumbernauld

Garrowhill

Blairhill

Coatbridge
Sunnyside

Airdrie

leston

Easterhouse

Coatdyke

Drumgelloch

Coatbridge
Central

RIVER CLYDE

Whifflet

Uddingston

Bellshill

Holytown

Cleland

Shotts

Carfin

Hartwood

EDINBURGH

ntyre

ilton
West

Motherwell

Shieldmuir

Hamilton
Central

Airbles

Wishaw

Carluke

Lanark

Carstairs

EDINBURGH

CARLISLE

RAIL NETWORK

    Interchange with
British Rail

   (U)   Glasgow Underground

Travelator Link between
Buchanan St (U) and
Queen Street

    Prestwick Airport

    Glasgow Airport

AIRLINK BUS
Glasgow Airport from
Paisley Gilmour Street

Inter-terminal Bus Link

    Interchange with Ferries
(---- Summer Only)

    Park-and-Ride
Station car parks

Public Transport

The City of Glasgow has one of the most advanced, fully integrated public transport systems in the whole of Europe. The Strathclyde Transport network consists of; the local British Rail network, the local bus services and the fully modernised Glasgow Underground, with links to Glasgow Airport and the Steamer and Car Ferry Services.
Note: Although the information in this section is correct at the time of printing it should be checked before use.

Bus Services and Tours

Long Distance Coach Service
Buchanan Bus Station 041 332 9191
Scottish City Link Coaches Ltd provide express services to London and most parts of Scotland including Campbeltown, Tarbert, Ardrishaig, Inveraray, Oban, Fort William, Skye, Stirling, Perth, Dundee, Arbroath, Montrose, Aberdeen, Aviemore, Inverness and Edinburgh.

Local Bus Services
A comprehensive network of local bus services is provided by a variety of operators within the City of Glasgow and also direct to the following destinations:
Airdrie, Ardrossan, Ayr, Balfron, Barrhead, Bearsden, Beith, Bellshill, Bishopbriggs, Bishopton, Blantyre, Bo'ness, Caldercruix, Cambuslang, Campsie Glen, Carluke, Clydebank, Coatbridge, Cumbernauld, Denny, Drymen, Dunfermline, Duntocher, Eaglesham, East Kilbride, Erskine, Falkirk, Glenrothes, Grangemouth, Hamilton, Irvine, Johnstone, Kilbarchan, Kilbirnie, Killearn, Kilmarnock, Kilsyth, Kirkintilloch, Kirkcaldy, Lanark, Largs, Larkhall, Lennoxtown, Lochwinnoch, Motherwell, Milngavie, Newton Mearns, Old Kilpatrick, Paisley, Prestwick, Renfrew, Saltcoats,
Shotts, Stirling, Strathblane, Strathaven, Uddingston, Wishaw.

These services depart from City Centre bus stops or from Anderston or Buchanan Bus Station. For information contact St. Enoch Travel Centre 041 226 4826; lines open 7 a.m. - 9 p.m. Monday - Saturday and 0900 - 1930 Sundays.

Coach Hire and Day, Half Day and Extended Tours
Scottish City Link Coaches
Buchanan Bus Station
041 332 8055
Private hire and seasonal tours
041 332 8055

Haldane's of Cathcart
Delvin Road, G44 041 637 2234

Strathclyde Buses Ltd.
197 Victoria Road, G42 7AD
041 636 3190
Private hire and seasonal tours

British Rail

Passenger enquiries: 041 204 2844
Sleeper reservations: 041 221 2305

Local Strathclyde Transport trains serve over 170 stations in Glasgow and Strathclyde (see map). ScotRail services operate to most destinations in Scotland. InterCity services operate to England.

Glasgow Queen Street Station
for services to Cumbernauld, Edinburgh, Falkirk, Stirling, Perth, Dundee, Arbroath, Montrose, Aberdeen, Pitlochry, Aviemore, Inverness, Dumbarton, Balloch, Helensburgh, Oban, Fort William, Mallaig, Coatbridge, Airdrie.

Glasgow Central Station
for services to Gourock (ferry connection to Dunoon), Greenock, Wemyss Bay (ferry connection to Rothesay), Paisley, Johnstone, Largs, Ardrossan (ferry connection to Brodick), Irvine, Ayr, Girvan, Stranraer, East Kilbride, Kilmarnock, Dumfries, Motherwell, Hamilton, Lanark, Carlisle, Shotts, Edinburgh, Berwick, Newcastle.
London and destinations on West and East Coast Main Lines.

INDEX TO STREETS

General Abbreviations

All.	Alley	Dr.	Drive	Mkt.	Market	St.	Street/Saint
App.	Approach	E.	East	Ms.	Mews	Sta.	Station
Arc.	Arcade	Esp.	Esplanade	Mt.	Mount	Ter.	Terrace
Av.	Avenue	Ex.	Exchange	N.	North	Trd.	Trading
Bk.	Bank	Fm.	Farm	Par.	Parade	Twr.	Tower
Bldgs.	Buildings	Gdns.	Gardens	Pas.	Passage	Vill.	Villa
Boul.	Boulevard	Gra.	Grange	Pk.	Park	Vills.	Villas
Bri.	Bridge	Grn.	Green	Pl.	Place	Vw.	View
Cft.	Croft	Gro.	Grove	Prom.	Promenade	W.	West
Circ.	Circus	Ho.	House	Quad.	Quadrant	Wd.	Wood
Clo.	Close	Ind.	Industrial	Rd.	Road	Wds.	Woods
Cor.	Corner	La.	Lane	Ri.	Rise	Wf.	Wharf
Cotts.	Cottages	Ln.	Loan	S.	South	Wk.	Walk
Cres.	Crescent	Lo.	Lodge	Sch.	School	Yd.	Yard
Ct.	Court	Mans.	Mansions	Sq.	Square		

District Abbreviations

Bail.	Baillieston	Clark.	Clarkston	Giff.	Giffnock	Pais.	Paisley
Barr.	Barrhead	Clyde.	Clydebank	John.	Johnstone	Renf.	Renfrew
Bear.	Bearsden	Coat.	Coatbridge	Kilb.	Kilbarchan	Ruth.	Rutherglen
Bish.	Bishopbriggs	Cumb.	Cumbernauld	Kirk.	Kirkintilloch	Step.	Stepps
Blan.	Blantyre	Dalm.	Dalmuir	Lenz.	Lenzie	Thorn.	Thornliebank
Both.	Bothwell	E.K.	East Kilbride	Linw.	Linwood	Udd.	Uddingston
Chr.	Chryston	Gart.	Gartcosh	Old K.	Old Kilpatrick		

NOTES

The figures and letters following a street name indicate the postal district for that street with the page number and square where it will be found in the atlas. Thus the postal district for Abbey Drive is G14, and it will be found on page 19 in square H12.

A street name followed by the name of another street in italics does not appear on the map, but will be found adjoining or near the latter.

Abbey Clo., Pais.	46	K14	Aberuthven Dr. G32	54	BB14	Afton Rd., Cumb.	71	PP2
Abbey Dr. G14	19	R10	Abiegail Pl., Blan.	68	FF19	Afton St. G41	51	U16
Abbey Rd., John.	44	F15	Abington St. G20	21	V10	Agamemnon St., Dalm.	4	K7
Abbeycraig Rd. G34	40	FF11	Aboukir St. G51	33	R12	Aigas Cotts. G13	19	R9
Abbeydale Way G73	65	Z18	Aboyne Dr., Pais.	46	K15	*Crow Rd.*		
Neilvaig Dr.			Aboyne St. G51	33	R13	Aikenhead Rd. G42	51	V14
Abbeyhill St. G32	38	AA12	Acacia Dr. G78	59	L17	Ailean Dr. G32	55	DD14
Abbot St. G41	51	U15	Acacia Dr., Pais.	45	H15	Ailean Gdns. G32	55	DD14
Frankfort St.			Acacia Pl., John.	44	E16	Ailort Av. G44	63	V17
Abbot St., Pais.	30	K13	Academy Rd., Giff.	62	T19	*Lochinver Dr.*		
Abbotsburn Way, Pais.	30	J12	Academy St. G32	54	BB14	Ailsa Dr. G42	51	U16
Abbotsford, Bish.	11	Z7	Acer Cres. G78	45	H15	Ailsa Dr. G73	64	X17
Abbotsford Av. G73	53	Y16	Achamore Pl. G15	6	N6	Ailsa Dr., Clyde.	5	M5
Abbotsford Ct., Cumb.	70	NN4	*Achamore Rd.*			Ailsa Dr., Pais.	46	J16
Abbotsford Cres., Pais.	44	F16	Achamore Rd. G15	6	N6	Ailsa Dr., Udd.	69	HH18
Abbotsford La. G5	51	V14	Achray Dr., Pais.	45	H15	Ailsa Rd., Bish.	11	Y7
Cumberland St.			Acorn Ct. G40	52	X14	Ailsa Rd., Renf.	31	M11
Abbotsford Pl. G5	51	V14	*Acorn St.*			Ainslie Rd. G52	32	P12
Abbotsford Pl., Cumb.	70	NN4	Acorn St. G40	52	X14	Ainslie Rd., Cumb.	71	QQ2
Abbotsford Rd., Bear.	7	Q5	Acre Dr. G20	8	T7	Airdale Rd., Giff.	62	T19
Abbotsford Rd., Clyde.	5	L7	Acre Rd. G20	8	S7	Aird's La. G1	36	W13
Abbotsford Rd., Cumb.	70	NN4	Acredyke Cres. G21	23	Z8	*Bridgegate*		
Abbotshall Av. G15	6	N6	Acredyke Pl. G21	23	Z9	Airgold Dr. G15	6	N6
Abbotsinch Rd., Pais.	30	K11	Acredyke Rd. G21	23	Y8	Airgold Pl. G15	6	N6
Abbott Cres., Clyde.	17	M8	Acredyke Rd. G73	52	X16	Airlie Gdns. G73	65	Z18
Aberconway St., Clyde.	17	M8	Acrehill St. G33	37	Z11	Airlie Rd., Bail.	56	EE14
Abercorn Av. G52	32	N12	Adams Ct. La. G2	35	V12	Airlie St. G12	20	S10
Abercorn Pl. G23	9	U7	*Howard St.*			Airlour Rd. G43	63	U17
Abercorn St., Pais.	30	K13	Adamswell St. G21	22	X10	Airth Dr. G52	49	R14
Abercrombie Cres.,	41	GG13	Adamswell Ter., Chr.	15	HH7	Airth La. G51	49	R14
Bail.			Addiewell St. G32	38	BB12	Airth Pl. G51	49	R14
Abercromby Dr. G40	36	X13	Addison Gro., Thorn.	61	R18	Airthrey Av. G14	19	R10
Abercromby Sq. G40	36	X13	Addison Pl., Thorn.	61	R18	Aitken St. G31	37	Z12
Abercromby St. G40	36	X13	Addison Rd. G12	20	T10	Aitkenhead Av., Coat.	57	HH14
Aberdalgie Path G34	40	EE12	Addison Rd., Thorn.	61	R18	Aitkenhead Rd., Udd.	57	HH16
Aberdalgie Rd. G34	40	EE12	Adelphi St. G5	36	W13	Alasdair Ct., Barr.	59	M19
Aberdour St. G31	37	Z12	Admiral St. G41	35	U13	Albany Av. G32	39	CC13
Aberfeldy St. G31	37	Z12	Advie Pl. G42	51	V16	Albany Cotts. G13	19	R9
Aberfoyle St. G31	37	Z12	*Prospecthill Rd.*			*Crow Rd.*		
Aberlady Rd. G51	33	R12	Affric Dr., Pais.	47	L15	Albany Dr. G73	65	Y17
Abernethy Dr., Linw.	28	E13	Afton Cres., Bear.	8	S6	Albany Pl., Both.	69	HH19
Abernethy St. G31	37	Z12	Afton Dr., Renf.	18	N10	*Marguerite Gdns.*		

Street	Page	Grid
Albany Quad. G32	39	CC13
Mansionhouse Dr.		
Albany St. G40	53	Y14
Albany Ter. G72	66	AA18
Albany Way, Pais.	30	K12
Abbotsburn Way		
Albert Av. G42	51	U15
Albert Ct. G41	51	U14
Albert Dr.		
Albert Cross G41	51	U14
Albert Dr. G41	50	T15
Albert Dr. G73	65	Y17
Albert Dr., Bear.	8	S7
Albert Rd. G42	51	V15
Albert Rd., Clyde.	5	L6
Albert Rd., Lenz.	13	CC6
Albert Rd., Renf.	17	M10
Alberta Ter. G12	20	T10
Saltoun St.		
Albion St. G1	36	W12
Albion St., Bail.	55	DD14
Albion St., Pais.	30	K13
Alcaig Rd. G52	49	R15
Alder Av., Lenz.	12	BB5
Alder Ct., Barr.	59	M19
Alder Pl. G43	62	T17
Alder Pl., John.	44	E15
Alder Rd. G43	62	T17
Alder Rd., Cumb.	71	QQ3
Alder Rd., Dalm.	4	K5
Alderman Pl. G13	19	Q9
Alderman Rd. G13	18	N8
Aldersdyke Pl., Blan.	68	FF19
Alderside Dr., Udd.	57	GG16
Alexander St., Clyde.	5	L7
Alexandra Av. G33	25	CC9
Alexandra Av., Lenz.	13	CC6
Alexandra Ct. G31	37	Y12
Roebank St.		
Alexandra Cross G31	37	Y12
Duke St.		
Alexandra Dr., Pais.	45	H14
Alexandra Dr., Renf.	17	M10
Alexandra Gdns., Lenz.	13	CC6
Alexandra Par. G31	37	Y12
Alexandra Pk. St. G31	37	Y12
Alexandra Rd., Lenz.	13	CC6
Alford St. G21	22	W10
Alfred Ter. G52	20	T10
Cecil St.		
Algie St. G41	51	U16
Alice St. G5	52	W14
Alice St., Pais.	46	K15
Aline Ct., Barr.	59	L18
Allan Av., Renf.	32	N11
Allan Pl. G40	53	Y14
Allan St. G40	53	Y15
Allander Gdns., Bish.	10	X6
Allander Rd., Bear.	7	Q6
Allander St. G22	22	W10
Allands Av., Renf.	16	J9
Allanfauld Rd., Cumb.	70	NN2
Allanton Av., Pais.	48	N14
Allanton Dr. G52	32	P13
Allerton Gdns., Bail.	55	DD14
Alleysbank Rd. G73	53	Y15
Allison Dr. G72	66	BB17
Allison Pl. G42	51	V15
Prince Edward St.		
Allison Pl., Gart.	27	GG10
Allison St. G42	51	V15
Allnach Pl. G34	41	GG12
Alloway Cres. G73	64	X17
Alloway Dr. G73	64	X17
Alloway Dr., Clyde.	5	M6
Alloway Rd. G43	62	T17
Alma St. G40	37	Y13
Almond Av., Renf.	32	N11
Almond Cres., Pais.	45	G15
Almond Dr., Lenz.	12	BB5
Almond Rd. G33	25	CC9
Almond Rd., Bear.	7	Q7
Almond St. G33	37	Z11
Almond Vale, Udd.	57	HH16
Hamilton Vw.		
Alness Cres. G52	49	R14
Alpatrick Gdns., John.	44	E14
Alpine Gro., Udd.	57	GG16
Alsatian Av., Clyde.	5	M7
Alston La. G40	36	X13
Claythorn St.		
Altnacreag Gdns., Chr.	15	HH6
Alton Gdns. G12	20	T10
Great George St.		
Alton Rd., Pais.	47	M14
Altyre St. G32	54	AA14
Alva Gdns. G52	49	R15
Alva Gate G52	49	R15
Alva Pl., Lenz.	13	DD6
Alyth Gdns. G52	49	R14
Ambassador Way, Renf.	31	M11
Cockels Ln.		
Amisfield St. G20	21	U9
Amochrie Dr., Pais.	45	H16
Amochrie Rd., Pais.	45	G15
Amulree Pl. G32	54	BB14
Amulree St. G32	38	BB13
Ancaster Dr. G13	19	R9
Ancaster La. G13	19	Q8
Great Western Rd.		
Anchor Av., Pais.	47	L14
Anchor Cres., Pais.	47	L14
Anchor Dr., Pais.	47	L14
Anchor Wynd, Pais.	47	L14
Ancroft St. G20	21	V10
Anderson Dr., Renf.	17	M10
Anderson Gdns., Blan.	69	GG19
Station Rd.		
Anderson Quay G3	35	U13
Anderson St. G11	34	S11
Andrew Av., Lenz.	13	CC6
Andrew Av., Renf.	18	N10
Andrew Dr., Clyde.	17	M8
Andrew Sillars Av. G72	67	CC17
Andrews St., Pais.	30	K13
Anglegate G14	19	Q10
Angus Av. G52	49	Q14
Angus Av., Bish.	23	Z8
Angus Gdns., Udd.	57	GG16
Angus La. G64	11	Z7
Angus Oval G52	48	P14
Angus Pl. G52	48	P14
Angus St. G21	22	X10
Angus St., Clyde.	18	N8
Angus Wk., Udd.	57	HH16
Annan Dr. G73	53	Z16
Annan Dr., Bear.	7	Q6
Annan Dr., Pais.	45	G15
Annan Pl., John.	43	C16
Annan St. G42	51	V16
Annandale St. G42	51	V14
Annbank St. G31	36	X13
Anne Av., Renf.	17	M10
Anne Cres., Lenz.	13	CC6
Annette St. G42	51	V15
Annfield Gdns., Blan.	68	FF19
Annfield Pl. G31	36	X12
Annick Dr., Bear.	7	Q7
Annick St. G32	38	BB13
Annick St. G72	67	CC17
Anniesdale Av. G33	25	CC9
Anniesland Cres. G14	18	P9
Anniesland Mans. G13	19	R9
Ancaster Dr.		
Anniesland Rd. G13	19	Q9
Anniesland Rd. G14	18	P9
Anson St. G40	52	X14
Anson Way, Renf.	31	M11
Britannia Way		
Anstruther St. G32	38	AA13
Anthony St. G2	35	V12
Cadogan St.		
Antonine Gdns., Clyde.	5	L5
Antonine Rd., Bear.	6	P5
Anworth St. G32	54	BB14
Appin Rd. G31	37	Y12
Appin Ter. G73	65	Z18
Lochaber Dr.		
Appin Way, Udd.	69	HH18
Bracken Ter.		
Appleby St. G22	21	V10
Applecross Gdns., Chr.	15	GG6
Applecross St. G22	21	V10
Appledore Cres., Udd.	69	HH18
Apsley La. G11	34	S11
Apsley St. G11	34	S11
Aray St. G20	20	T9
Arbroath Av. G52	48	P14
Arcadia St. G40	36	X13
Arcan Cres. G15	6	P7
Archerfield Av. G32	54	BB15
Archerfield Cres. G32	54	BB15
Archerfield Dr. G32	54	BB15
Archerfield Gro. G32	54	BB15
Archerhill Av. G13	18	N8
Archerhill Cotts. G13	18	P8
Archerhill Rd.		
Archerhill Cres. G13	18	P8
Archerhill Gdns. G13	18	P8
Archerhill Rd.		
Archerhill Rd. G13	18	P8
Archerhill Sq. G13	18	P8
Kelso St.		
Archerhill St. G13	18	P8
Archerhill Rd.		
Archerhill Ter. G13	18	P8
Archerhill Rd.		
Ard Pl. G42	52	X16
Ard Rd., Renf.	17	L10
Ard St. G32	54	BB14
Ardagie Dr. G32	55	CC16
Ardagie Pl. G32	55	CC16
Ardbeg Av. G73	66	AA18
Ardbeg Av., Bish.	11	Z7
Ardbeg St. G42	51	V15
Ardconnel St. G46	61	R18
Arden Av. G46	61	R19
Arden Dr., Giff.	62	S19
Arden Pl. G46	61	R19
Stewarton Rd.		
Ardencraig Cres. G44	64	W19
Ardencraig Dr. G45	64	X19
Ardencraig La. G45	64	W19
Ardencraig Rd.		
Ardencraig Quad. G45	64	X19
Ardencraig Rd. G45	64	W19
Ardencraig St. G45	65	Y19
Ardencraig Ter. G45	64	X19
Ardenlea Rd., Udd.	57	GG16
Ardenlea St. G40	53	Y14
Ardery St. G11	34	S11
Apsley St.		
Ardessie Pl. G20	20	T9
Ardessie St. G23	8	T7
Torrin Rd.		
Ardfern St. G32	54	BB14
Ardgay Pl. G32	54	BB14
Ardgay St. G32	54	BB14
Ardgay Way G73	65	Y18
Ardgour Dr., Linw.	28	E13
Ardgowan Av., Pais.	46	K14
Ardgowan Dr., Udd.	57	GG16
Ardgowan St., Pais.	46	K15
Ardholm St. G32	38	BB13
Ardhu Pl. G15	6	N6
Ardlamont Sq., Linw.	28	F13
Ardlaw St. G51	33	R13
Ardle Rd. G43	63	U17
Ardlui St. G32	54	AA14
Ardmaleish Cres. G45	64	X19
Ardmaleish Rd. G45	64	W19
Ardmaleish St. G45	64	X19
Ardmaleish Ter. G45	64	X19
Ardmay Cres. G44	52	W16
Ardmillan St. G33	38	AA12
Ardmore Oval, Pais.	29	H13
Ardmory Av. G42	52	W16
Ardmory La. G42	52	X16
Ardnacross Dr. G33	39	CC11
Ardnahoe Av. G42	52	W16
Ardnahoe Pl. G42	52	W16
Ardneil Rd. G51	33	R13
Ardnish St. G51	33	R12
Ardo Gdns. G51	34	S13
Ardoch Gro. G72	66	AA17

Street	Page	Grid
Ardoch Rd., Bear.	8	S5
Ardoch St. G22	22	W10
Ardoch Way, Chr.	15	GG7
Braeside Av.		
Ardshiel Rd. G51	33	R12
Ardsloy La. G14	18	P10
Ardsloy Pl.		
Ardsloy Pl. G14	18	P10
Ardtoe Cres. G33	25	DD9
Ardtoe Pl. G33	25	DD9
Arduthie Rd. G51	33	R12
Ardwell Rd. G52	49	R14
Argosy Way, Renf.	31	M11
Britannia Way		
Argyle St. G3	34	T11
Argyle St., Pais.	46	J14
Argyll Arc. G2	35	V12
Argyll Av., Pais.	30	K11
Argyll Av., Renf.	17	L10
Argyll Rd., Clyde.	5	M7
Arisaig Dr. G52	49	R14
Arisaig Dr., Bear.	8	S6
Arisaig Pl. G52	49	R14
Ark La. G31	36	X12
Arkle Ter. G72	66	AA18
Arkleston Cres., Pais.	31	L12
Arkleston Rd., Pais.	31	L12
Arklet Rd. G51	33	R13
Arlington St. G3	35	U11
Armadale Ct. G31	37	Y12
Townmill Rd.		
Armadale Path G31	37	Y12
Armadale Pl. G31	37	Y12
Armadale St. G31	37	Y12
Armaleish Dr. G45	64	X19
Armour Pl., John.	44	E14
Armour St. G31	36	X13
Armour St., John.	44	E14
Arngask Rd. G51	33	R12
Arnhall Pl. G52	49	R14
Arnholm Pl. G52	49	R14
Arnisdale Pl. G34	40	EE12
Arnisdale Rd. G34	40	EE12
Arnisdale Way G73	65	Y18
Shieldaig Dr.		
Arniston St. G32	38	AA12
Arnol Pl. G33	39	DD12
Arnold Av., Bish.	11	Y7
Arnold St. G20	21	V9
Arnott Way G72	66	BB17
Arnprior Gdns., Chr.	15	GG7
Braeside Av.		
Arnprior Quad. G45	64	W18
Arnprior Rd. G45	64	W18
Arnprior St. G45	64	W18
Arnside Av., Giff.	62	T18
Arnthern St. G72	67	CC17
Arnwood Dr. G12	20	S9
Aron Ter. G72	66	AA18
Aros Dr. G52	49	R15
Arran Av., Pais.	30	K11
Arran Dr. G52	49	R14
Arran Dr., Cumb.	70	MM4
Arran Dr., Giff.	62	S19
Arran Dr., John.	43	C15
Arran Dr., Pais.	46	K16
Arran La., Chr.	15	HH7
Burnbrae Av.		
Arran Pl., Clyde.	5	M7
Arran Pl., Linw.	28	E13
Arran Rd., Renf.	31	M11
Arran Ter. G73	64	X17
Arranthrue Cres., Renf.	17	M10
Arranthrue Dr., Renf.	17	M10
Arriochmill Rd. G20	20	T10
Kelvin Dr.		
Arrochar Ct. G23	21	U8
Sunningdale Rd.		
Arrochar Dr. G23	8	T7
Arrochar St. G23	20	T8
Arrol Pl. G40	53	Y14
Arrol St. G52	32	N12
Arrowchar Ct. G23	21	U8
Arrowchar St.		
Arrowchar St. G23	20	T8
Arrowsmith Av. G13	19	Q8
Arthur Av., Barr.	59	L19
Arthur Rd., Pais.	46	K16
Arthur St. G3	34	T11
Arthur St., Pais.	30	J13
Arthurlie Av., Barr.	59	M19
Arthurlie Dr., Giff.	62	T19
Arthurlie St. G51	33	R12
Arthurlie St., Barr.	59	M19
Arundel Dr. G42	51	V16
Arundel Dr., Bish.	11	Y6
Asbury Ct., Linw.	28	F13
Ascaig Cres. G52	49	R15
Ascog Rd., Bear.	7	R7
Ascog St. G42	51	V15
Ascot Av. G12	19	R9
Ascot Ct. G12	20	S9
Ash Gro., Bish.	11	Y7
Ash Gro., Lenz.	12	BB5
Ash Gro., Udd.	57	HH16
Douglas Cres.		
Ash Pl., John.	44	E15
Ash Rd., Bail.	56	EE14
Ash Rd., Cumb.	71	QQ1
Ash Rd., Dalm.	4	K5
Ash Wk. G73	65	Z18
Ashburton Rd. G12	20	S9
Ashby Cres. G13	7	R7
Ashcroft Dr. G44	64	X17
Ashdale Dr. G52	49	R14
Ashdene Rd. G22	21	V8
Ashfield, Bish.	11	Y6
Ashfield St. G22	22	W10
Ashgill Pl. G22	22	W9
Ashgill Rd. G22	21	V9
Ashgrove, Bail.	41	GG13
Ashgrove St. G40	53	Y15
Ashkirk Dr. G52	49	R14
Ashlea Dr., Giff.	62	T18
Ashley La. G3	35	U11
Woodlands Rd.		
Ashley St. G3	35	U11
Ashmore Rd. G43	63	U17
Ashton Gdns. G12	34	T11
Ashton Rd.		
Ashton La. G12	34	T11
University Av.		
Ashton Pl. G12	20	T10
Byres Rd.		
Ashton Rd. G12	34	T11
University Av.		
Ashton Rd. G73	53	Y15
Ashton Ter. G12	34	T11
University Av.		
Ashton Way G78	45	G16
Ashtree Rd. G43	50	T16
Ashvale Cres. G21	22	X10
Aspen Dr. G21	23	Y10
Foresthall Dr.		
Aspen Pl., John.	44	E15
Aster Dr. G45	65	Y18
Aster Gdns. G53	61	Q18
Waukglen Cres.		
Athelstane Dr., Cumb.	70	MM4
Athelstane Rd. G13	19	Q8
Athena Way, Udd.	57	HH16
Athol Av. G52	32	N12
Athol Ter., Udd.	57	GG15
Lomond Rd.		
Athole Gdns. G12	20	T10
Athole La. G12	20	T10
Saltoun St.		
Atholl Cres., Pais.	32	N13
Atholl Gdns. G73	66	AA18
Atholl Gdns., Bish.	11	Y6
Atholl La., Chr.	15	HH7
Atholl Pl., Linw.	28	E13
Atlas Pl. G21	22	X10
Atlas Rd. G21	22	X10
Attlee Av., Clyde.	5	M7
Attlee Pl., Clyde.	5	M7
Attlee Av.		
Attow Rd. G43	62	S17
Auburn Dr., Barr.	59	M19
Auburn Pl. G31	37	Z13
Auchans Rd., Linw.	28	E11
Auchencrow St. G34	40	FF12
Auchendale, Lenz.	13	DD5
Auchengeich Rd., Chr.	14	FF6
Auchengill Path G34	40	FF11
Auchengill Rd.		
Auchengill Pl. G34	40	FF11
Auchengill Rd. G34	40	FF11
Auchenglen Dr., Chr.	15	GG7
Auchengreoch Av., John.	43	C16
Auchengreoch Rd., John.	43	C16
Auchenlodment Rd., John.	44	E15
Auchentorlie Quad., Pais.	47	L14
Auchentorlie St. G11	33	R11
Dumbarton Rd.		
Auchentoshan Av., Clyde.	4	K5
Auchentoshan Ter. G21	36	X11
Auchentoshen Cotts., Old K.	4	J5
Auchinairn Rd., Bish.	22	X8
Auchinbee Way, Cumb.	70	MM2
Eastfield Rd.		
Auchinlea Rd. G34	39	DD11
Auchinleck Av. G33	24	AA9
Auchinleck Cres. G33	24	AA9
Auchinleck Dr. G33	24	AA9
Auchinleck Gdns. G33	24	AA9
Auchinleck Rd. G33	24	AA8
Auchinloch Rd., Lenz.	13	CC6
Auchinloch St. G21	22	X10
Auchmannoch Av., Pais.	32	N13
Auckland Pl., Dalm.	4	J6
Auckland St. G22	21	V10
Auld Kirk Rd. G72	67	CC18
Auld Rd., The, Cumb.	71	PP2
Auld St., Dalm.	4	K6
Auldbar Rd. G52	49	R14
Auldbar Ter., Pais.	47	L15
Auldburn Rd. G43	62	S17
Auldearn Rd. G21	23	Z8
Auldgirth Rd. G52	49	R14
Auldhouse Av. G42	62	S17
Harriet St.		
Auldhouse Rd. G43	62	S17
Auldhouse Ter. G43	62	T17
Auldhouse Rd.		
Aultbea St. G22	21	V8
Aultmore Rd. G33	39	DD12
Aurs Cres., Barr.	59	M19
Aurs Dr., Barr.	59	M19
Aurs Glen, Barr.	59	M19
Aurs Pl., Barr.	59	M19
Aurs Rd., Barr.	59	M18
Aursbridge Dr., Barr.	59	M19
Austen La. G13	19	R9
Skaterig La.		
Austen La. G13	19	R9
Woodend Dr.		
Austen Rd. G13	19	R9
Avenel Rd. G13	7	R7
Avenue, The, Kilb.	42	B15
Low Barholm		
Avenue End Rd. G33	24	BB10
Avenue St. G40	37	Y13
Avenue St. G73	53	Y15
Avenuehead Rd., Chr.	15	GG6
Avenuehead Rd., Gart.	27	HH8
Avenuepark St. G20	21	U10
Aviemore Gdns., Bear.	8	S5
Aviemore Rd. G52	49	R15
Avoch Dr. G46	61	R18
Avoch St. G34	40	EE11
Avon Av., Bear.	8	S6
Avon Dr. G64	23	Y8
Avon Dr., Linw.	28	E13
Avon Rd., Bish.	23	Y8
Avon Rd., Giff.	62	S19
Avon St. G5	35	U13
Avonbank Rd. G73	52	X16

Avondale Dr., Pais.	31	L13
Avondale St. G33	38	BB11
Avonhead Av. G67	70	MM4
Avonhead Gdns. G67	70	MM4
Avonhead Pl. G67	70	MM4
Avonhead Rd. G67	70	MM4
Avonspark St. G21	23	Y10
Aylmer Rd. G43	63	U17
Ayr Rd., Giff.	62	S19
Ayr St. G21	22	X10
Aytoun Rd. G41	50	T14
Back Causeway G31	37	Z13
Back Sneddon St., Pais.	30	M13
Backmuir Rd. G15	6	P6
Bagnell St. G21	22	X9
Baillie Dr., Both.	69	HH18
Baillieston Rd. G32	55	CC14
Baillieston Rd., Udd.	56	EE15
Bain Sq. G40	36	X13
Bain St.		
Bain St. G40	36	X13
Bainsford St. G32	38	AA13
Baird Av. G52	32	N12
Baird Dr., Bear.	7	Q5
Baird St. G4	36	W11
Bairdsbrae G4	21	V10
Possil Rd.		
Baker Pl. G41	51	U15
Baker St.		
Baker St. G41	51	U15
Bakewell Rd., Bail.	40	EE13
Balaclava St. G2	35	V13
McAlpine St.		
Balado Rd. G33	39	DD12
Balbeg St. G51	33	R13
Balbeggie Pl. G32	55	CC14
Balbeggie St. G32	55	CC14
Balblair Rd. G52	49	R15
Balcarres Av. G12	20	T9
Balcomie St. G33	38	BB11
Balcurvie Rd. G34	40	EE11
Baldinnie Rd. G34	40	EE12
Baldorran Cres., Cumb.	70	LL2
Baldoven Cres. G33	39	DD12
Baldovie Rd. G52	49	Q14
Baldragon Rd. G34	40	EE11
Baldric Rd. G13	19	Q9
Baldwin Av. G13	7	Q7
Balerno Dr. G52	49	R14
Balfluig St. G34	39	DD11
Balfour St. G20	20	T9
Balfron Rd. G51	33	R12
Balfron Rd., Pais.	31	M13
Balgair Dr., Pais.	31	L13
Balgair St. G22	21	V9
Balgair Ter. G32	38	BB13
Balglass St. G22	21	V10
Balgonie Av. G78	45	H15
Balgonie Av., Pais.	45	H15
Balgonie Dr., Pais.	46	J15
Balgonie Rd. G52	49	R14
Balgonie Wds., Pais.	46	J15
Balgownie Cres., Thorn.	62	S19
Balgray Cres., Barr.	60	N19
Balgrayhill Rd. G21	23	Y10
Balgrayhill Rd. G21	22	X9
Balintore St. G32	38	BB13
Baliol La. G3	35	U11
Woodlands Rd.		
Baliol St. G3	35	U11
Ballaig Av., Bear.	7	Q5
Ballaig Cres. G33	25	CC9
Ballantay Quad. G45	65	Y18
Ballantay Rd. G45	65	Y18
Ballantay Ter. G45	65	Y18
Ballantyne Rd. G52	32	P12
Ballater Dr., Bear.	7	R7
Ballater Dr., Pais.	47	L15
Ballater Dr., Renf.	16	J8
Ballater Pl. G5	52	W14
Ballater St. G5	36	W13
Ballayne Dr., Chr.	15	HH7
Ballindalloch Dr. G31	37	Y12

Balloch Gdns. G52	49	R14
Balloch Rd., Cumb.	70	MM3
Balloch Vw., Cumb.	70	NN3
Ballochmill Rd. G73	53	Z16
Ballogie Rd. G44	51	V16
Balmarino Pl. G64	11	Z7
Balmartin Rd. G23	8	T7
Balmerino Pl., Bish.	23	Z8
Angus Av.		
Balmoral Cres. G42	51	V15
Queens Dr.		
Balmoral Cres., Renf.	16	K9
Balmoral Dr. G32	54	BB16
Balmoral Dr. G72	66	AA17
Balmoral Dr., Bear.	8	S7
Balmoral Gdns., Blan.	68	FF19
Balmoral Gdns., Udd.	57	GG15
Balmoral Rd., John.	44	E15
Balmoral St. G14	18	P10
Balmore Pl. G22	21	V9
Balmore Rd.		
Balmore Rd. G23	9	U5
Balmore Sq. G22	21	V9
Balmuildy Rd., Bish.	9	V6
Balornock Rd. G21	23	Y9
Balruddery Pl. G64	23	Z8
Balshagray Av. G11	19	R10
Balshagray Cres. G11	19	R10
Balshagray Dr. G11	19	R10
Balshagray La. G11	19	R10
Balshagray Pl. G11	19	R10
Balshagray Dr.		
Baltic Ct. G40	53	Y14
Baltic St.		
Baltic La. G40	53	Y14
Baltic Pl. G40	52	X14
Baltic St. G40	53	Y14
Balure St. G31	37	Z12
Balvaird Cres. G73	53	Y16
Balvaird Dr. G73	53	Y16
Balveny St. G33	39	CC11
Balvicar Dr. G42	51	U15
Balvicar St. G42	51	U15
Balvie Av. G15	6	P7
Balvie Av., Giff.	62	T19
Banavie Rd. G11	20	S10
Banchory Av. G43	62	S17
Banchory Av., Renf.	16	J8
Banchory Cres., Bear.	8	S7
Banff St. G33	38	BB11
Bangorshill St. G46	61	R18
Bank Rd. G32	55	CC16
Bank St. G12	35	U11
Bank St. G72	66	BB17
Bank St., Barr.	59	M19
Bank St., Pais.	46	K14
Bankbrae Av. G53	60	P17
Bankend St. G33	38	BB11
Bankfoot Dr. G52	48	P14
Bankfoot Rd. G52	48	P14
Bankfoot Rd., Pais.	29	H13
Bankglen Rd. G15	6	P6
Bankhall St. G42	51	V15
Bankhead Av. G13	18	P9
Bankhead Dr. G73	53	Y16
Bankhead Rd. G73	64	X17
Bankier St. G40	36	X13
Banknock St. G32	38	AA13
Bankside Av., John.	43	D14
Banktop Pl., John.	43	D14
Banling Grn. Rd. G44	63	V17
Clarkston Rd.		
Bannatyne Av. G31	37	Y12
Banner Dr. G13	7	Q7
Banner Rd. G13	7	Q7
Bannercross Av., Bail.	40	EE13
Bannercross Dr., Bail.	40	EE13
Bannercross Gdns., Bail.	40	EE13
Bannercross Dr.		
Bannerman Pl., Clyde.	5	M7
Bannerman St., Clyde.	5	L7
Bantaskin St. G20	20	T8
Banton Pl. G33	40	EE12
Barassie Ct., Both.	69	GG19
Barassie Cres., Cumb.	70	NN1

Barbae Pl., Udd.	69	HH18
Hume Dr.		
Barberry Av. G53	60	P19
Barberry Gdns. G53	60	P19
Barberry Av.		
Barberry Pl. G53	60	P19
Barberry Av.		
Barbreck Rd. G42	51	U15
Pollokshaws Rd.		
Barcaldine Av., Chr.	14	EE7
Barclay Av., John.	44	E15
Barclay Sq., Renf.	31	L11
Barclay St. G21	22	X9
Balgrayhill Rd.		
Barcraigs Dr., Pais.	46	K16
Bard Av. G13	18	P8
Bardowie St. G22	21	V10
Bardrain Av., John.	44	F15
Bardrain Rd., Pais.	46	J16
Bardrill Dr., Bish.	10	X7
Bardykes Rd., Blan.	68	FF19
Barfillan Dr. G52	33	R13
Barfillan Rd. G52	33	R13
Bargaran Rd. G53	48	P14
Bargarron Dr., Pais.	31	L12
Bargeddie St. G33	37	Z11
Barhill Cres., Kilb.	42	B15
Barholm Sq. G33	39	CC11
Barke Rd., Cumb.	71	PP2
Barlanark Av. G32	39	CC12
Barlanark Pl. G32	39	CC13
Hallhill Rd.		
Barlanark Pl. G33	39	DD12
Barlanark Rd. G33	39	CC12
Barlia Dr. G45	64	X18
Barlia St. G45	64	X18
Barlia Ter. G45	64	X18
Barloch St. G22	22	W10
Barlogan Av. G52	33	R13
Barlogan Quad. G52	33	R13
Barmill Rd. G43	62	S17
Barmulloch Rd. G21	23	Y10
Barn Grn. G78	42	B14
Barnard Gdns., Bish.	11	Y6
Barnard Ter. G40	53	Y14
Barnbeth Rd. G53	48	P15
Barnes Rd. G20	21	V9
Barnes St., Barr.	59	L19
Barnflat St. G73	53	Y15
Barnhill Dr. G21	23	Y10
Foresthall Dr.		
Barnkirk Av. G15	6	P6
Barns St., Clyde.	5	M7
Barnsford Av., Renf.	16	J9
Barnsford Rd., Pais.	29	H11
Barnton St. G32	38	AA12
Barnwell Ter. G51	33	R12
Barochan Cres., Pais.	45	H14
Barochan Rd. G53	48	P14
Baron Rd., Pais.	31	L13
Baron St., Renf.	31	M11
Baronald Dr. G12	20	S9
Baronald Gate G12	20	S9
Baronald St. G73	53	Y15
Baronhill, Cumb.	71	PP1
Barons Ct. Dr., John.	45	G14
Barons Ct. Gdns., John.	45	G14
Barons Ct. Rd., John.	45	G14
Barons Gate, Both.	69	GG18
Barony Dr., Bail.	40	EE13
Barony Gdns., Bail.	40	EE13
Barony Dr.		
Barr Cres., Clyde.	5	L5
Barr Pl., Pais.	46	J14
Barr St. G20	21	V10
Barra Av., Renf.	31	M11
Barra Cres., Old K.	4	J5
Barra Gdns., Old K.	4	J5
Barra Rd.		
Barra St. G20	20	T8
Barra St., Old K.	4	J5
Barrachnie Ct., Bail.	39	DD13
Barrachnie Cres.		
Barrachnie Cres., Bail.	39	DD13
Barrachnie Rd., Bail.	39	DD13

Name		Grid	Name		Grid	Name		Grid
Barrack St. G4	36	X13	Beeches Av., Clyde.	4	K5	Ben Ledi Av., Pais.	47	M15
Barrhead Rd. G43	48	N16	Beeches Rd., Clyde.	4	K5	Ben Lui Dr., Pais.	47	M15
Barrhead Rd., Pais.	47	L14	Beeches Ter., Clyde.	4	K5	Ben,More Dr., Pais.	47	M15
Barrie Quad., Clyde.	5	L6	Beechgrove St. G40	53	Y15	Ben Nevis Rd., Pais.	47	M15
Barrie Rd. G52	32	P12	Beechlands Av., Giff.	63	U19	Ben Venue Way, Pais.	47	M15
Barrington Dr. G4	35	U11	Beechmount Cotts. G14	18	N9	Ben Wyvis Dr., Pais.	47	M15
Barrisdale Rd. G20	20	T8	*Dumbarton Rd.*			Benalder St. G11	34	T11
Barrisdale Way G73	65	Y18	Beechmount Rd., Lenz.	13	CC6	Benarty Gdns., Bish.	11	Y7
Barrland Dr., Giff.	62	T18	Beechwood Av. G11	19	R10	Bencroft Dr. G44	64	X17
Barrland St. G41	51	V14	*Beechwood Dr.*			Bengairn St. G31	37	Z12
Barrochan Rd., John.	43	D14	Beechwood Av. G73	65	Z17	Bengal Pl. G43	50	T16
Barrowfield St. G40	37	Y13	Beechwood Ct., Bear.	7	R6	*Christian St.*		
Barrwood St. G33	38	AA11	Beechwood Dr. G11	19	R10	Bengal St. G43	50	T16
Barscube Ter., Pais.	47	L14	Beechwood Dr., Renf.	31	L11	Benhar Pl. G33	38	AA12
Barshaw Dr., Pais.	31	L13	Beechwood Gro., Barr.	59	M19	Benholme St. G32	54	AA14
Barshaw Pl., Pais.	31	M13	*Arthurlie Av.*			Benhope Av., Pais.	47	M15
Barshaw Rd. G52	32	N13	Beechwood La., Bear.	7	R6	Benlawers Dr., Pais.	47	M15
Barterholm Rd., Pais.	46	K15	*Beechwood Ct.*			Benloyal Av., Pais.	47	M15
Bartholomew St. G40	53	Y14	Beechwood Pl. G11	19	R10	Benmore St. G21	22	X9
Bartiebeith Rd. G33	39	DD12	*Beechwood Dr.*			Bennan Sq. G42	52	W15
Basset Av. G13	18	P8	Beechwood Rd., Cumb.	70	NN3	Benston Pl., John.	43	D15
Basset Cres. G13	18	P8	Beil Dr. G13	18	N8	Benston Rd., John.	43	D15
Bath La. G2	35	V12	Beith Rd., John.	42	B16	Bentall St. G5	52	W14
Blythswood St.			Beith St. G11	34	S11	Bentinck St. G3	35	U11
Bath La. W. G3	35	U12	Belgrave La. G12	21	U10	Bents Rd., Bail.	40	EE13
North St.			*Belgrave Ter.*			Benvane Av., Pais.	47	M15
Bath St. G2	35	V12	Belgrave Ter. G12	21	U10	Benvie Gdns., Bish.	11	Y7
Bathgate St. G31	37	Y13	Belhaven Cres. La. G12	20	T10	Benview St. G20	21	U10
Bathgo Av., Pais.	48	N14	*Lorraine Rd.*			Benview Ter., Pais.	47	L15
Batson St. G42	51	V15	Belhaven Ter. G12	20	T10	Berelands Cres. G73	52	X16
Battle Pl. G41	51	U16	Belhaven Ter. W. G12	20	T10	Berelands Pl. G73	52	X16
Battleburn St. G32	54	BB14	Bell St. G1	36	W13	Beresford Av. G14	19	R10
Battlefield Av. G42	51	V16	Bell St., Clyde.	17	M8	Berkeley St. G3	35	U12
Battlefield Cres. G42	51	V16	Bell St., Renf.	17	M10	Berkeley Ter. La. G3	35	U11
Battlefield Gdns.			Bellahouston Dr. G52	49	R14	*Elderslie St.*		
Battlefield Gdns. G42	51	V16	Bellahouston La. G52	49	R14	Berkley Dr., Blan.	68	FF19
Battlefield Rd. G42	51	V16	Bellairs Pl., Blan.	68	FF19	Bernard Path G40	53	Y14
Bavelaw St. G33	39	CC11	Belleisle Av., Udd.	57	GG16	Bernard St. G40	53	Y14
Bayfield Av. G15	6	P6	Belleisle St. G42	51	V15	Bernard Ter. G40	53	Y14
Bayfield Ter. G15	6	P6	Bellevue Pl. G21	36	X11	Berneray St. G22	22	W8
Beaconsfield Rd. G12	20	S9	Bellfield Cres., Barr.	59	L18	Berridale Av. G44	63	V17
Beard Cres., Gart.	27	GG9	Bellfield St. G31	37	Y13	Berriedale Av., Bail.	56	EE14
Beardmore Cotts., Renf.	16	K9	Bellfield St., Barr.	59	L18	Berryburn Rd. G21	23	Z10
Beardmore St., Dalm.	4	J6	Bellflower Gdns. G53	61	Q18	Berryhill Dr., Giff.	62	S19
Beardmore Way, Dalm.	4	J6	Bellgrove St. G31	36	X13	Berryhill Rd., Cumb.	70	NN3
Bearford Dr. G52	32	P13	Bellrock Cres. G33	38	BB12	Berryhill Rd., Giff.	62	S19
Bearsden Rd. G13	19	R8	Bellrock St. G33	38	BB12	Berryknowes Av. G52	33	Q13
Beaton Rd. G41	51	U15	Bellscroft Av. G73	52	X16	Berryknowes La. G52	33	Q13
Beattock St. G31	37	Z13	Bellshaugh Gdns. G12	20	T9	Berryknowes Rd. G52	49	Q14
Beaufort Av. G43	62	T17	Bellshaugh La. G12	20	T9	Berryknowes Rd., Chr.	26	FF8
Beaufort Gdns., Bish.	10	X7	Bellshaugh Pl. G12	20	T9	Bertram St. G41	51	U15
Beauly Dr., Pais.	45	G15	Bellshaugh Rd. G12	20	T9	Bertrohill Ter. G33	39	CC12
Beauly Pl. G20	20	T9	Bellshill Rd., Both.	69	HH19	*Stepps Rd.*		
Beauly Pl., Bish.	11	Z7	Bellshill Rd., Udd.	69	GG17	Bervie St. G51	33	R13
Beauly Pl., Chr.	14	FF7	Belltrees Cres., Pais.	45	H14	Berwick Cres., Linw.	28	E12
Beauly Rd., Bail.	56	EE14	Bellwood St. G41	51	U16	Berwick Dr. G52	48	P14
Beaumont Gate G12	34	T11	Belmar Ct., Linw.	28	F13	Berwick Dr. G73	53	Z16
Bedale Rd., Bail.	55	DD14	Belmont Av., Udd.	57	GG16	Betula Dr., Dalm.	5	L5
Bedford Av., Clyde.	5	M7	Belmont Cres. G12	21	U10	Bevan Gro., John.	43	C16
Onslow Rd.			Belmont Dr. G73	53	Y16	Beverley Rd. G43	62	T17
Bedford La. G5	35	V13	Belmont Dr., Barr.	59	M19	Bevin Av., Clyde.	5	M7
Bedford Row G5	35	V13	Belmont Dr., Giff.	62	S18	Bideford Cres. G32	55	CC14
Dunmore St.			Belmont La. G12	20	T10	Biggar Pl. G31	37	Y13
Bedford St. G5	35	V13	*Great Western Rd.*			Biggar St. G31	37	Y13
Bedlay Ct., Chr.	15	HH6	Belmont Rd. G21	22	X9	Bigton St. G33	38	BB11
Bedlay St. G21	22	X10	Belmont Rd. G72	66	AA18	Bilbao St. G5	52	W14
Mollinsburn St.			Belmont Rd., Pais.	31	L13	Bilsland Dr. G20	21	V9
Bedlay St. G21	22	X10	Belmont St. G12	21	U10	*Bilsland Dr.*		
Petershill Rd.			Belmont St., Clyde.	17	L8	Bilsland Dr. G20	21	U9
Bedlay Wk., Chr.	15	HH6	Belses Dr. G52	33	Q13	Binend Rd. G53	49	Q16
Beech Av. G41	50	S14	Belstane Pl., Udd.	69	HH18	Binnie Pl. G40	36	X13
Beech Av. G72	66	AA17	*Appledore Cres.*			Binniehill Rd., Cumb.	70	MM2
Beech Av. G73	65	Z18	Belsyde Av. G15	6	P7	Binns Rd. G33	39	CC11
Beech Av., Bail.	40	EE13	Beltane St. G3	35	U12	Birch Cres., John.	44	E15
Beech Av., John.	44	F15	Beltrees Av. G53	48	P15	Birch Dr., Lenz.	13	CC5
Beech Av., Pais.	47	L15	Beltrees Cres. G53	48	P15	Birch Gro., Udd.	57	HH16
Beech Dr., Dalm.	5	L5	Beltrees Rd. G53	48	P15	*Burnhead St.*		
Beech Gdns., Bail.	40	EE13	Belvidere Cres., Bish.	11	Y6	Birch Knowle, Bish.	23	Y8
Beech Gro., Barr.	59	M19	Bemersyde, Bish.	11	Z7	Birch Rd., Dalm.	5	L5
Arthurlie Av.			Bemersyde Av. G43	62	S17	Birch Vw., Bear.	8	S5
Beech Pl., Bish.	23	Y8	Bemersyde Rd. G78	45	G16	Birchfield Dr. G14	18	P10
Beech Rd., Bish.	23	Y8	Ben Alder Dr., Pais.	47	M15	Birchlea Dr., Giff.	62	T18
Beech Rd., John.	43	C15	Ben Buie Way, Pais.	47	M15	Birchwood Av. G32	55	DD14
Beech Rd., Lenz.	13	CC5	Ben Lawers Dr., Cumb.	70	MM3	Birchwood Dr., Pais.	45	H15
Beechcroft Pl., Blan.	69	GG19	*Balloch Rd.*			Birchwood Pl. G32	55	DD14

Street	No.	Grid
Birdston Rd. G21	23	Z9
Birgidale Av. G45	64	W19
Birgidale Rd. G45	64	W19
Birgidale Ter. G45	64	W19
Birkdale Ct., Both.	69	GG19
Birken Rd., Lenz.	13	DD6
Birkenshaw St. G31	37	Y12
Birkenshaw Way, Pais.	30	K12
Abbotsburn Way		
Birkhall Av. G52	48	N14
Birkhall Av., Renf.	16	J8
Birkhall Dr., Bear.	7	R7
Birkhill Av., Bish.	11	Y6
Birkhill Gdns., Bish.	11	Z6
Birkmyre Rd. G51	33	R13
Birks Rd., Renf.	31	L11
Tower Dr.		
Birkwood St. G40	53	Y15
Birmingham Rd., Renf.	31	L11
Birnam Av., Bish.	11	Y6
Birnam Cres., Bear.	8	S5
Birnam Gdns., Bish.	11	Y7
Birnam Rd. G31	53	Z14
Birness Dr. G43	50	T16
Birness St. G43	50	T16
Birnie Ct. G21	23	Z10
Birnie Rd. G21	23	Z10
Birnock Av., Renf.	32	N11
Birsay Rd. G22	21	V8
Bishop Gdns., Bish.	10	X7
Bishop St. G2	35	V12
Bishopmill Pl. G21	23	Z10
Bishopmill Rd. G21	23	Z10
Bisset Cres., Clyde.	4	K5
Black St. G4	36	W11
Blackburn Sq., Barr.	59	M19
Blackburn St. G51	34	T13
Blackbyres Rd., Barr.	59	M17
Blackcraig Av. G15	6	P6
Blackcroft Gdns. G32	55	CC14
Blackcroft Rd. G32	55	CC14
Blackfaulds Rd. G73	52	X16
Blackford Cres. G32	55	CC14
Blackford Pl. G32	55	CC14
Blackford Rd., Pais.	47	L14
Blackfriars St. G1	36	W12
Blackhall La., Pais.	46	K14
Blackhall St., Pais.	46	K14
Blackhill Cotts. G23	9	V7
Blackhill Pl. G33	37	Z11
Blackhill Rd. G23	8	T7
Blackie St. G3	34	T11
Blacklands Pl., Lenz.	13	DD6
Blacklaw La., Pais.	30	K13
Blackstone Av. G53	49	Q16
Blackstone Cres. G53	49	Q15
Blackstone Rd., Candren	29	G12
Blackstoun Av., Linw.	28	E13
Blackstoun Oval, Pais.	29	H13
Blackstoun Rd., Pais.	29	H13
Blackthorn Av., Lenz.	12	BB5
Blackthorn Gro., Lenz.	12	BB5
Blackthorn Rd., Cumb.	71	QQ2
Blackthorn St. G22	22	X9
Blackwood Av., Linw.	28	E13
Blackwood St. G13	19	R8
Blackwood St., Barr.	59	L19
Blackwoods Cres., Chr.	15	GG7
Blacurvie Rd. G34	40	EE11
Bladda La., Pais.	46	K14
Blades Ct., Gart.	27	HH9
Bladnoch Dr. G15	7	Q7
Moraine Av.		
Blaeloch Av. G45	64	W19
Blaeloch Dr. G45	64	W19
Blaeloch Ter. G45	64	W19
Blair Cres., Bail.	56	EE14
Blair Rd., Pais.	32	N13
Blair St. G32	38	AA13
Blairatholl Av. G11	20	S10
Blairatholl Gdns. G11	20	S10
Blairbeth Dr. G44	51	V16
Blairbeth Rd. G73	65	Y17
Blairbeth Ter. G73	65	Y18
Blairdardie Rd. G15	6	P7
Blairdenan Av., Chr.	15	HH6
Blairdenon Dr., Cumb.	70	MM2
Blairgowrie Rd. G52	49	Q14
Blairhall Av. G41	51	U16
Blairhill Av., Chr.	14	EE5
Blairlogie St. G33	38	BB11
Blairston Av., Both.	69	HH19
Blairston Gdns., Both.	69	HH19
Blairston Av.		
Blairtum Dr. G73	65	Y17
Blairtummock Rd. G32	39	CC12
Blake Rd., Cumb.	71	PP3
Blane St. G4	36	W11
Blantyre Fm. Rd., Blan.	68	FF19
Blantyre Mill Rd., Both.	69	GG19
Blantyre Rd., Both.	69	HH19
Blantyre St. G3	34	T11
Blaven Ct., Bail.	56	FF14
Bracadale Rd.		
Blawarthill St. G14	18	N9
Blenheim Av. G33	25	CC9
Blenheim Ct. G33	25	DD9
Blenheim Av.		
Blenheim La. G33	25	DD9
Blesdale Ct., Clyde.	5	L7
Blochairn Rd. G21	37	Y11
Bluebell Gdns. G45	65	Y19
Bluevale St. G31	37	Y13
Blyth Pl. G32	39	CC13
Blyth Rd. G33	39	DD13
Blythswood Av., Renf.	17	M10
Blythswood Ct. G2	35	V12
Cadogan St.		
Blythswood Dr., Pais.	30	K13
Blythswood Rd., Renf.	17	M9
Blythswood Sq. G2	35	V12
Blythswood St. G2	35	V12
Boclair Av., Bear.	7	R6
Boclair Cres., Bear.	8	S6
Boclair Cres., Bish.	11	Y7
Boclair Rd., Bear.	8	S6
Boclair Rd., Bish.	11	Y7
Boclair St. G13	19	R8
Boden St. G40	53	Y14
Bodmin Gdns., Chr.	15	GG6
Gartferry Rd.		
Bogany Ter. G45	64	X19
Bogbain Rd. G34	40	EE12
Boggknowe, Udd.	56	FF16
Old Edinburgh Rd.		
Boghall Rd., Udd.	56	EE15
Boghall St. G33	38	BB11
Boghead Rd. G21	23	Y10
Boghead Rd., Lenz.	12	BB6
Bogleshole Rd. G72	54	AA16
Bogmoor Rd. G51	33	Q12
Bogside Pl., Bail.	40	FF12
Whamflet Av.		
Bogside Rd. G33	24	BB9
Bogside St. G40	53	Y14
Bogton Av. G44	63	U18
Bogton Av. La. G44	63	U18
Bogton Av.		
Boleyn Rd. G41	51	U15
Bolivar Ter. G42	52	W16
Bolton Dr. G42	51	V16
Bon Accord St., Clyde.	17	L8
Bonawe St. G20	21	U10
Boness St. G40	53	Y14
Bonhill St. G22	21	V10
Bonnar St. G40	53	Y14
Bonnaughton Rd., Bear.	6	P5
Bonnyholm Av. G53	48	P14
Bonnyrigg Dr. G43	62	S17
Bonyton Av. G13	18	N9
Boon Dr. G15	6	P7
Boquhanran Pl., Clyde.	5	L6
Albert Rd.		
Boquhanran Rd., Clyde.	4	K7
Borden La. G13	19	R9
Borden Rd. G13	19	R9
Boreland Dr. G13	18	P8
Boreland Pl. G13	18	P9
Borgie Cres. G72	66	BB17
Borland Rd., Bear.	8	S6
Borron St. G4	22	W10
Borthwick St. G33	38	BB11
Boswell Sq. G52	32	N12
Botanic Cres. G20	20	T10
Bothlyn Cres., Gart.	27	GG8
Bothlyn Dr. G33	25	CC9
Bothlynn Rd., Chr.	26	FF8
Bothwell La. G2	35	V12
West Campbell St.		
Bothwell Pk. Rd. G71	69	HH19
Bothwell Rd., Udd.	69	GG17
Bothwell St. G2	35	V12
Bothwell St. G72	66	AA17
Bothwell Ter. G12	35	U11
Bank St.		
Bothwick Way, Pais.	45	G16
Crosbie Dr.		
Boundary Rd. G73	52	X15
Bourne Ct., Renf.	16	J8
Bourne Cres., Renf.	16	J8
Bourock Sq., Barr.	60	N19
Bourtree Dr. G73	65	Z18
Bouverie St. G14	18	N9
Bouverie St. G73	52	X16
Bowden Dr. G52	32	P13
Bower St. G12	21	U10
Bowerwalls St., Barr.	60	N18
Bowes Cres., Bail.	55	DD14
Bowfield Av. G52	32	N13
Bowfield Cres. G52	32	N13
Bowfield Dr. G52	32	N13
Bowfield Pl. G52	32	N13
Bowfield Ter. G52	32	N13
Bowfield Cres.		
Bowhouse Way G73	65	Y18
Bowling Grn. La. G14	19	Q10
Westland Dr.		
Bowling Grn. Rd. G14	19	Q10
Bowling Grn. Rd. G32	55	CC14
Bowling Grn. Rd. G44	63	V17
Bowling Grn. Rd., Chr.	26	FF8
Bowman St. G42	51	V15
Bowmont Gdns. G12	20	T10
Bowmont Hill, Bish.	11	Y6
Bowmont Ter. G12	20	T10
Bowmore Gdns. G73	66	AA18
Bowmore Gdns., Udd.	57	GG16
Bowmore Rd. G52	33	R13
Boyd St. G42	51	V15
Boydstone Pl. G46	61	R17
Boydstone Rd. G43	61	R17
Boyle St., Clyde.	17	M8
Boyleston Rd., Barr.	59	L18
Boyndie Path G34	40	EE12
Boyndie St. G34	40	EE12
Brabloch Cres., Pais.	30	K13
Bracadale Dr., Bail.	56	FF14
Bracadale Gdns., Bail.	56	FF14
Bracadale Gro., Bail.	56	FF14
Bracadale Rd., Bail.	56	FF14
Bracken St. G22	21	V9
Bracken Ter., Udd.	69	HH18
Brackenbrae Av., Bish.	10	X7
Brackenbrae Rd., Bish.	10	X7
Brackenrig Rd. G46	61	R19
Brackla Av. G13	18	N8
Bracora Pl. G20	20	T9
Glenfinnan Dr.		
Bradan Av. G13	18	N8
Bradda Av. G73	65	Z18
Bradfield Av. G12	20	T9
Braeface Rd., Cumb.	70	NN3
Braefield Dr., Thorn.	62	S18
Braefoot Cres., Pais.	46	K16
Braehead Rd., Cumb.	71	PP2
Braehead Rd., Pais.	58	J17
Braehead St. G5	52	W14
Braemar Av., Dalm.	4	K6
Braemar Cres., Bear.	7	R7
Braemar Dr., John.	44	E15
Braemar Rd. G73	66	AA18
Braemar Rd., Renf.	16	J9

Street	No.	Ref.
Braemar St. G42	51	U16
Braemar Vw., Dalm.	4	K5
Braemount Av., Pais.	58	J17
Braes Av., Clyde.	17	M8
Braeside Av. G73	53	Z16
Braeside Av., Chr.	15	GG7
Braeside Cres., Bail.	41	GG13
Braeside Cres., Barr.	60	N19
Braeside Dr., Barr.	59	M19
Braeside Pl. G72	66	BB18
Braeside St. G20	21	U10
Braeview Av., Pais.	45	H16
Braeview Dr., Pais.	45	H16
Braeview Gdns., Pais.	45	H16
Braeview Rd., Pais.	45	H16
Braid Sq. G4	35	V11
Braid St. G4	35	V11
Braidbar Fm. Rd., Giff.	62	T18
Braidbar Rd., Giff.	62	T18
Braidcraft Rd. G53	49	Q15
Braidfauld Gdns. G32	54	AA14
Braidfauld Pl. G32	54	AA15
Braidfauld St. G32	54	AA15
Braidfield Rd., Clyde.	5	L5
Braidholm Cres., Giff.	62	T18
Braidholm Rd., Giff.	62	T18
Braidpark Cres., Giff.	62	T18
Braidpark Dr., Giff.	62	T18
Braids Rd., Pais.	46	K15
Bramley Pl., Lenz.	13	DD6
Branchock Av. G72	67	CC18
Brand St. G51	34	T13
Brandon Gdns. G72	66	AA17
Brandon St. G31	36	X13
Branscroft G78	42	B14
Brassey St. G20	21	U9
Breadalbane Gdns. G73	65	Z18
Breadalbane St. G3	35	U12
Brech Av., Bail.	41	GG13
Brechin Rd., Bish.	11	Z7
Brechin St. G3	35	U12
Breck Av. G78	44	F16
Brediland Rd., Linw.	28	E13
Brediland Rd., Pais.	45	G15
Bredisholm Dr., Bail.	56	FF14
Bredisholm Rd., Bail.	57	GG14
Bredisholm Ter., Bail.	56	FF14
Brenfield Av. G44	63	U18
Brenfield Dr. G44	63	U18
Brentwood Av. G53	60	P18
Brentwood Dr. G53	60	P18
Brentwood Sq. G53	60	P18
Brentwood Dr.		
Brereton St. G42	52	W15
Bressey Rd. G33	39	DD13
Brewery St., John.	43	D14
Brewster Av., Pais.	31	L12
Briar Dr., Clyde.	5	L6
Briar Neuk, Bish.	23	Y8
Briar Rd. G43	62	T17
Briarlea Dr., Giff.	62	T18
Briarwood Ct. G32	55	DD15
Briarwood Gdns. G32	55	DD15
Woodend Rd.		
Brick La., Pais.	30	K13
Bridge of Weir Rd., Linw.	28	E13
Bridge St. G72	66	BB17
Bridge St., Dalm.	4	K6
Bridge St., Linw.	28	F13
Bridge St., Pais.	46	K14
Bridgebar St., Barr.	60	N18
Bridgeburn Dr., Chr.	15	GG7
Bridgegate G1	36	W13
Bridgend Rd. G53	49	Q16
Bridgeton Cross G40	36	X13
Brigham Pl. G23	21	U8
Broughton Rd.		
Brighton Pl. G51	34	S13
Brighton St. G51	34	S13
Brightside Av., Udd.	69	HH17
Brisbane Ct., Giff.	62	T18
Braidpark Dr.		
Brisbane St. G42	51	V16
Brisbane St., Dalm.	4	J6
Britannia Way, Clyde.	5	L7
Britannia Way, Renf.	31	M11
Briton St. G51	34	S13
Broad Pl. G40	36	X13
Broad St.		
Broad St. G40	36	X13
Broadford St. G4	36	W11
Harvey St.		
Broadholm St. G22	21	V9
Broadleys Av., Bish.	10	X6
Broadlie Dr. G13	18	P9
Broadloan, Renf.	31	M11
Broadwood Dr. G44	63	V17
Brock Oval G53	61	Q17
Brock Pl. G53	49	Q16
Brock Rd. G53	49	Q16
Brock Ter. G53	61	Q17
Brock Way G67	71	PP3
North Carbrain Rd.		
Brockburn Rd. G53	48	P15
Brockburn Ter. G53	49	Q16
Brockville St. G32	38	AA13
Brodick Sq. G64	23	Y8
Brodick St. G21	37	Y11
Brodie Pk. Av., Pais.	46	K15
Brodie Pk. Gdns., Pais.	46	K15
Brodie Pl., Renf.	31	L11
Brodie Rd. G21	23	Z8
Brogknowe, Udd.	56	FF16
Glasgow Rd.		
Brook St. G40	36	X13
Brooklands Av., Udd.	57	GG16
Brooklea Dr., Giff.	62	T17
Brookside St. G40	37	Y13
Broom Cres., Barr.	59	L17
Broom Dr., Clyde.	5	L6
Broom Gdns., Lenz.	12	BB5
Broom Path, Bail.	55	DD14
Tudor St.		
Broom Rd. G43	62	T17
Broom Rd. G67	71	QQ1
Broom Ter., John.	44	E15
Broomdyke Way, Pais.	30	J12
Broomfield Av. G21	23	Y10
Broomfield Rd.		
Broomfield Av. G72	53	Z16
Broomfield Pl. G21	22	X9
Broomfield Rd.		
Broomfield Rd. G21	22	X9
Broomfield Ter., Udd.	57	GG15
Broomhill Av. G11	33	R11
Broomhill Av. G32	54	BB16
Broomhill Cres. G11	19	R10
Broomhill Dr. G11	19	R10
Broomhill Dr. G73	65	Y17
Broomhill Gdns. G11	19	R10
Broomhill La. G11	19	R10
Broomhill Path G11	33	R11
Broomhill Pl. G11	19	R10
Broomhill Rd. G11	33	R11
Broomhill Ter. G11	33	R11
Broomieknowe Dr. G73	65	Y17
Broomieknowe Rd. G73	65	Y17
Broomielaw G1	35	V13
Broomknowe, Cumb.	70	MM2
Broomknowe Pl. G66	13	DD6
Broomknowes Rd. G21	23	Y10
Broomlands Av., Renf.	16	J8
Broomlands Cres., Renf.	16	J8
Broomlands Gdns., Renf.	16	J8
Broomlands Rd., Cumb.	71	PP4
Broomlands St., Pais.	46	J14
Broomlands Way, Renf.	16	K8
Broomlea Cres., Renf.	16	J8
Broomley Dr. G46	62	T19
Broomley La., Giff.	62	T19
Broomloan Ct. G51	34	S13
Broomloan Pl. G51	34	S13
Broomloan Rd. G51	34	S13
Broompark Circ. G31	36	X12
Broompark Dr. G31	36	X12
Broompark Dr., Renf.	16	J8
Broompark St. G31	36	X12
Broomton Rd. G21	23	Z8
Broomward Dr., John.	44	E14
Brora Dr., Bear.	8	S6
Brora Dr., Giff.	62	T19
Brora Dr., Renf.	18	N10
Brora Gdns., Bish.	11	Y7
Brora La. G31	37	Z11
Brora St.		
Brora Rd., Bish.	11	Y7
Brora St. G33	37	Z11
Broughton Dr. G23	21	U8
Broughton Gdns. G23	9	U7
Broughton Rd. G23	21	U8
Brown Av., Clyde.	17	M8
Brown Pl. G72	66	BB17
Allison Dr.		
Brown Rd., Cumb.	70	NN3
Brown St. G2	35	V12
Brown St., Pais.	30	J13
Brown St., Renf.	31	L11
Brownhill Rd. G43	62	S18
Brownlie St. G42	51	V16
Browns La., Pais.	46	K14
Brownsdale Rd. G73	52	X16
Brownside Av. G72	66	AA17
Brownside Av., Barr.	59	L17
Brownside Av., Pais.	46	J16
Brownside Cres., Barr.	59	L17
Brownside Dr. G13	18	N9
Brownside Dr., Barr.	59	L17
Brownside Gro., Barr.	59	L17
Brownside Rd. G72	65	Z17
Brownside Rd. G73	65	Z17
Bruce Av., John.	43	D16
Bruce Av., Pais.	31	L12
Bruce Rd. G41	51	U14
Bruce Rd., Pais.	31	L13
Bruce Rd., Renf.	31	L11
Bruce St., Clyde.	5	L7
Bruce Ter., Blan.	69	GG19
Brucefield Pl. G34	40	FF12
Brunstane Rd. G34	40	EE11
Brunswick Ho., Dalm.	4	J5
Perth Cres.		
Brunswick St. G1	36	W12
Brunton St. G44	63	V17
Brunton Ter. G44	63	U18
Bruntsfield Av. G53	60	P18
Bruntsfield Gdns. G53	60	P18
Bruntsfield Av.		
Brydson Pl., Linw.	28	E13
Fulwood Av.		
Buccleuch Av. G52	32	N12
Buccleuch La. G3	35	V11
Scott St.		
Buccleuch St. G3	35	V11
Buchan St. G5	35	V13
Norfolk St.		
Buchan Ter. G72	66	AA18
Buchanan Cres. G64	23	Z8
Buchanan Dr. G64	23	Z8
Buchanan Dr. G72	66	AA17
Buchanan Dr. G73	65	Y17
Buchanan Dr., Bear.	8	S6
Buchanan Dr., Bish.	23	Z8
Buchanan Dr., Lenz.	13	CC6
Buchanan Gdns. G32	55	DD15
Buchanan St. G1	35	V12
Buchanan St., Bail.	56	EE14
Buchanan St., John.	43	D15
Buchlyvie Gdns., Bish.	22	X8
Hillcroft Ter.		
Buchlyvie Path G34	40	EE12
Buchlyvie Rd., Pais.	32	N13
Buchlyvie St. G34	40	EE12
Buckingham Bldgs. G12	20	T10
Great Western Rd.		
Buckingham Dr. G32	54	BB16
Buckingham Dr. G73	53	Z16
Buckingham St. G12	20	T10
Buckingham Ter. G12	20	T10
Great Western Rd.		
Bucklaw Gdns. G52	49	Q14
Bucklaw Pl. G52	49	Q14·
Bucklaw Ter. G52	49	Q14
Buckley St. G22	22	W9
Bucksburn Rd. G21	23	Z10

Street	Page	Ref
Buckthorne Pl. G53	60	P18
Buddon St. G40	53	Z14
Budhill Av. G32	38	BB13
Bulldale St. G14	18	N9
Bullionslaw Dr. G73	65	Z17
Bulloch Av., Giff.	62	T19
Bullwood Av. G53	48	N15
Bullwood Ct. G53	48	N15
Bullwood Dr. G53	48	N15
Bullwood Gdns. G53	48	N15
Bullwood Pl. G53	48	N15
Bunessan St. G52	33	R13
Bunhouse Rd. G3	34	T11
Burgh Hall La. G11	34	S11
Fortrose St.		
Burgh Hall St. G11	34	S11
Burgh La. G12	20	T10
Vinicombe St.		
Burghead Dr. G51	33	R12
Burghead Pl. G51	33	R12
Burgher St. G31	37	Z13
Burleigh Rd., Udd.	69	HH18
Burleigh St. G51	34	S12
Burlington Av. G12	20	S9
Burmola St. G22	21	V10
Burmouth Rd. G33	39	DD13
Burn Gdns., Blan.	68	FF19
Burn Ter. G72	54	AA16
Burn Vw., Cumb.	71	QQ2
Burnacre Gdns., Udd.	57	GG16
Burnbank Dr., Barr.	59	M19
Burnbank Gdns. G20	35	U11
Burnbank Pl. G4	36	X12
Drygate		
Burnbank Ter. G20	35	U11
Burnbrae, Clyde.	5	L5
Burnbrae Av., Chr.	15	HH7
Burnbrae Av., Linw.	28	F13
Bridge St.		
Burnbrae Ct., Lenz.	13	CC6
Auchinloch Rd.		
Burnbrae Dr. G73	65	Z17
East Kilbride Rd.		
Burnbrae Rd., John.	44	F14
Burnbrae Rd., Lenz.	13	DD7
Burnbrae St. G21	23	Y10
Burncleuch Av. G72	66	BB18
Burncrooks Ct., Clyde.	4	K5
Burndyke Ct. G51	34	T12
Burndyke Sq. G51	34	T12
Burndyke St. G51	34	S12
Burnett Rd. G33	39	DD12
Burnfield Av., Giff.	62	S18
Burnfield Cotts., Giff.	62	S18
Burnfield Dr. G43	62	S18
Burnfield Gdns., Giff.	62	T18
Burnfield Rd.		
Burnfield Rd., Giff.	62	S17
Burnfoot Cres. G73	65	Z17
Burnfoot Cres., Pais.	46	J16
Burnfoot Dr. G52	32	P13
Burngreen Ter., Cumb.	71	PP1
Burnham Rd. G14	18	P10
Burnham Ter. G14	18	P10
Burnham Rd.		
Burnhead Rd. G43	63	U17
Burnhead Rd., Cumb.	70	MM3
Burnhead St., Udd.	57	HH16
Burnhill Quad. G73	52	X16
Burnhill St. G73	52	X16
Burnhouse St. G20	20	T9
Burnmouth Ct. G33	39	DD13
Pendeen Rd.		
Burnpark Av., Udd.	56	FF16
Burns Dr., John.	43	D16
Burns Gro., Thorn.	62	S19
Burns Rd., Cumb.	71	PP3
Burns St. G4	35	V11
Burns St., Dalm.	4	K6
Burnside Av., Barr.	59	L18
Burnside Ct., Dalm.	4	K6
Scott St.		
Burnside Gdns., Kilb.	42	B15
Burnside Gate G73	65	Z17
Burnside Rd. G73	65	Z17
Burnside Rd., John.	44	F15
Burnside Ter. G72	67	DD18
Burntbroom Dr., Bail.	55	DD14
Burntbroom Gdns., Bail.	55	DD14
Burntbroom Rd., Udd.	55	DD14
Burntbroom St. G33	39	CC12
Burntshields Rd., Kilb.	42	A15
Burr Gdns., Bish.	11	Z7
Solway Rd.		
Burrells La. G4	36	X12
High St.		
Burrelton Rd. G43	63	U17
Burton La. G43	51	V15
Langside Rd.		
Bushes Av., Pais.	46	J15
Busheyhill St. G72	66	BB17
Bute Av., Renf.	31	M11
Bute Cres., Bear.	7	R7
Bute Cres., Pais.	46	J16
Bute Dr., John.	43	C15
Bute Gdns. G12	34	T11
Bute Gdns. G44	63	U18
Bute Rd., Pais.	30	J11
Bute Ter. G73	65	Y17
Bute Ter., Udd.	57	HH16
Butterbiggins Rd. G42	51	V14
Butterfield Pl. G41	51	U15
Pollokshaws Rd.		
Byrebush Rd. G53	49	Q15
Byres Av., Pais.	31	L13
Byres Cres.		
Byres Cres., Pais.	31	L13
Byres Rd. G11	34	T11
Byres Rd., John.	44	F15
Byron Ct., Udd.	69	HH19
Shelley Dr.		
Byron La. G11	33	R11
Sandeman St.		
Byron St. G11	33	R11
Byron St., Clyde.	4	K6
Byshot St. G22	22	W10
Cable Depot Rd., Dalm.	4	K7
Cadder Ct., Bish.	11	Y5
Cadder Gro. G20	21	U8
Cadder Rd.		
Cadder Pl. G20	21	U8
Cadder Rd. G20	21	U8
Cadder Rd., Bish.	11	Y5
Cadder Way, Bish.	11	Y5
Cadoc St. G72	66	BB17
Cadogan St. G2	35	V12
Cadzow Dr. G72	66	AA17
Cadzow St. G2	35	V12
Cadogan St.		
Caird Dr. G11	34	S11
Cairn Av., Renf.	32	N11
Cairn Dr., Linw.	28	E13
Cairn La., Pais.	30	J12
Mosslands Rd.		
Cairn St. G21	22	X9
Cairnban St. G51	33	Q13
Cairnbrook Rd. G34	40	FF12
Cairncraig St. G31	53	Z14
Cairndow Av. G44	63	U18
Cairndow Ct. G44	63	U18
Cairngorm Cres., Barr.	59	M19
Cairngorm Cres., Bear.	6	P5
Cairngorm Cres., Pais.	46	K15
Cairngorm Rd. G43	62	T17
Cairnhill Circ. G52	48	N14
Cairnhill Dr. G52	48	N14
Cairnhill Pl. G52	48	N14
Cairnhill Circ.		
Cairnhill Rd. G61	7	R7
Cairnlea Dr. G51	34	S13
Cairnmuir Rd. G72	66	AA19
Cairns Av. G72	66	BB17
Cairns Rd. G72	66	BB18
Cairnsmore Pl. G15	6	N7
Cairnsmore Rd. G15	6	N7
Cairnswell Av. G72	67	CC18
Cairnswell Pl. G72	67	CC18
Cairntoul Dr. G14	18	P9
Cairntoul Pl. G14	18	P9
Caithness St. G20	21	U10
Calcots Path G34	40	FF11
Auchengill Rd.		
Calcots Pl. G34	40	FF11
Caldarvan St. G22	21	V10
Calder Av., Barr.	59	M19
Calder Dr. G72	66	BB17
Calder Gate, Bish.	10	X6
Calder Pl., Bail.	56	EE14
Calder Rd., Pais.	29	H13
Calder Rd., Udd.	68	FF17
Calder St. G42	51	V15
Calderbank Vw., Bail.	56	FF14
Calderbraes Av., Udd.	57	GG16
Caldercuilt Rd. G20	20	T8
Caldercuilt St. G20	20	T8
Calderpark Av., Udd.	56	EE15
Calderpark Cres., Udd.	56	EE15
Caldervale, Udd.	68	FF17
Calderwood Av., Bail.	56	EE14
Calderwood Dr., Bail.	56	EE14
Calderwood Gdns., Bail.	56	EE14
Calderwood Rd. G43	62	T17
Calderwood Rd. G73	53	Z16
Caldwell Av. G13	18	P9
Caldwell Av., Linw.	28	E13
Caledon La. G12	34	T11
Highburgh Rd.		
Caledon St. G12	34	T11
Caledonia Av. G5	52	W14
Caledonia Av. G73	53	Y16
Caledonia Dr., Bail.	56	EE14
Caledonia Rd. G5	52	W14
Caledonia Rd., Bail.	56	EE14
Caledonia St. G5	52	W14
Caledonia St., Dalm.	4	K7
Caledonia St., Pais.	30	J13
Caledonia Way W., Pais.	30	J11
Caledonian Circuit G72	67	CC17
Caledonian Cres. G12	20	T10
Great Western Rd.		
Caledonian Cres. G12	35	U11
Caledonian Mans. G12	20	T10
Great Western Rd.		
Caledonian Pl. G72	67	DD17
Caley Brae, Udd.	69	GG17
Calfhill Rd. G53	48	P14
Calfmuir Rd., Chr.	14	EE5
Calgary St. G4	36	W11
Callander St. G20	21	V10
Callieburn Rd., Bish.	23	Y8
Cally Av. G15	6	P6
Calside, Pais.	46	K15
Calside Av., Pais.	46	J14
Calton Entry G40	36	X13
Gallowgate		
Calvay Cres. G33	39	CC12
Calvay Pl. G33	39	DD13
Calvay Rd. G33	39	CC12
Cambourne Rd., Chr.	15	GG6
Cambridge Av., Clyde.	5	L6
Cambridge Dr. G20	20	T9
Glenfinnan Dr.		
Cambridge La. G3	35	V11
Cambridge St.		
Cambridge Rd., Renf.	31	M11
Cambridge St. G3	35	V12
Camburn St. G32	38	AA13
Cambus Pl. G32	39	CC11
Cambusdoon Rd. G32	39	CC11
Cambuskenneth Gdns. G32	39	DD13
Cambuskenneth Pl. G32	39	CC11
Cambuslang Rd. G32	54	AA16
Cambuslang Rd. G72	53	Z16
Cambuslang Rd. G73	53	Y15
Cambusmore Pl. G32	39	CC11
Camden St. G5	52	W14
Camelon St. G32	38	AA13
Cameron Dr., Bear.	8	S6
Cameron Dr., Udd.	57	HH16
Cameron Sq., Clyde.	5	M5
Glasgow Rd.		

Cameron St. G20	21	V10	Cardwell St. G41	51	V14	Carrington St. G4	35	U11
Cameron St. G52	32	N12	Cardyke St. G21	23	Y10	Carroglen Gdns. G32	39	CC13
Cameron St., Clyde.	17	M8	Careston Pl., Bish.	11	Z7	Carroglen Gro. G32	39	CC13
Camlachie St. G31	37	Y13	Carfin St. G42	51	V15	Carron Ct. G72	67	CC17
Camp Rd. G73	52	X15	Carfrae St. G3	34	T12	Carron Cres. G22	22	W9
Camp Rd., Bail.	40	EE13	Cargill St. G31	54	AA14	Carron Cres. G66	13	DD6
Campbell Dr., Barr.	59	M19	Cargill St. G64	23	Y8	Carron Cres., Bear.	7	Q6
Campbell Dr., Bear.	7	Q5	Carham Cres. G52	33	Q13	Carron Cres., Bish.	11	Y7
Campbell St. G20	20	T8	Carham Dr. G52	33	Q13	Carron La., Pais.	31	L12
Campbell St., John.	43	D15	Carillon Rd. G51	34	T13	*Kilearn Rd.*		
Campbell St., Renf.	17	M10	Carisbrooke Cres., Bish.	11	Y6	Carron Pl. G22	22	X9
Camperdown St. G20	21	V10	Carlaverock Rd. G43	62	T17	Carron St. G22	22	X9
Garscube Rd.			Carleith Av., Clyde.	4	K5	Carrour Gdns., Bish.	10	X7
Camphill, Pais.	46	J14	Carleith Quad. G51	33	Q12	Carsaig Dr. G52	33	R13
Camphill Av. G41	51	U16	Carleith Ter., Clyde.	4	K5	Carse Vw. Dr., Bear.	8	S5
Camps Cres., Renf.	32	N11	*Carleith Av.*			Carsebrook Av., Chr.	14	EE5
Campsie Av., Barr.	59	M19	Carleston St. G21	22	X10	*Chryston Rd.*		
Campsie Dr., Pais.	31	L12	*Atlas Rd.*			Carsegreen Av., Pais.	45	H16
Campsie Dr., Pais.	46	J16	Carleton Dr., Giff.	62	T18	Carstairs St. G40	53	Y15
Campsie Dr., Pais.	30	K11	Carleton Gate, Giff.	62	T18	Carswell Gdns. G41	51	U15
Campsie Pl., Chr.	26	FF8	Carlibar Av. G13	18	N9	Cart St., Clyde.	17	L8
Campsie St. G21	22	X9	Carlibar Dr., Barr.	59	M18	Cartcraigs Rd. G43	62	S17
Campsie Vw., Bail.	41	GG13	Carlibar Gdns., Barr.	59	M18	Cartha Cres., Pais.	47	L14
Campsie Vw., Chr.	26	FF8	*Commercial Rd.*			Cartha St. G41	51	U16
Campsie Vw., Cumb.	71	PP2	Carlibar Rd., Barr.	59	L18	Cartside Av., John.	43	C15
Campsie Vw G33	25	CC10	Carlile La., Pais.	30	K13	Cartside Quad. G42	51	V16
Campston Pl. G33	38	BB11	*New Sneddon St.*			Cartside St. G42	51	U16
Camstradden Dr. E., Bear.	7	Q6	Carlile Pl., Pais.	30	K13	Cartside Ter., Kilb.	43	C15
Camstradden Dr. W., Bear.	7	Q6	Carlisle St. G21	22	W10	*Kilbarchan Rd.*		
Camus Pl. G15	6	N6	Carlowrie Av., Blan.	68	FF19	Cartvale La., Pais.	30	K13
Canal Av., John.	44	E14	Carlton Ct. G5	35	V13	Cartvale Rd. G42	51	U16
Canal Rd., John.	43	D15	Carlton Pl. G5	35	V13	Caskie Dr., Blan.	69	GG19
Canal St. G4	36	W11	Carlton Ter. G20	21	U10	Cassley Av., Renf.	32	N11
Canal St., Clyde.	17	L8	*Wilton St.*			Castle Av., Both.	69	GG19
Canal St., John.	44	F14	Carlyle Av. G52	32	N12	Castle Av., John.	44	E15
Canal St., Pais.	46	J14	Carlyle Rd., Pais.	30	K13	Castle Av., Udd.	69	GG17
Canal St., Renf.	17	M10	Carlyle Ter. G73	53	Y15	Castle Chimmins Av.	67	CC18
Canal Ter., Pais.	46	K14	Carmaben Rd. G33	39	DD12	G72		
Canberra Av., Dalm.	4	J6	Carment Dr. G41	50	T16	Castle Chimmins Rd.	67	CC18
Canberra Ct., Giff.	62	T18	Carment La. G41	50	T16	G72		
Braidpark Dr.			Carmichael Pl. G42	51	U16	Castle Cres. N. Ct. G1	36	W12
Cander Rigg, Bish.	11	Y6	Carmichael St. G51	34	S13	*Royal Ex. Sq.*		
Candleriggs G1	36	W13	Carmunnock Bypass	64	W19	Castle Gait, Pais.	46	K14
Candren Rd., Linw.	28	F13	G44			Castle Gdns., Chr.	15	GG7
Candren Rd., Pais.	45	H14	Carmunnock La. G44	63	V17	Castle Gate, Both.	69	GG17
Canmore Pl. G31	53	Z14	*Madison Av.*			Castle Pl., Udd.	69	GG17
Canmore St. G31	53	Z14	Carmunnock Rd. G44	51	V16	*Ferry Rd.*		
Cannich Dr., Pais.	47	L15	Carmyle Av. G32	54	BB15	Castle Rd. G78	44	F14
Canniesburn Rd., Bear.	7	Q6	Carna Dr. G44	64	W17	*Main Rd.*		
Canniesburn Sq., Bear.	7	R7	Carnarvon St. G3	35	U11	Castle Rd., John.	44	F14
Macfarlane Rd.			Carnbooth Ct. G45	64	X19	Castle Sq., Dalm.	4	K6
Canniesburn Toll, Bear.	7	R6	Carnbroe St. G20	35	V11	Castle St. G4	36	X12
Canonbie St. G34	40	FF11	Carnegie Rd. G52	32	P13	Castle St. G73	53	Y16
Canting Way G51	34	T12	Carnock Cres., Barr.	59	L19	Castle St., Bail.	56	EE14
Capelrig St. G46	61	R18	Carnock Rd. G53	49	Q16	Castle St., Dalm.	4	K6
Caplaw Rd., Pais.	58	J17	Carnoustie Ct., Both.	69	GG19	Castle St., Pais.	46	J14
Caplethill Rd., Pais.	46	K16	Carnoustie Cres., Bish.	11	Z7	Castle Vw., Clyde.	5	L6
Caprington St. G33	38	BB11	Carnoustie St. G5	35	U13	*Granville St.*		
Cara Dr. G51	33	R12	Carntyne Gdns. G32	38	AA12	Castle Way, Cumb.	71	QQ2
Caravelle Way, Renf.	31	M11	*Abbeyhill St.*			Castlebank Ct. G13	19	R9
Friendship Way			Carntyne Pl. G32	37	Z12	Castlebank Cres. G11	34	S11
Carberry Rd. G41	50	T15	Carntyne Rd. G31	37	Z13	*Meadowside St.*		
Carbeth St. G22	21	V10	Carntynehall Rd. G32	38	AA12	Castlebank Gdns. G13	19	R9
Carbisdale St. G22	22	X9	Carnwadric Rd. G46	61	R18	Castlebank St. G11	33	R11
Carbost St. G23	8	T7	Carnwath Av. G43	63	U17	Castlebank Vill. G13	19	R9
Torgyle St.			Caroline St. G31	38	AA13	Castlebay Dr. G22	10	W7
Carbrook St. G21	37	Y11	Carolside Dr. G15	6	P6	Castlebay Pl. G22	22	W8
Carbrook St., Pais.	46	J14	Carradale Gdns., Bish.	11	Z7	Castlebay St. G22	22	W8
Cardarrach St. G21	23	Y10	*Thrums Av.*			Castlecroft Gdns., Udd.	69	GG17
Cardell Dr., Pais.	45	H14	Carradale Pl., Linw.	28	E13	Castlefern Rd. G73	65	Y18
Cardell Rd., Pais.	45	H14	Carrbridge Dr. G20	20	T9	Castlehill Cres., Renf.	17	M10
Carding La. G3	35	U12	*Glenfinnan Dr.*			*Ferry Rd.*		
Argyle St.			Carriagehill Dr., Pais.	46	K15	Castlehill Rd., Bear.	6	P5
Cardonald Dr. G52	48	P14	Carrick Cres., Giff.	62	T19	Castlelaw Gdns. G32	38	BB13
Cardonald Gdns. G52	48	P14	Carrick Dr. G32	55	DD14	Castlelaw Pl. G32	38	BB13
Cardonald Pl. Rd. G52	48	P14	Carrick Dr. G73	65	Y17	Castlelaw St. G32	38	BB13
Cardow Rd. G21	23	Z10	Carrick Gro. G32	55	DD14	Castlemilk Cres. G44	64	X17
Cardowan Dr. G33	25	CC9	Carrick Rd. G73	64	X17	Castlemilk Dr. G45	64	X18
Cardowan Rd. G33	25	DD9	Carrick Rd., Bish.	11	Z7	Castlemilk Ms. G44	64	X17
Cardowan Rd. G32	38	AA13	Carrick Rd., Cumb.	71	PP2	*Castlemilk Rd.*		
Cardrona St. G33	24	BB10	Carrick St. G2	35	V12	Castlemilk Rd. G44	52	X16
Cardross Ct. G31	36	X12	Carrickarden Rd., Bear.	7	R6	Castleton Av. G21	22	X8
Cardross St. G31	36	X12	Carrickstone Vw., Cumb.	70	NN1	*Colston Rd.*		
			Carriden Pl. G33	39	DD12	Castleton Ct. G45	64	X19
						Cathay St. G22	22	W8

Street	No.	Grid
Cathcart Cres., Pais.	47	L14
Cathcart Pl. G73	52	X16
Cathcart Rd. G42	51	V16
Cathcart Rd. G73	52	X16
Cathedral Ct. G4	36	W12
Rottenrow E.		
Cathedral La. G4	36	W12
Cathedral St.		
Cathedral Sq. G4	36	X12
Cathedral St. G1	36	W12
Cathedral St. G4	36	X12
Catherine Pl. G3	35	U12
Hydepark St.		
Cathkin Av. G72	66	AA17
Cathkin Av. G73	53	Z16
Cathkin Bypass G73	65	Z18
Cathkin Ct. G45	64	X19
Cathkin Gdns., Udd.	57	GG15
Cathkin Pl. G72	66	AA17
Cathkin Rd. G42	51	U16
Cathkin Rd., E.K.	65	Y19
Cathkin Rd., Udd.	57	GG15
Cathkin Vw. G32	54	BB16
Cathkinview Rd. G42	51	V16
Catrine Av., Clyde.	5	M6
Causewayside St. G32	54	BB15
Causeyside St., Pais.	46	K14
Cavendish Pl. G5	51	V14
Cavendish St. G5	51	V14
Cavin Dr. G45	64	X18
Cavin Rd. G45	64	X18
Caxton St. G13	19	R9
Cayton Gdns., Bail.	55	DD14
Cecil Pl. G51	35	U13
Paisley Rd. W.		
Cecil St. G12	20	T10
Cedar Av. G78	44	E16
Cedar Av., Dalm.	4	J6
Cedar Ct. G20	35	V11
Cedar Ct. G78	42	B14
Cedar Dr., Lenz.	13	CC5
Cedar Gdns. G73	65	Z18
Cedar Pl., Barr.	59	M19
Cedar Pl., Blan.	68	FF19
Cedar Rd., Bish.	23	Y8
Cedar Rd., Cumb.	71	QQ2
Cedar St. G20	35	V11
Cedar Wk., Bish.	23	Y8
Cedric Pl. G13	19	Q8
Cedric Rd. G13	19	Q8
Celtic Pl. G20	20	T8
Maryhill Rd.		
Cemetery Rd. G32	39	CC13
Cemetery Rd. G52	49	Q14
Paisley Rd. W.		
Central Av. G11	33	R11
Broomhill Ter.		
Central Av. G32	55	CC14
Central Av. G72	66	AA17
Central Av., Clyde.	5	L7
Central Chambers G2	35	V12
Hope St.		
Central Path G32	55	DD14
Central Way, Cumb.	70	NN4
Central Way, Pais.	30	K13
Centre, The, Barr.	59	L19
Centre St. G5	35	V13
Ceres Gdns. G64	11	Z7
Cessnock Rd. G33	24	BB9
Cessnock St. G51	34	T13
Cessnock St., Clyde.	5	M6
Chachan Dr. G51	33	R12
Skipness Dr.		
Chalmers Ct. G40	36	X13
Chalmers Gate G40	36	X13
Claythorn St.		
Chalmers Pl. G40	36	X13
Claythorn St.		
Chalmers St. G40	36	X13
Chalmers St., Clyde.	5	L7
Chamberlain La. G13	19	R9
Chamberlain Rd. G13	19	R9
Chancellor St. G11	34	S11
Chapel Rd., Clyde.	5	L5
Chapel St. G20	21	U9
Chapel St. G73	52	X16
Chapelhill Rd., Pais.	47	L15
Chapelton Av., Bear.	7	R6
Chapelton Gdns., Bear.	7	R6
Chapelton St. G22	21	V9
Chaplet Av. G13	19	Q8
Chapman St. G42	51	V15
Allison St.		
Chappel St., Barr.	59	L18
Charing Cross G2	35	U11
Charing Cross La. G3	35	U12
Granville St.		
Charles Av., Renf.	17	M10
Charles Cres., Lenz.	13	CC6
Charles St. G21	36	X11
Charlotte La. G1	36	W13
London Rd.		
Charlotte La. S. G1	36	W13
Charlotte St.		
Charlotte Pl., Pais.	46	K15
Charlotte St. G1	36	W13
Chatelherault Av. G72	66	AA17
Chatton St. G23	8	T7
Cheapside St. G3	35	U12
Chelmsford Dr. G12	20	S9
Cherry Bk., Lenz.	12	BB5
Cherry Cres., Clyde.	5	L6
Cherry Pl., Bish.	23	Y8
Cherry Pl., John.	44	E15
Cherrybank Rd. G43	63	U17
Cherrywood Rd., John.	44	F15
Chester St. G32	38	BB13
Chesterfield Av. G12	20	S9
Chesters Pl. G73	53	Y16
Chesters Rd., Bear.	7	Q6
Chestnut Dr., Dalm.	5	L5
Chestnut Dr., Lenz.	12	BB5
Chestnut Pl., John.	44	E16
Chestnut St. G22	22	W9
Cheviot Av., Barr.	59	M19
Cheviot Rd. G43	62	T17
Cheviot Rd., Pais.	46	K16
Chirnside Pl. G52	32	P13
Chirnside Rd. G52	32	P13
Chisholm St. G1	36	W13
Christian St. G43	50	T16
Christie La., Pais.	30	K13
New Sneddon St.		
Christie Pl. G72	66	BB17
Christie St., Pais.	30	K13
Christopher St. G21	37	Y11
Chryston Rd., Chr.	26	FF8
Chryston Rd., Chr.	14	FF5
Chryston Rd., Waterside	14	EE5
Church Av. G33	25	CC9
Church Av. G73	65	Z17
Church Dr., Lenz.	13	CC5
Church Hill, Pais.	30	K13
Church La. G42	51	V15
Victoria Rd.		
Church Rd., Chr.	26	FF8
Church Rd., Giff.	62	T19
Church Rd. G11	34	T11
Church St., Bail.	56	FF14
Church St., Clyde.	5	L6
Church St., John.	43	D14
Church St., Kilb.	42	B14
Church St., Udd.	69	GG17
Church Vw. G72	54	BB16
Churchill Av., John.	43	C16
Churchill Cres., Udd.	69	HH18
Churchill Dr. G11	19	R10
Churchill Pl., Kilb.	42	B14
Churchill Way, Bish.	10	X7
Kirkintilloch Rd.		
Circus Dr. G31	36	X12
Circus Pl. G31	36	X12
Circus Pl. La. G31	36	X12
Circus Pl.		
Cityford Cres. G73	52	X16
Cityford Dr. G73	52	X16
Clachan Dr. G51	33	R12
Skipness Dr.		
Claddens Pl., Lenz.	13	DD6
Claddens Quad. G22	22	W9
Claddens St. G22	21	V9
Claddens Wynd G66	13	DD6
Claddon Vw., Clyde.	5	M6
Kirkoswald Dr.		
Clair Rd., Bish.	11	Z7
Clairmont Gdns. G3	35	U11
Clare St. G21	37	Y11
Claremont Av., Giff.	62	T19
Claremont Pl. G3	35	U11
Claremont Ter.		
Claremont St. G3	35	U12
Claremont Ter. G3	35	U11
Claremont Ter. La. G3	35	U11
Clifton St.		
Clarence Dr. G11	20	S10
Clarence Gdns. G11	20	S10
Clarence St., Clyde.	5	M6
Clarence St., Pais.	31	L13
Clarendon La. G20	35	V11
Clarendon St.		
Clarendon Pl. G20	35	V11
Clarendon St. G20	35	V11
Clarion Cres. G13	18	P8
Clarion Rd. G13	18	P8
Clark St. G41	35	U13
Tower St.		
Clark St., Dalm.	4	K6
Clark St., John.	43	D14
Clark St., Pais.	30	J13
Clark St., Renf.	17	L10
Clarkston Av. G44	63	U18
Clarkston Rd. G44	63	U19
Clathic Av., Bear.	8	S6
Claude Av. G72	67	DD18
Claude Rd., Pais.	31	L13
Claudhall Av., Gart.	27	GG8
Clavens Rd. G52	32	N13
Claverhouse Pl., Pais.	47	L14
Claverhouse Rd. G52	32	N12
Clavering St. E., Pais.	30	J13
Well St.		
Clavering St. W., Pais.	30	J13
King St.		
Clayhouse Rd. G33	25	DD9
Claypotts Pl. G33	38	BB11
Claypotts Rd. G33	38	BB11
Clayslaps Rd. G3	34	T11
Argyle St.		
Claythorn Av. G40	36	X13
Claythorn Circ. G40	36	X13
Claythorn Av.		
Claythorn Ct. G40	36	X13
Claythorn Pk.		
Claythorn Pk. G40	36	X13
Claythorn St. G40	36	X13
Claythorn Ter. G40	36	X13
Claythorn Pk.		
Clayton Ter. G31	36	X12
Cleddans Cres., Clyde.	5	M5
Cleddans Rd., Clyde.	5	M5
Cleddens Ct., Bish.	11	Y7
Cleeves Pl. G53	60	P17
Cleeves Quad. G53	60	P17
Cleeves Rd. G53	60	P17
Cleghorn St. G22	21	V10
Cleland La. G5	36	W13
Cleland St.		
Cleland St. G5	36	W13
Clelland Av., Bish.	23	Y8
Clerwood St. G32	37	Z13
Cleveden Cres. G12	20	S9
Cleveden Cres. La. G12	20	S9
Cleveden Dr.		
Cleveden Dr. G12	20	S9
Cleveden Dr. G73	65	Z17
Cleveden Gdns. G12	20	T9
Cleveden Pl. G12	20	S9
Cleveden Rd. G12	20	S9
Cleveland St. G3	35	U12
Cliff Rd. G3	35	U11
Clifford Gdns. G51	34	S13
Clifford La. G51	34	T13
Gower St.		

Street	Page	Grid
Clifford Pl. G51	34	T13
Clifford St.		
Clifford St. G51	34	S13
Clifton Pl. G3	35	U11
Clifton St.		
Clifton Rd., Giff.	62	S18
Clifton St. G3	35	U11
Clifton Ter. G72	66	AA18
Clifton Ter., John.	44	E15
Clincart Rd. G42	51	V16
Clincarthill Rd. G73	53	Y16
Clinton Av., Udd.	69	GG17
Clippens Rd., Linw.	28	E13
Cloan Av. G15	6	P7
Cloan Cres., Bish.	11	Y6
Cloberhill Rd. G13	7	Q7
Cloch St. G33	38	BB12
Clochoderick Av., Kilb.	42	B15
Mackenzie Dr.		
Clonbeith St. G33	39	DD11
Closeburn St. G22	22	W9
Cloth St., Barr.	59	M19
Clouden Rd., Cumb.	71	PP3
Cloudhowe Ter., Blan.	68	FF19
Clouston Ct. G20	21	U10
Clouston La. G20	20	T10
Clouston St.		
Clouston St. G20	20	T10
Clova Pl., Udd.	69	GG17
Clova St. G46	61	R18
Clover Av., Bish.	10	X7
Cloverbank St. G21	37	Y11
Clovergate, Bish.	10	X7
Clunie Rd. G52	49	R14
Cluny Av., Bear.	8	S7
Cluny Dr., Bear.	8	S7
Cluny Dr., Pais.	31	L13
Cluny Gdns. G14	19	R10
Cluny Gdns., Bail.	56	EE14
Cluny Vill. G14	19	Q10
Westland Dr.		
Clutha St. G51	35	U13
Paisley Rd. W.		
Clyde Av., Barr.	59	M19
Clyde Av., Both.	69	GG19
Clyde Ct., Dalm.	4	K6
Little Holm		
Clyde Pl. G5	35	V13
Clyde Pl. G72	67	CC18
Clyde Pl., John.	43	C16
Clyde Rd., Pais.	31	L12
Clyde St. G1	35	V13
Clyde St., Clyde.	17	M8
Clyde St., Renf.	17	M9
Clyde Ter., Both.	69	HH19
Clyde Vale G71	69	HH19
Clyde Vw., Pais.	47	L15
Clydebrae Dr. G71	69	HH19
Clydebrae St. G51	34	S12
Clydeford Dr. G32	54	AA14
Clydeford Dr., Udd.	56	FF16
Clydeford Rd. G72	54	BB16
Clydeholm Rd. G14	33	Q11
Clydeholm Ter., Clyde.	17	M8
Clydeneuk Dr., Udd.	56	FF16
Clydesdale Av., Pais.	31	L11
Clydeside Expressway G3	34	T11
Clydeside Expressway G14	19	Q10
Clydeside Rd. G73	52	X15
Clydesmill Dr. G32	54	BB16
Clydesmill Gro. G32	54	BB16
Clydesmill Pl. G32	54	BB16
Clydesmill Rd. G32	54	BB16
Clydeview G11	34	S11
Dumbarton Rd.		
Clydeview La. G11	33	R11
Broomhill Ter.		
Clydeview Ter. G32	55	CC16
Clydeview Ter. G40	52	X14
Newhall St.		
Clynder St. G51	34	S13
Clyth Dr., Giff.	62	T19
Coalhill St. G31	37	Y13
Coatbridge Rd., Bail.	41	GG13
Coatbridge Rd., Gart.	27	GG10
Coates Cres. G53	49	Q16
Coats Cres., Bail.	40	EE13
Coats Dr., Pais.	45	H14
Coatshill Av., Blan.	68	FF19
Cobbleriggs Way, Udd.	69	GG17
Cobinshaw St. G32	38	BB13
Cobinton Pl. G33	38	BB11
Coburg St. G5	35	V13
Cochno St., Clyde.	17	M8
Cochran St., Pais.	46	K14
Cochrane St. G1	36	W12
Cochrane St., Barr.	59	L19
Cochranemill Rd., John.	43	C15
Cockels Ln., Renf.	31	L11
Cockenzie St. G32	38	BB13
Cockmuir St. G21	23	Y10
Cogan Rd. G43	62	T17
Cogan St. G43	50	T16
Cogan St., Barr.	59	L19
Colbert St. G40	52	X14
Colbreggan Ct., Clyde.	5	M5
St. Helena Cres.		
Colbreggan Gdns., Clyde.	5	M5
Colchester Dr. G12	20	S9
Coldingham Av. G14	18	N9
Coldstream Dr. G73	65	Z17
Coldstream Dr., Pais.	45	H15
Coldstream Pl. G21	22	W10
Keppochhill Rd.		
Coldstream Rd., Clyde.	5	L7
Colebrook St. G72	66	BB17
Colebrook Ter. G12	21	U10
Colebrooke St.		
Colebrooke La. G12	21	U10
Colebrooke St.		
Colebrooke Pl. G12	21	U10
Belmont St.		
Colebrooke St. G12	21	U10
Colegrove Cres. G32	54	AA14
Coleridge, Udd.	69	HH18
Colfin St. G34	40	FF11
Colgrain St. G20	21	V9
Colinbar Circle, Barr.	59	L19
Colinslee Av., Pais.	46	K15
Colinslee Cres., Pais.	46	K15
Colinslee Dr., Pais.	46	K15
Colinslie Rd. G53	49	Q16
Colinton Pl. G32	38	BB12
Colintraive Av. G33	24	AA10
Coll Av., Renf.	31	M11
Coll Pl. G21	37	Y11
Coll St. G21	37	Y11
Colla Gdns., Bish.	11	Z7
College La. G1	36	W13
High St.		
College St. G1	36	W12
Collessie Dr. G33	39	CC11
Collier St., John.	43	D14
Collina St. G20	20	T9
Collins St. G4	36	X12
Collylin Rd., Bear.	7	R6
Colmonell Av. G13	18	N8
Colonsay Av., Renf.	31	M11
Colonsay Rd. G52	33	R13
Colonsay Rd., Pais.	46	J16
Colquhoun Av. G52	32	P12
Colquhoun Dr., Bear.	7	Q5
Colston Av., Bish.	22	X8
Colston Dr., Bish.	22	X8
Colston Gdns., Bish.	22	X8
Colston Path, Bish.	22	X8
Colston Gdns.		
Colston Pl., Bish.	22	X8
Colston Rd., Bish.	22	X8
Coltmuir Av., Bish.	22	X8
Coltmuir Dr.		
Coltmuir Cres., Bish.	22	X8
Coltmuir Dr., Bish.	22	X8
Coltmuir Gdns., Bish.	22	X8
Coltmuir Dr.		
Coltmuir St. G22	21	V9
Coltness La. G33	39	CC12
Coltness St. G33	39	CC12
Coltpark Av., Bish.	22	X8
Coltpark La., Bish.	22	X8
Coltsfoot Dr. G53	60	P18
Columba Path, Clyde.	5	M7
Onslow Rd.		
Columba St. G51	34	S12
Colvend Dr. G73	65	Y18
Colvend St. G40	52	X14
Colville Dr. G73	65	Z17
Colwood Av. G53	60	P18
Colwood Gdns. G53	60	P18
Colwood Av.		
Colwood Path G53	60	P18
Parkhouse Rd.		
Colwood Pl. G53	60	P18
Colwood Sq. G53	60	P18
Colwood Av.		
Comedie Rd. G33	25	DD10
Comely Pk. St. G31	37	Y13
Comley Pl. G31	37	Y13
Gallowgate		
Commerce St. G5	35	V13
Commercial Ct. G5	36	W13
Commercial Rd. G5	52	W14
Commercial Rd., Barr.	59	M18
Commonhead Rd. G34	40	FF12
Commonhead Rd., Bail.	41	GG12
Commore Av., Barr.	59	M19
Commore Dr. G13	18	P8
Comrie Rd. G33	25	CC9
Comrie St. G32	54	BB14
Cona St. G46	61	R18
Conan Ct. G72	67	CC17
Condorrat Ring Rd., Cumb.	70	MM4
Congleton St. G53	60	N17
Nitshill Rd.		
Congress Rd. G3	35	U12
Conifer Pl., Lenz.	12	BB5
Conisborough Path G34	39	DD11
Balfluig St.		
Conisborough Rd. G34	39	DD11
Connal St. G40	53	Y14
Conniston St. G32	38	AA12
Conon Av., Bear.	7	Q6
Consett La. G33	39	CC12
Consett St. G33	39	CC12
Consett La.		
Contin Pl. G12	20	T9
Convair Way, Renf.	31	M11
Lismore Av.		
Conval Way, Pais.	30	J12
Abbotsburn Way		
Cook St. G5	35	V13
Coopers Well La. G11	34	T11
Dumbarton Rd.		
Coopers Well St. G11	34	T11
Dumbarton Rd.		
Copland Pl. G51	34	S13
Copland Quad. G51	34	S13
Copland Rd. G51	34	S13
Coplaw St. G42	51	V14
Copperfield La., Udd.	57	HH16
Hamilton Vw.		
Corbett St. G32	54	BB14
Corbiston Way, Cumb.	71	PP3
Cordiner St. G44	51	V16
Corkerhill Gdns. G52	49	R14
Corkerhill Pl. G52	49	Q15
Corkerhill Rd. G52	49	Q15
Corlaich Av. G42	52	X16
Corlaich Dr. G42	52	X16
Corn St. G4	35	V11
Cornaig Rd. G53	48	P16
Cornalee Gdns. G53	48	P16
Cornalee Pl. G53	48	P16
Cornalee Rd. G53	48	P16
Cornhill St. G21	23	Y9
Cornoch St. G23	8	T7
Torrin Rd.		
Cornock Cres., Clyde.	5	L6
Cornock St., Clyde.	5	L6
Cornwall Av. G73	65	Z17
Cornwall St. G41	34	T13

Name	Page	Grid
Croftpark Av. G44	64	W18
Croftside Av. G44	64	X18
Croftspar Av. G32	39	CC13
Croftspar Dr. G32	39	CC13
Croftspar Pl. G32	39	CC13
Croftwood, Bish.	11	Y6
Croftwood Av. G44	64	W18
Cromart Pl., Chr.	14	FF7
Cromarty Av. G43	63	U17
Cromarty Av., Bish.	11	Z7
Cromarty Gdns., Clark.	63	V19
Crombie Gdns., Bail.	56	EE14
Cromdale St. G51	33	R13
Cromer La., Pais.	30	J12
Abbotsburn Way		
Cromer St. G20	21	U9
Cromer Way, Pais.	30	J12
Mosslands Rd.		
Crompton Av. G44	63	V17
Cromwell La. G20	35	V11
Cromwell St.		
Cromwell St. G20	35	V11
Cronberry Quad. G52	48	N14
Cronberry Ter. G52	48	N14
Crookedshields Rd. G72	66	BB19
Crookston Av. G52	48	P14
Crookston Ct. G52	48	P14
Crookston Dr. G52	48	N14
Crookston Gdns. G52	48	N14
Crookston Gro. G52	48	P14
Crookston Pl. G52	48	N14
Crookston Quad. G52	48	N14
Crookston Rd. G52	48	P15
Crookston Ter. G52	48	P14
Crookston Rd.		
Crosbie Dr. G78	45	G16
Crosbie St. G20	20	T8
Crosbie Wds., Pais.	45	H15
Cross, The G1	36	W13
Cross, The, Pais.	30	K13
Cross Arthurlie St., Barr.	59	L19
Cross Rd., Pais.	45	H15
Cross St. G32	55	CC15
Cross St., Pais.	46	J14
Crossbank Av. G42	52	X15
Crossbank Dr. G42	52	X15
Crossbank Rd. G42	52	W15
Crossbank Ter. G42	52	W15
Crossflat Cres., Pais.	31	L13
Crossford Dr. G23	9	U7
Crosshill Av. G42	51	V15
Crosshill Av., Lenz.	13	CC5
Crosshill Dr. G73	65	Y17
Crosshill Rd., Bish.	11	Z5
Crosshill Sq., Bail.	56	FF14
Crosslee St. G52	33	R13
Crosslees Ct., Thorn.	61	R18
Main St.		
Crosslees Dr., Thorn.	61	R18
Crosslees Pk., Thorn.	61	R18
Crosslees Rd., Thorn.	61	R19
Crossloan Pl. G51	33	R12
Crossloan Rd. G51	33	R12
Crossloan Ter. G51	33	R12
Crossmill Av., Barr.	59	M18
Crossmyloof Gdns. G41	50	T15
Crosspoint Dr. G23	9	U7
Invershiel Rd.		
Crosstobs Rd. G53	48	P15
Crossview Av., Bail.	40	FF13
Swinton Av.		
Crossview Pl., Bail.	40	FF13
Crovie Rd. G53	48	P16
Crow Ct., The, Bish.	10	X7
Kenmure Av.		
Crow La. G13	19	R9
Crow Rd. G11	19	R10
Crow Wd. Rd., Chr.	26	EE8
Crow Wd. Ter., Chr.	26	EE8
Crowflats Rd., Udd.	69	GG17
Lady Isle Cres.		
Crowhill Rd. G64	22	X8
Crowhill St. G22	22	W9
Crowlin Cres. G33	38	BB12
Crown Av., Clyde.	5	L6
Crown Circ. G12	20	S10
Crown Rd. S.		
Crown Ct. G1	36	W12
Virginia St.		
Crown Gdns. G12	20	S10
Crown Rd. N.		
Crown Mans. G11	20	S10
North Gardner St.		
Crown Rd. N. G12	20	S10
Crown Rd. S. G12	20	S10
Crown St. G5	52	W14
Crown St., Bail.	55	DD14
Crown Ter. G12	20	S10
Crown Rd. S.		
Crownpoint Rd. G40	36	X13
Crowpoint Rd. G40	37	Y13
Alma St.		
Croy Pl. G21	23	Z9
Rye Rd.		
Croy Pl. G21	23	Z9
Croy Rd.		
Croy Rd. G21	23	Z9
Cruachan Av., Renf.	31	M11
Cruachan Cres., Pais.	46	K16
Cruachan Dr., Barr.	59	M19
Cruachan Rd. G73	65	Z18
Cruachan St. G46	61	R18
Cruachan Way, Barr.	59	M19
Cruden St. G51	33	R13
Crum Av., Thorn.	62	S18
Crusader Av. G13	7	Q7
Cubie St. G40	36	X13
Cuilhill Rd., Bail.	41	GG12
Cuillin Way, Barr.	59	M19
Cuillins, The, Udd.	56	FF15
Cuillins Rd. G73	65	Z18
Culbin Dr. G13	18	N8
Cullen St. G32	54	BB14
Cullins, The, Chr.	15	HH6
Culloden St. G31	37	Y12
Coventry Dr.		
Culrain Gdns. G32	38	BB13
Culrain St. G32	38	BB13
Culross La. G32	55	CC14
Culross St. G32	55	CC14
Cult Rd., Lenz.	13	DD6
Cults St. G51	33	R13
Culzean Cres., Bail.	56	EE14
Huntingtower Rd.		
Culzean Dr. G32	39	CC13
Cumberland Ct. G1	36	W13
Gallowgate		
Cumberland La. G5	51	V14
Cumberland St.		
Cumberland Pl. G5	52	W14
Cumberland Pl., Pais.	46	K14
Laigh Kirk La.		
Cumberland St. G5	35	V13
Cumbernauld Rd. G31	37	Z12
Cumbrae Ct., Clyde.	5	L7
Montrose St.		
Cumbrae Rd., Pais.	46	K16
Cumbrae Rd., Renf.	31	M11
Cumbrae St. G33	38	BB12
Cumlodden Dr. G20	20	T8
Cumming Dr. G42	51	V16
Cumnock Dr., Renf.	59	M19
Cumnock Rd. G33	24	AA9
Cunard St., Clyde.	17	M8
Cunningham Dr., Clyde.	4	K5
Cunningham Dr., Giff.	63	U18
Cunningham Rd. G52	32	N12
Cunningham Rd. G73	53	Z16
Cunninghame Rd., Kilb.	42	B14
Curfew Rd. G13	7	Q7
Curle St. G14	33	Q11
Curlew Pl., John.	43	C16
Curling Cres. G44	52	W16
Currie St. G20	21	U9
Curtis Av. G44	52	W16
Curzon St. G20	21	U9
Cut, The, Udd.	69	GG17
Cuthbert St., Udd.	57	HH16
Oakdene Av.		
Cuthbertson St. G42	51	V15
Cuthelton Dr. G31	54	AA14
Cuthelton St.		
Cuthelton St. G31	53	Z14
Cuthelton Ter. G31	53	Z14
Cypress Av., Blan.	68	FF19
Cypress Av., Udd.	57	HH16
Myrtle Rd.		
Cypress Ct., Lenz.	12	BB5
Cypress St. G22	22	W9
Cyprus Av., John.	44	E15
Cyprus St., Clyde.	17	M8
Cyril St., Pais.	47	L14
Daer Av., Renf.	32	N11
Dairsie Gdns., Bish.	23	Z8
Dairsie St. G44	63	U18
Daisy St. G42	51	V15
Dakota Way, Renf.	31	M11
Friendship Way		
Dalbeth Rd. G32	54	AA15
Dalchurn Path G34	40	EE12
Dalchurn Pl.		
Dalchurn Pl. G34	40	EE12
Dalcraig Cres., Blan.	68	FF19
Dalcross La. G11	34	T11
Byres Rd.		
Dalcross St. G11	34	T11
Dalcruin Gdns. G69	15	HH6
Daldowie Av. G32	55	CC14
Dale Path G40	52	X14
Dale St. G40	52	X14
Dale Way G73	65	Y18
Daleview Av. G12	20	S9
Dalfoil Ct. G52	48	N14
Dalgarroch Av. G13	18	N8
Dalgleish Av., Clyde.	4	K5
Dalhouse Rd., Udd.	56	EE15
Dalhousie Gdns., Bish.	10	X7
Dalhousie La. G3	35	V11
Scott St.		
Dalhousie La. W. G3	35	V11
Buccleuch St.		
Dalhousie Rd., Kilb.	42	B15
Dalhousie St. G3	35	V11
Dalilea Dr. G34	40	FF11
Dalilea Path G34	40	FF11
Dalilea Dr.		
Dalilea Pl. G34	40	FF11
Dalintober St. G5	35	V13
Dalkeith Av. G41	50	S14
Dalkeith Av., Bish.	11	Y6
Dalkeith Rd., Bish.	11	Y6
Dalmahoy St. G32	38	AA12
Dalmally St. G20	21	U10
Dalmarnock Bri. G40	53	Y15
Dalmarnock Ct. G40	53	Y14
Baltic St.		
Dalmarnock Rd. G40	52	X14
Dalmary Dr., Pais.	31	L13
Dalmeny Av., Giff.	62	T18
Dalmeny Dr., Barr.	59	L19
Dalmeny St. G5	52	X15
Dalmuir Ct., Dalm.	4	K6
Stewart St.		
Dalnair St. G3	34	T11
Dalness Pas. G32	54	BB14
Ochil St.		
Dalness St. G32	54	BB14
Dalreoch Av., Bail.	40	FF13
Dalriada St. G40	53	Z14
Dalry Rd., Udd.	57	HH16
Myrtle Rd.		
Dalry St. G32	54	BB14
Dalserf Cres., Giff.	62	S19
Dalserf St. G31	37	Y13
Dalsetter Av. G15	6	N7
Dalsetter Pl. G15	6	P7
Dalsholm Rd. G20	20	S8
Dalskeith Av., Pais.	29	H13
Dalskeith Cres., Pais.	29	H13
Dalskeith Rd., Pais.	45	H14
Dalswinton Pl. G34	40	FF12
Dalswinton St.		

Street	No.	Grid
Dalswinton St. G34	40	FF12
Dalton Av., Clyde.	6	N7
Dalton St. G31	38	AA13
Dalveen Av., Udd.	57	GG16
Dalveen Ct., Barr.	59	M19
Dalveen St. G32	38	AA13
Dalveen Way G73	65	Z18
Dalwhinnie Av., Blan.	68	FF19
Daly Gdns., Blan.	69	GG19
Dalziel Dr. G41	50	T14
Dalziel Quad. G41	50	T14
Dalziel Dr.		
Dalziel Rd. G52	32	N12
Damshot Cres. G53	49	Q15
Damshot Rd. G53	49	Q16
Danby Rd., Bail.	55	DD14
Danes Cres. G14	18	P9
Danes Dr. G14	18	P9
Danes La. S. G14	19	Q10
Dunglass Av.		
Dargarvel Av. G41	50	S14
Darkwood Cres., Pais.	29	H13
Darleith St. G32	38	AA13
Darluith Rd., Linw.	28	E13
Darnaway Av. G33	39	CC11
Darnaway St. G33	39	CC11
Darnick St. G21	23	Y10
Hobden St.		
Darnley Cres., Bish.	10	X6
Darnley Gdns. G41	51	U15
Darnley Path G41	61	R17
Kennisholm Av.		
Darnley Pl. G41	51	U15
Darnley Rd.		
Darnley Rd. G41	51	U15
Darnley Rd., Barr.	60	N18
Darnley St. G41	51	U15
Darroch Way, Cumb.	71	PP2
Dartford St. G22	21	V10
Darvaar Rd., Renf.	31	M11
Darvel Cres., Pais.	47	M14
Darvel St. G53	60	N17
Darwin Pl., Dalm.	4	J6
Dava St. G51	34	S12
Davaar Rd., Pais.	46	K16
Davaar St. G40	53	Y14
Daventry Dr. G12	20	S9
David Pl., Bail.	55	DD14
David Pl., Pais.	31	L12
Killarn Way		
David St. G40	37	Y13
David Way, Pais.	31	L12
Killarn Way		
Davidson Gdns. G14	19	Q10
Westland Dr.		
Davidson St. G40	53	Y15
Davidson St., Clyde.	18	N8
Davidston Pl., Lenz.	13	DD6
Davieland Rd., Giff.	62	S19
Daviot St. G51	33	Q13
Dawes La. N. G14	19	Q10
Upland Rd.		
Dawson Pl. G4	21	V10
Dawson Rd.		
Dawson Rd. G4	21	V10
Dealston Rd., Barr.	59	L18
Dean Pk. Dr. G72	67	CC18
Dean Pk. Rd., Renf.	32	N11
Dean St., Clyde.	5	M7
Deanbrae St., Udd.	69	GG17
Deanfield Quad. G52	32	N13
Deanpark Av., Udd.	69	HH18
Deans Av. G72	67	CC18
Deanside La. G4	36	W12
Rottenrow		
Deanside Rd., Renf.	32	P12
Deanston Dr. G41	51	U16
Deanwood Av. G44	63	U18
Deanwood Rd. G44	63	U18
Debdale Cotts. G13	19	R9
Whittingehame Dr.		
Dechmont Av. G72	67	CC18
Dechmont Gdns., Blan.	68	FF19
Dechmont Gdns., Udd.	57	GG15
Dechmont Pl. G72	67	CC18
Dechmont Rd., Udd.	57	GG15
Dechmont St. G31	53	Z14
Dechmont Vw., Udd.	57	HH16
Hamilton Vw.		
Dee Av. G78	45	G15
Dee Av., Renf.	18	N10
Dee Dr., Pais.	45	G15
Dee Pl., John.	43	C16
Dee St. G33	37	Z11
Deepdene Rd., Bear.	7	Q7
Deepdene Rd., Chr.	15	HH7
Delburn St. G31	53	Z14
Delhi Av., Dalm.	4	J6
Delhmont Vw., Udd.	57	HH16
Hamilton Vw.		
Delny Pl. G33	39	DD12
Delvin Rd. G44	63	V17
Denbeck St. G32	38	AA13
Denbrae St. G32	38	AA13
Dene Wk., Bish.	23	Z8
Denewood Av., Pais.	46	J16
Denham St. G22	21	V10
Denholme Dr., Giff.	62	T19
Denkenny Sq. G15	6	N6
Denmark St. G22	22	W10
Denmilne Path G34	40	FF12
Denmilne Pl. G34	40	FF12
Denmilne St. G34	40	FF12
Derby St. G3	35	U12
Derby Ter. La. G3	35	U12
Derby St.		
Derwent St. G22	21	V10
Despard Av. G32	55	DD14
Despard Gdns. G32	55	DD14
Deveron Av., Giff.	62	T19
Deveron Rd., Bear.	7	Q7
Deveron St. G33	37	Z11
Devol Cres. G53	48	P16
Devon Gdns. G12	20	S10
Hyndland Rd.		
Devon Gdns., Bish.	10	X6
Devon Pl. G42	51	V14
Devon St. G5	51	V14
Devondale Av., Blan.	68	FF19
Devonshire Gdns. G12	20	S10
Devonshire Gdns. La. G12	20	S10
Hyndland Rd.		
Devonshire Ter. G12	20	S10
Devonshire Ter. La. G12	20	S10
Hughenden Rd.		
Diana Av. G13	18	P8
Dick St. G20	21	U10
Henderson St.		
Dickens Av., Clyde.	4	K6
Dilwara Av. G14	33	R11
Dimity St., John.	43	D15
Dinard Dr., Giff.	62	T18
Dinart St. G33	37	Z11
Dinduff St. G34	40	FF11
Dingwall St. G3	34	T12
Kelvinhaugh St.		
Dinmont Pl. G41	51	U15
Norham St.		
Dinmont Rd. G41	50	T15
Dinwiddie St. G21	37	Z11
Dipple Pl. G15	6	P7
Dirleton Av. G41	51	U16
Dirleton Dr., Pais.	45	H15
Dirleton Gate, Bear.	7	Q7
Dixon Av. G42	51	V15
Dixon Rd. G42	52	W15
Dixon St. G1	35	V13
Dixon St., Pais.	46	K14
Dobbies Ln. G4	35	V11
Dobbies Ln. Pl. G4	36	W12
Dochart Av., Renf.	32	N11
Dochart St. G33	38	AA11
Dock St., Clyde.	17	M8
Dodhill Pl. G13	18	P9
Dodside Gdns. G32	55	CC14
Dodside Pl. G32	55	CC14
Dodside St. G32	55	CC14
Dolan St., Bail.	40	EE13
Dollar Ter. G20	20	T8
Crosbie St.		
Dolphin Rd. G41	50	T15
Don Av., Renf.	32	N11
Don Dr., Pais.	45	G15
Don Pl., John.	43	C16
Don St. G33	37	Z12
Donald Way, Udd.	57	HH16
Donaldson Dr., Renf.	17	M10
Ferguson St.		
Donaldswood Rd., Pais.	46	J16
Doncaster St. G20	21	V10
Doon Cres., Bear.	7	Q6
Doon Side, Cumb.	71	PP3
Doon St., Clyde.	5	M6
Doonfoot Rd. G43	62	T17
Dora St. G40	53	Y14
Dorchester Av. G12	20	S9
Dorchester Ct. G12	20	S9
Dorchester Av.		
Dorchester Pl. G12	20	S9
Dorlin Rd. G33	25	DD9
Dormanside Rd. G53	48	P14
Dornal Av. G13	18	N8
Dornford Av. G32	55	CC15
Dornford Rd. G32	55	CC15
Dornie Dr. G32	55	CC16
Dornie Dr. G46	61	R18
Dornoch Av., Giff.	62	T19
Dornoch Pl., Bish.	11	Z7
Dornoch Pl., Chr.	14	FF7
Dornoch Rd., Bear.	7	Q7
Dornoch St. G40	36	X13
Dornoch Way, Cumb.	71	PP1
Dorset Sq. G3	35	U12
Dorset St.		
Dorset St. G3	35	U12
Dosk Av. G13	18	N8
Dosk Pl. G13	18	N8
Douglas Av. G32	54	BB15
Douglas Av. G73	65	Z17
Douglas Av., Giff.	62	T19
Douglas Av., John.	44	E15
Douglas Av., Lenz.	13	CC5
Douglas Ct., Lenz.	13	CC5
Douglas Cres., Udd.	57	HH16
Douglas Dr. G15	6	N7
Douglas Dr. G72	66	AA17
Douglas Dr., Bail.	39	DD13
Douglas Dr., Both.	69	HH19
Douglas Gdns., Bear.	7	R6
Douglas Gdns., Giff.	62	T19
Douglas Gdns., Lenz.	13	CC5
Douglas Gdns., Udd.	69	GG17
Douglas La. G2	35	V12
West George St.		
Douglas Pk. Cres., Bear.	8	S5
Douglas Pl., Bear.	7	R5
Douglas Pl., Lenz.	13	CC5
Douglas Rd., Pais.	31	L12
Douglas St. G2	35	V12
Douglas St., Pais.	30	J13
Douglas St., Udd.	57	HH16
Douglas Ter. G41	51	U14
Shields Rd.		
Douglas Ter., Pais.	30	K11
Douglaston Rd. G23	9	U7
Dougray Pl., Barr.	59	M19
Dougrie Dr. G45	64	W18
Dougrie Pl. G45	64	X18
Dougrie Rd. G45	64	W19
Dougrie St. G45	64	X18
Dougrie Ter. G45	64	W18
Doune Cres., Bish.	11	Y6
Doune Gdns. G20	21	U10
Doune Quad. G20	21	U10
Dove St. G53	60	P17
Dovecot G43	50	T16
Shawhill Rd.		
Dovecothall St., Barr.	59	M18
Dover St. G3	35	U12
Downanfield Rd., Cumb.	70	NN3
Downhill Pl. G11	34	T11
Old Dumbarton Rd.		

Street	No.	Grid
Dowanhill St. G11	34	T11
Dowanside La. G12	20	T10
Byres Rd.		
Dowanside Rd. G12	20	T10
Dowanvale Ter. G11	34	S11
White St.		
Downcraig Dr. G45	64	W19
Downcraig Rd. G45	64	W19
Downcraig Ter. G45	64	W19
Downfield Gdns., Both.	69	GG19
Downfield St. G32	54	AA14
Downiebrae Rd. G73	53	Y15
Downs St. G21	22	X10
Dowrie Cres. G53	48	P15
Dows Pl. G4	21	V10
Possil Rd.		
Drainie St. G34	40	EE12
Westerhouse Rd.		
Drake St. G40	36	X13
Drakemire Av. G45	64	W18
Drakemire Dr. G45	64	W18
Dreghorn St. G31	37	Z12
Drem Pl. G11	34	S11
Merkland St.		
Drimnin Rd. G33	25	DD9
Drive Gdns., John.	45	G14
Drive Rd. G51	33	R12
Drochil St. G34	40	EE11
Drumbeg Dr. G53	60	P17
Drumbeg Pl. G53	60	P17
Drumbottie Rd. G21	23	Y9
Drumby Cres., Clark.	62	T19
Drumcavel Rd., Chr.	26	FF8
Drumcavel Rd., Gart.	26	FF8
Drumchapel Gdns. G15	6	P7
Drumchapel Pl. G15	6	P7
Drumchapel Rd. G15	6	P7
Drumclog Gdns. G33	24	AA9
Drumclutha Dr., Both.	69	HH19
Drumcross Rd. G53	49	Q15
Drumhead Pl. G32	54	AA15
Drumhead Rd. G32	54	AA15
Drumilaw Rd. G73	65	Y17
Drumilaw Way G73	65	Y17
Drumlaken Av. G23	8	T7
Drumlaken Ct. G23	8	T7
Drumlaken St. G23	8	T7
Drumlanrig Av. G34	40	FF11
Drumlanrig Pl. G34	40	FF11
Drumlanrig Quad. G34	40	FF11
Drumlochy Rd. G33	38	BB11
Drummond Av. G73	52	X16
Drummond Dr., Pais.	47	M14
Drummond Gdns. G13	19	R9
Crow Rd.		
Drummore Rd. G15	6	P6
Drumover Dr. G31	54	AA14
Drumoyne Av. G51	33	R12
Drumoyne Circ. G51	33	R13
Drumoyne Dr. G51	33	R12
Drumoyne Pl. G51	33	R13
Drumoyne Circ.		
Drumoyne Quad. G51	33	R13
Drumoyne Rd. G51	33	R13
Drumoyne Sq. G51	33	R12
Drumpark St. G46	61	R18
Drumpark St., Coat.	57	HH14
Dunnachie Dr.		
Drumpeller Rd., Bail.	56	EE14
Drumpellier Av., Bail.	56	EE14
Drumpellier Pl., Bail.	56	EE14
Drumpellier St. G33	37	Z11
Drumreoch Dr. G42	52	X16
Drumreoch Pl. G42	52	X16
Drumry Pl. G15	6	N7
Drumry Rd., Clyde.	5	L6
Drumry Rd. E. G15	6	N7
Drums Av., Pais.	30	J13
Drums Cres., Pais.	30	J13
Drums Rd. G53	48	P14
Drumsack Av., Chr.	26	FF8
Drumsargard Rd. G73	65	Z17
Drumshaw Dr. G32	55	CC16
Drumvale Dr., Chr.	15	GG7
Drury St. G2	35	V12
Dryad St. G46	61	R17
Dryborough Av., John.	45	H15
Dryburgh Av. G73	53	Y16
Dryburgh Gdns. G20	21	U10
Dryburgh Rd., Bear.	7	Q5
Dryburgh Av. G52	32	P13
Drygate G4	36	X12
Drygrange Rd. G33	39	CC11
Drymen Pl., Lenz.	13	CC6
Drymen Rd., Bear.	7	Q5
Drymen St. G52	33	R13
Morven St.		
Drymen Wynd, Bear.	7	R6
Drynoch Pl. G22	21	V8
Drysdale St. G14	18	N9
Duart Dr., John.	44	E15
Duart St. G20	20	T8
Dubs Rd., Barr.	60	N18
Dubton Path G34	40	EE11
Dubton St. G34	40	EE11
Duchall Pl. G14	18	P10
Duchess Pl. G73	53	Z16
Duchess Rd. G73	53	Z15
Duchray Dr., Pais.	48	N14
Duchray La. G31	37	Z11
Duchray St.		
Duchray St. G33	37	Z11
Ducraig St. G32	38	BB13
Dudhope St. G33	39	CC11
Dudley Dr. G12	20	S10
Duffus Pl. G32	55	CC16
Duffus St. G34	40	EE11
Duffus Ter. G32	55	CC16
Duich Gdns. G23	9	U7
Duisdale Rd. G32	55	CC16
Duke St. G4	36	X12
Duke St. G31	36	X12
Duke St., Linw.	28	F13
Duke St., Pais.	46	K15
Dukes Gate, Both.	69	GG18
Dukes Rd. G72	65	Z17
Dukes Rd. G73	65	Z17
Dukes Rd., Bail.	41	HH13
Dulnain St. G72	67	DD17
Dulsie Rd. G21	23	Z9
Dumbarton Rd. G11	34	S11
Dumbarton Rd. G14	18	N9
Dumbarton Rd., Clyde.	4	K5
Dumbarton Rd., Clyde.	4	J6
Dumbarton Rd., Dalm.	4	J6
Dumbarton Rd., Old K.	4	J6
Dumbreck Av. G41	50	S14
Dumbreck Ct. G41	50	S14
Dumbreck Pl., Lenz.	13	DD6
Dumbreck Rd. G41	50	S14
Dumbreck Sq. G41	50	S14
Dumbreck Av.		
Dunagoil Rd. G45	64	W19
Dunagoil St. G45	64	X19
Dunagoil Ter. G45	64	X19
Dunalastair Dr. G33	24	BB9
Dunan Pl. G33	39	DD12
Dunard Rd. G73	53	Y16
Dunard St. G20	21	U10
Dunard Way, Pais.	30	J12
Mosslands Rd.		
Dunaskin St. G11	34	T11
Dunbar Av. G73	53	Z16
Dunbar Av., John.	43	D16
Dunbar Rd., Pais.	45	H15
Dunbeith Pl. G20	20	T9
Dunblane St. G4	35	V11
Dunbrach Rd., Cumb.	70	MM2
Duncan Av. G14	19	Q10
Duncan La. G14	19	Q10
Duncan Av.		
Duncan La. N. G14	19	Q10
Ormiston Av.		
Duncan St., Clyde.	5	L6
Duncansby Rd. G33	39	CC13
Dunchatt St. G31	36	X12
Dunchattan Pl. G31	36	X12
Duke St.		
Dunchurch Rd., Pais.	31	M13
Dunclutha Dr., Both.	69	HH19
Dunclutha St. G40	53	Y15
Duncombe St. G20	20	T8
Duncombe Vw., Clyde.	5	M6
Kirkoswald Dr.		
Duncraig Cres., John.	43	C16
Duncrub Dr., Bish.	10	X7
Duncruin St. G20	20	T8
Duncryne Av. G32	55	CC14
Duncryne Gdns. G32	55	DD14
Duncryne Pl., Bish.	22	X8
Dundas La. G1	36	W12
Dundas St. G1	36	W12
Dundasvale Ct. G4	35	V11
Maitland St.		
Dundasvale Rd. G4	35	V11
Maitland St.		
Dundee Dr. G52	48	P14
Dundee Path G52	49	Q14
Dundee Dr.		
Dundonald Av., John.	43	C15
Dundonald Rd. G12	20	T10
Dundonald Rd., Pais.	31	L12
Dundrennan Rd. G42	51	U16
Dunearn Pl., Pais.	47	L14
Dunearn St. G4	35	U11
Dunegoin St. G51	34	S12
Sharp St.		
Dunellan St. G52	33	R13
Dungeonhill Rd. G34	40	FF12
Dunglass Av. G14	19	Q10
Dunglass La. N. G14	19	Q10
Verona Av.		
Dungoil Av., Cumb.	70	LL2
Dungoil Rd., Lenz.	13	DD6
Dungoyne St. G20	20	T8
Dunira St. G32	54	AA14
Dunivaig St. G33	39	DD12
Dunkeld Av. G73	53	Y16
Dunkeld Dr., Bear.	8	S6
Dunkeld Gdns., Bish.	11	Y7
Dunkeld La., Chr.	15	HH7
Burnbrae Av.		
Dunkeld St. G31	53	Z14
Dunkenny Pl. G15	6	N6
Dunkenny Rd. G15	6	N6
Dunlop Cres., Both.	69	HH19
Dunlop Cres., Renf.	17	M10
Hairst St.		
Dunlop St. G1	36	W13
Dunlop St. G72	67	DD17
Dunlop St., Linw.	28	F13
Dunlop St., Renf.	17	M10
Hairst St.		
Dunmore La. G5	35	V13
Norfolk St.		
Dunmore St. G5	35	V13
Dunmore St., Clyde.	17	M8
Dunn St. G40	53	Y14
Dunn St., Clyde.	4	K5
Dunn St., Dalm.	4	K6
Dunn St., Pais.	47	L14
Dunnachie Dr., Coat.	57	HH14
Dunnichen Pl., Bish.	11	Z7
Dunning St. G31	53	Z14
Dunolly St. G21	37	Y11
Dunottar St. G33	38	BB11
Dunottar St., Bish.	11	Z7
Dunphail Dr. G34	40	FF12
Dunphail Rd. G34	40	FF12
Dunragit St. G31	37	Z12
Dunrobin Av., John.	44	E15
Dunrobin St. G31	37	Y13
Dunrod St. G32	54	BB14
Dunside Dr. G53	60	P17
Dunskaith Pl. G34	40	FF12
Dunskaith St. G34	40	FF12
Dunsmuir St. G51	34	S12
Dunster Gdns., Bish.	11	Y6
Dunswin Av., Dalm.	4	K6
Dunswin Ct., Dalm.	4	K6
Dunswin Av.		
Dunsyre Pl. G23	9	U7
Dunsyre St. G33	38	AA12
Duntarvie Cres. G34	40	FF12
Duntarvie Pl. G34	40	EE12

Name	No.	Grid
Duntarvie Quad. G34	40	FF12
Duntarvie Rd. G34	40	EE12
Dunterle Ct., Barr.	59	M18
Dunterlie Av. G13	18	P9
Duntiglennan Rd., Clyde.	5	L5
Duntocher Rd., Bear.	6	P5
Duntocher Rd., Clyde.	5	L5
Duntocher Rd., Dalm.	4	K6
Duntocher St. G21	22	X10
Northcroft Rd.		
Duntreath Av. G13	18	N8
Duntroon St. G31	37	Y12
Dunure Dr. G73	64	X17
Dunure St. G20	20	T8
Dunvegan Av., John.	44	F15
Dunvegan Ct. G13	18	P9
Kintillo Dr.		
Dunvegan Dr., Bish.	11	Y6
Dunvegan Quad., Renf.	17	L10
Kirklandneuk Rd.		
Dunvegan St. G51	34	S12
Sharp St.		
Dunwan Av. G13	18	N8
Dunwan Pl. G13	18	N8
Durban Av., Dalm.	4	J6
Durness Av., Bear.	8	S5
Durno Path G33	39	DD12
Duror St. G32	38	BB13
Durris Gdns. G32	55	CC14
Durrockstock Cres., Pais.	45	G16
Durward Av. G41	50	T15
Durward Cres., Pais.	45	G15
Durwood Ct. G41	50	T15
Duthil St. G51	33	Q13
Dyce La. G11	34	S11
Dyers La. G1	36	W13
Turnbull St.		
Dyers Wynd, Pais.	30	K13
Gilmour St.		
Dyke Pl. G13	18	P8
Dyke Rd. G13	18	N9
Dyke St., Bail.	40	FF13
Dykebar Av. G13	18	P9
Dykebar Cres., Pais.	47	L15
Dykefoot Dr. G53	49	Q16
Dykehead La. G33	39	CC12
Dykehead Rd., Bail.	41	GG13
Dykehead St. G33	39	CC12
Dykemuir Pl. G21	23	Y10
Dykemuir Quad. G21	23	Y10
Dykemuir St.		
Dykemuir St. G21	23	Y10
Eagle Cres., Bear.	6	P5
Eagle St. G4	36	W11
Eaglesham Ct. G51	35	U13
Blackburn St.		
Eaglesham Pl. G51	35	U13
Earl Haig Rd. G52	32	N12
Earl Pl. G14	19	Q10
Earl St. G14	18	P10
Earlbank Av. G14	19	Q10
Earlbank La. N. G14	19	Q10
Dunglass Av.		
Earlbank La. S. G14	19	Q10
Verona Av.		
Earls Ct., Chr.	15	GG7
Longdale Rd.		
Earls Gate, Both.	69	GG18
Earls Hill G68	70	LL2
Earlsburn Rd., Lenz.	13	DD6
Earlspark Av. G43	51	U16
Earn Av., Bear.	8	S6
Earn Av., Renf.	32	N11
Almond Av.		
Earn St. G33	38	AA11
Earnock St. G33	23	Z10
Earnside St. G32	38	BB13
Easdale Dr. G32	54	BB14
East Av., Renf.	17	M10
East Barns St., Clyde.	17	M8
East Bath La. G2	35	V12
Sauchiehall St.		
East Buchanan St., Pais.	30	K13
East Campbell St. G1	36	X13
East Fulton Holdings, Linw.	28	E12
East Greenlees Av. G72	67	CC18
East Greenlees Cres. G72	66	BB18
East Greenlees Dr. G72	66	BB18
East Greenlees Rd. G72	66	BB18
East Hallhill Rd., Bail.	40	EE13
East Kilbride Expressway G72	66	BB19
East Kilbride Rd. G73	65	Z17
East La., Pais.	47	L14
East Reid St. G73	53	Z16
East Springfield Ter., Bish.	23	Y8
East St., Kilb.	42	B14
East Thomson St., Clyde.	5	L6
East Whitby St. G31	53	Z14
Eastburn Rd. G21	23	Y9
Eastcote Av. G14	19	R10
Eastcroft G73	53	Y16
Eastcroft Ter. G21	23	Y10
Easter Av., Udd.	69	GG17
Easter Garngaber Rd. G66	13	DD5
Easter Ms., Udd.	69	GG17
Church St.		
Easter Queenslie Rd. G33	39	DD12
Eastercraigs G31	37	Y12
Easterhill Pl. G32	54	AA14
Easterhill St. G32	54	AA14
Easterhouse Path G34	40	FF12
Easterhouse Pl. G34	40	FF12
Easterhouse Quad. G34	40	FF12
Easterhouse Rd. G34	40	FF12
Eastfield Av. G72	66	AA17
Eastfield Rd. G21	22	X10
Eastgate, Gart.	27	HH9
Eastmuir St. G32	38	BB13
Eastvale Pl. G3	34	T12
Eastwood Av. G41	50	T16
Eastwood Av., Giff.	62	T19
Eastwood Ct., Thorn.	61	R18
Main St.		
Eastwood Cres., Thorn.	61	R18
Eastwood Rd., Chr.	15	GG7
Eastwood Vw. G72	67	DD17
Eastwoodmains Rd., Giff.	62	T19
Easwald Bk., Kilb.	42	B15
Eccles St. G22	22	X9
Eckford St. G32	54	BB14
Eday St. G22	22	W9
Edderton Pl. G33	40	EE12
Eddleston Pl. G72	67	DD17
Eddlewood Path G33	39	DD12
Eddlewood Rd. G33	39	DD12
Edelweiss Ter. G11	34	S11
Gardner St.		
Eden La. G33	37	Z11
Eden Pk., Both.	69	GG19
Eden Pl. G72	67	CC17
Eden Pl., Renf.	32	N11
Eden St. G33	37	Z11
Edenwood St. G33	38	AA13
Edgam Dr. G52	33	Q13
Edgefauld Av. G21	22	X10
Edgefauld Dr. G21	22	X10
Edgefauld Pl. G21	22	X9
Balgrayhill Rd.		
Edgefauld Rd. G21	22	X10
Edgehill La. G11	20	S10
Marlborough Av.		
Edgehill Rd. G11	20	S10
Edgehill Rd., Bear.	7	R5
Edgemont St. G41	51	U16
Edinbeg Av. G42	52	X16
Edinbeg Pl. G42	52	X16
Edinburgh Rd. G33	37	Z12
Edington Gdns., Chr.	15	GG6
Edington St. G4	35	V11
Edison St. G52	32	N12
Edmiston Dr. G51	33	R13
Edmiston Dr., Linw.	28	E13
Edmiston St. G31	53	Z14
Edmondstone Ct., Clyde.	17	M8
Yokerburn Ter.		
Edrom Path G32	38	AA13
Edrom St.		
Edrom St. G32	38	AA13
Edward Av., Renf.	18	N10
Edward St. G3	34	T12
Lumsden St.		
Edward St., Bail.	41	GG13
Edward St., Clyde.	17	M8
Edwin St. G51	34	T13
Edzell Ct. G14	33	Q11
Edzell Dr., John.	44	F15
Edzell Gdns., Bish.	23	Z8
Edzell Pl. G14	33	Q11
Edzell St. G14	33	Q11
Egidia Av., Giff.	62	S19
Egilsay Cres. G22	22	W8
Egilsay Pl. G22	22	W8
Egilsay St. G22	22	W8
Egilsay Ter. G22	22	W8
Eglinton Ct. G5	35	V13
Eglinton Dr., Giff.	62	T19
Eglinton La. G5	51	V14
Eglinton St.		
Eglinton St. G5	51	V14
Egunton Ct. G5	51	V14
Cumberland St.		
Eighth St., Udd.	57	GG15
Eildon Dr., Barr.	59	M19
Eileen Gdns., Bish.	11	Y7
Elba La. G31	37	Z13
Elcho St. G40	36	X13
Elder Gro., Udd.	57	HH16
Burnhead St.		
Elder St. G51	33	R12
Elderpark Gdns. G51	33	R12
Elderpark Gro. G51	33	R12
Elderpark St. G51	33	R12
Elderslie St. G3	35	U11
Eldon Gdns., Bish.	10	X7
Eldon Pl., John.	44	E15
Eldon St. G3	35	U11
Eldon Ter. G11	34	S11
Caird Dr.		
Elgin Dr., Linw.	28	E13
Elgin St. G40	37	Y13
Elibank St. G33	38	BB11
Elie St. G11	34	T11
Elizabeth Cres., Thorn.	62	S18
Elizabeth St. G51	34	T13
Elizabethan Way, Renf.	31	M11
Cockels Ln.		
Ellangowan Rd. G41	50	T16
Ellergreen Rd., Bear.	7	R6
Ellerslie St., John.	44	E14
Ellesmere St. G22	21	V10
Ellinger Ct., Dalm.	4	K6
Scott St.		
Elliot Av. G78	45	G16
Elliot Av., Giff.	62	T19
Elliot Dr., Giff.	62	T18
Elliot La. G3	35	U12
Elliot St.		
Elliot Pl. G3	35	U12
Elliot St. G3	35	U12
Ellisland Av., Clyde.	5	M6
Ellisland Cres. G73	64	X17
Ellisland Rd. G43	62	T17
Ellisland Rd., Cumb.	71	PP3
Ellismuir Fm. Rd., Bail.	56	FF14
Ellismuir Pl., Bail.	56	FF14
Ellismuir Rd., Bail.	56	FF14
Elliston Av. G53	61	Q17
Elliston Dr. G53	61	Q17
Elliston Pl. G53	61	Q17
Ravenscraig Dr.		
Elm Av., Lenz.	13	CC5
Elm Av., Renf.	17	M10
Elm Bk., Bish.	11	Y7
Elm Dr., John.	43	D16
Elm Gdns., Bear.	7	R5

Elm Rd. G73	65	Y18	Etive Cres., Bish.	11	Y7	Farm Pk., Lenz.	13	CC6
Elm Rd., Dalm.	5	L5	Etive Dr., Giff.	62	T19	Farm Rd. G41	50	S14
Elm Rd., Pais.	47	L15	Etive St. G32	38	BB13	Farm Rd., Blan.	68	FF19
Elm St. G14	19	Q10	Eton Gdns. G12	35	U11	Farm Rd., Clyde.	5	L5
Elm Wk., Bear.	7	R5	*Oakfield Av.*			Farm Rd., Dalm.	4	J6
Elmbank Av., Udd.	57	HH16	Eton La. G12	35	U11	Farme Cross G73	53	Y15
Elmbank Cres. G2	35	V12	*Great George St.*			Farmeloan Rd. G73	53	Y16
Elmbank St.			Eton Pl. G12	35	U11	Farmington Av. G32	39	CC13
Elmbank La. G3	35	U12	*Oakfield Av.*			Farmington Gdns. G32	39	CC13
North St.			Eton Ter. G12	35	U11	Farmington Gate G32	39	CC13
Elmbank St. G2	35	V12	*Oakfield Av.*			Farmington Gro. G32	39	CC13
Elmbank St. La. G3	35	U12	Ettrick Av., Renf.	32	N11	Farne Dr. G44	63	V18
North St.			Ettrick Ct. G72	67	DD18	Farnell St. G4	35	V11
Elmfoot St. G5	52	W15	*Gateside Av.*			Farrier Ct., John.	43	D14
Elmore Av. G44	63	V17	Ettrick Cres. G73	53	Z16	Faskally Av., Bish.	10	X6
Elmore La. G44	63	V17	Ettrick Oval, Pais.	45	G16	Faskin Cres. G53	48	N16
Elmslie Ct., Bail.	56	EE14	Ettrick Pl. G43	50	T16	Faskin Pl. G53	48	N16
Elmvale Row G21	22	X10	Ettrick Ter., John.	43	C16	Faskin Rd. G53	48	N16
Elmvale Row E. G21	22	X10	Ettrick Way, Renf.	32	N11	Fasque Pl. G15	6	N6
Elmvale Row			Evan Cres., Giff.	62	T19	Fastnet St. G33	38	BB12
Elmvale Row W. G21	22	X10	Evan Dr., Giff.	62	T19	Faulbswood Cres., Pais.	45	H15
Elmvale Row			Evanton Dr. G46	61	R19	Fauldhouse St. G5	52	W14
Elmvale St. G21	22	X9	Evanton Pl. G46	61	R18	Faulds, Bail.	40	FF13
Elmwood Av. G11	19	R10	*Evanton Dr.*			Faulds Gdns., Bail.	40	FF13
Elmwood Ct., Both.	69	HH19	Everard Ct. G21	22	X8	Fauldshead Rd., Renf.	17	M10
Blantyre Mill Rd.			Everard Dr. G21	22	X8	Fauldspark Cres., Bail.	40	FF13
Elmwood Gdns. G11	19	R10	Everard Pl. G21	22	X8	Fauldswood Cres., Pais.	45	H15
Randolph Rd.			Everard Quad. G21	22	X8	Fauldswood Dr., Pais.	45	H15
Elmwood Gdns., Kirk.	12	BB5	Everglades, The, Chr.	26	EE8	Fearnmore Rd. G20	20	T8
Elmwood La. G11	19	Q10	Eversley St. G32	54	BB14	Fendoch St. G32	54	BB14
Elmwood Av.			Everton Rd. G53	49	Q15	Fenella St. G32	38	BB13
Elmwood Ter. G11	19	R10	Ewart Pl. G3	34	T12	Fennsbank Av. G73	65	Z18
Crow Rd.			*Kelvinhaugh St.*			Fenwick Dr., Barr.	59	M19
Elphin St. G23	8	T7	Ewing Pl. G31	37	Z13	Fenwick Pl., Giff.	62	S19
Invershiel Rd.			Ewing St. G73	53	Y16	Fenwick Rd., Giff.	62	T19
Elphinstone Pl. G51	34	T12	Ewing St., Kilb.	42	B14	Fereneze Av., Barr.	59	L18
Elrig Rd. G44	63	V17	Exchange Pl. G1	36	W12	Fereneze Av., Pais.	31	L12
Elspeth Gdns., Bish.	11	Y7	*Buchanan St.*			Ferenze Cres. G13	18	P8
Eltham St. G22	21	V10	Exeter Dr. G11	34	S11	Ferenze Dr., Pais.	46	J16
Elvan Ct. G32	38	AA13	Exeter La. G11	34	S11	Fergus Ct. G20	21	U10
Edrom St.			*Exeter Dr.*			Fergus Dr. G20	21	U10
Elvan St. G32	38	AA13	Eynort St. G22	21	V8	Ferguslie, Pais.	45	H14
Embo Dr. G13	18	P9				Ferguslie Pk., Pais.	29	G13
Emerson Rd., Bish.	11	Y7				Ferguslie Pk. Av., Pais.	29	H13
Emerson St. G20	21	V9	Fagan Ct., Blan.	69	GG19	Ferguslie Wk., Pais.	45	H14
Emily Pl. G31	36	X13	Faifley Rd., Clyde.	5	L5	Ferguson Av., Renf.	17	M10
Endfield Av. G12	20	S9	Fairbairn Cres., Thorn.	62	S19	Ferguson St., John.	43	D14
Endrick Bk., Bish.	11	Y6	Fairbairn Path G40	53	Y14	Ferguson St., Renf.	17	M10
Endrick Dr., Bear.	7	R6	*Ruby St.*			Fergusson Rd., Cumb.	70	NN3
Endrick Dr., Pais.	31	L13	Fairbairn St. G40	53	Y14	Ferguston Rd., Bear.	7	R6
Endrick St. G21	22	W10	*Dalmarnock Rd.*			Fern Av., Bish.	23	Y8
Endsleigh Gdns. G11	20	S10	Fairburn St. G32	54	AA14	Fern Av., Lenz.	13	CC5
Partickhill Rd.			Fairfax Av. G44	64	W17	Fern Dr., Barr.	59	L18
Ensay St. G22	22	W8	Fairfield Gdns. G51	33	R12	Fern Hill Gra. G71	69	HH19
Enterkin St. G32	54	AA14	Fairfield Pl. G51	33	R12	Fernan St. G32	38	AA13
Ericht Rd. G43	62	T17	Fairfield Pl. G71	69	HH19	Fernbank Av. G72	67	CC18
Eriska Av. G14	18	P9	Fairfield St. G51	33	R12	Fernbank St. G22	22	X9
Erradale St. G22	21	V8	Fairhaven Dr. G23	20	T8	Fernbrae Rd. G46	65	Z18
Erriboll Pl. G22	21	V8	Fairhill Av. G53	49	Q16	Fernbrae Way G73	65	Y18
Erriboll St. G22	21	V8	Fairholm St. G32	54	AA14	Ferncroft Dr. G44	64	W17
Errogie St. G34	40	EE12	Fairley St. G51	34	S13	Ferndale Ct. G23	20	T8
Erskine Av. G41	50	S14	Fairlie Pk. Dr. G11	34	S11	*Rothes Dr.*		
Erskine Sq. G52	32	N12	Fairway Av., Pais.	46	J16	Ferndale Dr. G23	20	T8
Erskine Vw., Clyde.	5	L6	Fairways, Bear.	6	P5	Ferndale Gdns. G23	20	T8
Singer St.			Fairyknowe Gdns. G71	69	HH19	Ferndale Pl. G23	20	T8
Erskinefauld Rd., Linw.	28	E13	Falcon Cres., Pais.	29	H13	*Rothes Dr.*		
Ervie St. G34	40	FF12	Falcon Rd., John.	43	C16	Ferness Oval G21	23	Z8
Esk Av., Renf.	32	N11	Falcon Ter. G20	20	T8	Ferness Pl. G21	23	Z8
Esk Dr., Pais.	45	G15	Falfield St. G5	51	V14	Ferness Rd. G21	23	Z9
Esk St. G14	18	N9	Falkland Cres., Bish.	23	Z8	Ferngrove Av. G12	20	S9
Esk Way, Pais.	45	G15	Falkland Mans. G12	20	S10	Fernhill Rd. G73	65	Y18
Eskbank St. G32	38	BB13	*Clarence Dr.*			Fernleigh Pl., Chr.	15	GG7
Eskdale Dr. G73	53	Z16	Falkland St. G12	20	S10	Fernleigh Rd. G43	62	T17
Eskdale Rd., Bear.	7	Q7	Falloch Rd. G42	51	V16	Ferry Rd. G3	34	S12
Eskdale St. G42	51	V15	Falloch Rd., Bear.	7	Q7	Ferry Rd., Both.	69	HH19
Esmond St. G3	34	T11	Fallside Rd., Both.	69	HH19	Ferry Rd., Renf.	17	M10
Espedair St., Pais.	46	K14	Falside Av., Pais.	46	K15	Ferry Rd., Udd.	68	FF17
Essenside Av. G15	7	Q7	Falside Rd. G32	54	BB14	Ferryden St. G14	33	R11
Essex Dr. G14	19	R10	Falside Rd., Pais.	46	J15	Fersit St. G43	62	T17
Essex La. G14	19	R10	Fara St. G23	21	U8	Fetlar Dr. G44	64	W17
Esslemont Av. G14	18	P9	Farie St. G73	53	Y16	Fettercairn Av. G15	6	N6
Estate Quad. G32	55	CC16	Farm Ct., Both.	69	HH18	Fettercairn Gdns., Bish.	11	Z7
Estate Rd. G32	55	CC16	*Fallside Rd.*			Fettes St. G33	38	AA12
Etive Av., Bear.	8	S6	Farm La., Udd.	69	HH17	Fidra St. G33	38	AA12
Etive Ct., Clyde.	5	M5	*Myers Cres.*			Fielden Pl. G40	37	Y13

Name	No.	Grid
Fielden St. G40	37	Y13
Fieldhead Dr. G43	62	S17
Fieldhead Sq. G43	62	S17
Fife Av. G52	48	P14
Fife Cres., Both.	69	HH19
Fifeway, Bish.	23	Z8
Fifth Av. G12	19	R9
Fifth Av. G33	24	BB9
Fifth Av., Lenz.	13	CC7
Fifth Av., Renf.	31	M11
Finart Dr., Pais.	47	L15
Finch Pl., John.	43	C16
Findhorn Av., Renf.	18	N10
Findhorn Cres., Pais.	45	G15
Findhorn St. G33	37	Z12
Findochty St. G33	39	CC11
Fingal La. G20	20	T8
Fingal St.		
Fingal St. G20	20	T8
Fingask St. G32	55	CC14
Finglas Av., Pais.	47	L15
Fingleton Av., Barr.	59	M19
Finhaven St. G32	54	AA14
Finlarig St. G34	40	FF12
Finlas St. G22	22	W10
Finlay Dr. G31	37	Y12
Finnart Sq. G40	52	X14
Finnart St. G40	52	X14
Finnieston Pl. G3	35	U12
Finnieston St.		
Finnieston St. G3	35	U12
Finsbay St. G51	33	R13
Fintry Av., Pais.	46	K16
Fintry Cres., Barr.	59	M19
Fintry Cres., Bish.	11	Z7
Fintry Dr. G44	52	W16
Fir Pl. G72	67	CC17
Caledonian Circuit		
Fir Pl., Bail.	56	EE14
Fir Pl., John.	44	E15
Firbank Ter., Barr.	60	N19
Firdon Cres. G15	6	P7
Firhill Rd. G20	21	V10
Firhill St. G20	21	V10
Firpark Pl. G31	36	X12
Firpark St.		
Firpark Rd., Bish.	23	Y8
Firpark St. G31	36	X12
Firpark Ter. G31	36	X12
Ark La.		
First Av. G33	24	BB10
First Av. G44	63	U19
First Av., Bear.	8	S6
First Av., Lenz.	13	CC7
First Av., Renf.	31	M11
First Av., Udd.	57	GG16
First Gdns. G41	50	S14
First St., Udd.	57	GG16
First Ter., Clyde.	5	L6
Firwood Dr. G44	64	W17
Fischer Gdns., Pais.	29	G13
Fisher Av., Pais.	45	G14
Fisher Ct. G31	36	X12
Fisher Cres., Clyde.	5	L5
Fisher Dr., Pais.	45	G14
Fisher Way, Pais.	45	G14
Fisher Dr.		
Fishers Rd., Renf.	17	M9
Fishescoates Av. G73	65	Z18
Fishescoates Gdns. G73	65	Z17
Fishescoates Rd.		
Fishescoates Rd. G73	65	Z17
Fitzalan Dr., Pais.	31	L13
Fitzalan Rd., Renf.	31	L11
Fitzroy La. G3	35	U12
Claremont St.		
Fitzroy Pl. G3	35	U12
Claremont St.		
Fitzroy Pl. G3	35	U12
Sauchiehall St.		
Flax Rd., Udd.	69	HH17
Fleet Av., Renf.	32	N11
Fleet St. G32	54	BB14
Fleming Av., Chr.	26	FF8
Fleming Av., Clyde.	17	M8
Fleming Rd., Cumb.	70	NN3
Fleming St. G31	37	Y13
Fleming St., Pais.	30	K12
Flemington Rd. G72	67	DD19
Flemington St. G21	22	X10
Fleurs Av. G41	50	S14
Fleurs Rd. G41	50	S14
Floors St., John.	43	D15
Floorsburn Cres., John.	43	D15
Flora Gdns., Bish.	11	Z7
Florence Dr., Giff.	62	T19
Florence Gdns. G73	65	Z18
Florence St. G5	36	W13
Florentine Pl. G12	35	U11
Gibson St.		
Florentine Ter. G12	35	U11
Southpark Av.		
Florida Av. G42	51	V16
Florida Cres. G42	51	V16
Florida Dr. G42	51	V16
Florida Gdns., Bail.	40	EE13
Florida Sq. G42	51	V16
Florida St. G42	51	V16
Flowerdale Pl. G53	60	P19
Waukglen Dr.		
Flures Av., Renf.	16	K8
Flures Cres., Renf.	16	K8
Flures Dr., Renf.	16	K8
Flures Pl., Renf.	16	K8
Fochabers Dr. G52	33	Q13
Fogo Pl. G20	20	T9
Forbes Dr. G40	36	X13
Forbes Pl., Pais.	46	K14
Forbes St. G40	36	X13
Ford Rd. G12	20	T10
Fordneuk St. G40	37	Y13
Fordoun St. G34	40	FF12
Fordyce St. G11	34	S11
Fore St. G14	19	Q10
Forehouse Rd., Kilb.	42	A14
Forest Dr., Udd.	69	HH18
Forest Gdns., Lenz.	12	BB6
Forest Pl., Lenz.	12	BB6
Forest Pl., Pais.	46	K15
Brodie Pk. Av.		
Forest Rd., Cumb.	71	QQ3
Forest Vw., Cumb.	71	QQ2
Foresthall Cres. G21	23	Y10
Foresthall Dr. G21	23	Y10
Forfar Av. G52	48	P14
Forfar Cres., Bish.	23	Z8
Forgan Gdns., Bish.	23	Z8
Forge, The, Giff.	62	T18
Braidpark Dr.		
Forge St. G21	37	Y11
Forglen St. G34	40	EE11
Formby Dr. G23	8	T7
Forres Av. G46	62	T18
Forres Gate, Giff.	62	T19
Forres Av.		
Forres St. G23	9	U7
Tolsta Dr.		
Forrest St. G40	37	Y13
Forrestfield St. G21	37	Y11
Fortevoit Av., Bail.	40	FF13
Fortevoit Pl., Bail.	40	FF13
Forth Av., Pais.	45	G15
Forth Av., Renf.	31	M11
Third Av.		
Forth Pl., John.	43	C16
Forth Rd. G61	7	Q5
Forth Rd., Bear.	7	Q7
Forth St. G41	51	U14
Fortingall Av. G12	20	T9
Grandtully Dr.		
Fortingall Pl. G12	20	T9
Fortrose St. G11	34	S11
Foswell Pl. G15	6	N5
Fotheringay La. G41	51	U15
Beaton Rd.		
Fotheringay Rd. G41	50	T15
Foulis La. G13	19	R9
Foulis St. G13	19	R9
Foundary St. G21	22	X10
Foundry La., Barr.	59	L19
Main St.		
Foundry Open G31	37	Y13
Fountain St. G31	36	X13
Fountainwell Av. G21	36	W11
Fountainwell Dr. G21	36	W11
Fountainwell Pl. G21	36	W11
Fountainwell Rd. G21	36	W11
Fountainwell Sq. G21	36	X11
Fountainwell Ter. G21	36	X11
Fourth Av. G33	24	BB9
Fourth Av., Lenz.	13	CC7
Fourth Av., Renf.	31	M11
Third Av.		
Fourth Gdns. G41	50	S14
Fourth St., Udd.	57	GG15
Fox La. G1	36	W13
Fox St. G1	35	V13
Foxbar Cres., Pais.	45	G16
Foxbar Dr. G13	18	P9
Foxbar Dr. G78	45	G16
Foxbar Rd., Pais.	45	G16
Foxes Gro. G66	13	DD5
Foxglove Pl. G53	60	P18
Foxhills Pl. G23	9	U7
Foxley St. G32	55	CC15
Foyers Ct. G13	18	P9
Kirkton Av.		
Foyers Ter. G21	23	Y10
Francis St. G5	51	V14
Frankfield Rd. G33	25	DD9
Frankfield St. G33	37	Z11
Frankfort St. G41	51	U15
Franklin St. G40	52	X14
Fraser Av. G73	53	Z16
Fraser Av., John.	44	E15
Fraser St. G72	66	AA17
Fraserbank St. G21	22	W10
Keppochhill Rd.		
Frazer St. G31	37	Z13
Freeland Dr. G53	60	P17
Freeland Dr., Renf.	16	J9
Freelands Ct., Old K.	4	J5
Freelands Pl., Old K.	4	J6
Freelands Rd., Old K.	4	J5
French St. G40	52	X14
French St., Dalm.	4	K6
French St., Renf.	31	L11
Freuchie St. G34	40	EE12
Friar Av., Bish.	11	Y6
Friars Ct. Rd., Chr.	14	EE7
Friars Pl. G13	19	Q8
Friarscourt Av. G13	7	Q7
Friarscourt La. G13	19	Q8
Arrowsmith Av.		
Friarton Rd. G43	63	U17
Friendship Way, Renf.	31	M11
Fruin Pl. G22	22	W10
Fruin Rd. G15	6	N7
Fruin St. G22	22	W10
Fulbar Av., Renf.	17	M10
Fulbar Ct., Renf.	17	M10
Fulbar Av.		
Fulbar Cres., Pais.	45	G15
Fulbar Gdns., Pais.	45	G15
Peacock Dr.		
Fulbar La., Renf.	17	M10
Fulbar Rd. G51	33	Q12
Fulbar Rd., Pais.	45	G14
Fulbar St., Renf.	17	M10
Fullarton Av. G32	54	BB15
Fullarton Rd. G32	54	AA16
Fullerton St., Pais.	30	J12
Fullerton Ter., Pais.	30	K12
Fulmar Ct., Bish.	22	X8
Fulmar Pl., John.	43	C16
Fulton Cres., Kilb.	42	B14
Fulton St. G13	19	Q8
Fulwood Av. G13	18	N8
Fulwood Av., Linw.	28	E13
Fulwood Pl. G13	18	N8
Fyvie Av. G43	62	S17
Gadie Av., Renf.	32	N11

Name	Page	Grid
Gadie St. G33	37	Z12
Gadloch Av., Lenz.	13	CC7
Gadloch Gdns., Lenz.	13	CC6
Gadloch St. G22	22	W9
Gadlock Vw. G66	13	CC7
Gadsburn Ct. G21	23	Z9
Wallacewell Quad.		
Gadshill St. G21	36	X11
Gailes Pk., Both.	69	GG19
Gailes St. G40	53	Y14
Gairbraid Av. G20	20	T9
Gairbraid Ct. G20	20	T9
Gairbraid Pl. G20	20	T9
Gairbraid Ter., Bail.	41	HH13
Gairn St. G11	34	S11
Castlebank St.		
Gala Av., Renf.	32	N11
Gala St. G33	38	AA11
Galbraith Av. G51	33	R12
Burghead Dr.		
Galbraith Dr. G51	33	Q12
Galbraith St. G51	33	Q12
Moss Rd.		
Galdenoch St. G33	38	BB11
Gallacher Av., Pais.	45	H15
Gallan Av. G23	9	U7
Galloway Dr. G73	65	Y18
Galloway St. G21	22	X9
Gallowflat St. G73	53	Y16
Reid St.		
Gallowgate G1	36	W13
Gallowhill Av., Lenz.	13	CC5
Gallowhill Gro., Lenz.	13	CC5
Gallowhill Rd., Lenz.	13	CC5
Gallowhill Rd., Pais.	30	K13
Galston St. G53	60	N17
Gamrie Dr. G53	48	P16
Gamrie Gdns. G53	48	P16
Gamrie Rd. G53	48	P16
Gannochy Dr., Bish.	11	Z7
Gantock Cres. G33	38	BB12
Gardenside Av. G32	54	BB16
Gardenside Av., Udd.	69	GG17
Gardenside Cres. G32	54	BB16
Gardenside Pl. G32	54	BB16
Gardenside St., Udd.	69	GG17
Gardner La., Bail.	56	FF14
Church St.		
Gardner St. G11	34	S11
Gardyne St. G34	40	EE11
Garfield St. G31	37	Y13
Garforth Rd., Bail.	55	DD14
Gargrave Av., Bail.	55	DD14
Garion Dr. G13	18	P9
Talbot Dr.		
Garlieston Rd. G33	39	DD13
Garmouth Ct. G51	33	R12
Garmouth St.		
Garmouth Gdns. G51	33	R12
Garmouth St. G51	33	R12
Garnet La. G3	35	V11
Garnet St.		
Garnet St. G3	35	V11
Garnethill St. G3	35	V11
Garngaber Av., Lenz.	13	CC5
Garngaber Ct. G66	13	DD5
Woodilee Rd.		
Garnie Av., Renf.	16	J8
Garnie Cres., Renf.	4	J7
Garnie La., Renf.	4	J7
Garnie Oval, Renf.	4	J7
Garnie Pl., Renf.	4	J7
Garnieland Rd., Renf.	4	J7
Garnkirk La. G33	25	DD9
Garnkirk St. G21	36	X11
Garnock St. G21	36	X11
Garrell Way, Cumb.	70	NN3
Garrioch Cres. G20	20	T9
Garrioch Dr. G20	20	T9
Garrioch Gate G20	20	T9
Garrioch Quad. G20	20	T9
Garrioch Rd. G20	20	T10
Garriochmill Rd. G20	21	U10
Raeberry St.		
Garriochmill Way G20	21	U10
Woodside Rd.		
Garrowhill Dr., Bail.	55	DD14
Garry Av., Bear.	8	S7
Garry Dr., Pais.	45	H15
Garry St. G44	51	V16
Garscadden G13	18	P8
Garscadden Rd. G15	6	P7
Garscadden Vw., Clyde.	5	M6
Kirkoswald Dr.		
Garscube Rd. G20	21	V10
Gartartan Rd., Pais.	32	N13
Gartcarron Hill, Cumb.	70	MM2
Dunbrach Rd.		
Gartconnel Dr., Bear.	7	R5
Gartconnel Gdns., Bear.	7	R5
Gartconnel Rd., Bear.	7	R5
Gartcosh Rd., Bail.	41	HH12
Gartcraig Rd. G33	38	AA12
Gartferry Av., Chr.	15	GG7
Gartferry Rd., Chr.	15	GG7
Gartferry St. G21	23	Y10
Garth St. G1	36	W12
Garthamlock Rd. G33	39	DD11
Garthland Dr. G31	37	Y12
Garthland La., Pais.	30	K13
Gartliston Ter., Bail.	41	HH13
Gartloch Cotts., Chr.	26	EE9
Gartloch Cotts., Gart.	27	GG10
Gartloch Rd. G33	38	AA11
Gartly St. G44	63	U18
Clarkston Rd.		
Gartmore Gdns., Udd.	57	GG16
Gartmore La., Chr.	15	HH7
Gartmore Rd., Pais.	47	M14
Gartmore Ter. G72	66	AA18
Gartness St. G31	37	Y12
Gartocher Rd. G32	39	CC13
Gartochmill Rd. G20	21	U10
Gartons Rd. G21	23	Z10
Gartshore Rd.,	15	GG5
Drumbreck		
Garturk St. G42	51	V15
Garvald Ct. G40	53	Y14
Baltic St.		
Garvald St. G40	53	Y14
Garve Av. G44	63	V18
Garvel Cres. G33	39	DD13
Garvel Rd. G33	39	DD13
Garvock Dr. G43	62	S17
Gas St., John.	44	E14
Gask Pl. G13	18	N8
Gatehouse St. G32	38	BB13
Gateside Av. G72	67	CC17
Gateside Cres., Barr.	59	L19
Gateside Pl., Kilb.	42	B14
Gateside Rd., Barr.	59	L19
Gateside St. G31	37	Y13
Gauldry Av. G52	49	Q14
Gauze St., Pais.	30	K13
Gavins Rd., Clyde.	5	L5
Gavinton St. G44	63	U18
Gear Ter. G40	53	Y15
Geary St. G23	8	T7
Torrin Rd.		
Geddes Rd. G21	23	Z8
Gelston St. G32	54	BB14
General Terminus Quay G51	35	U13
Generals Gate, Udd.	69	GG17
Cobbleriggs Way		
Gentle Row, Clyde.	4	K5
George V., Clyde.	5	M6
Robert Burns Av.		
George Cres., Clyde.	5	M6
George Gray St. G73	53	Z16
George Mann Ter. G73	65	Y17
George Pl., Pais.	46	K14
George Reith Av. G12	19	R9
George Sq. G2	36	W12
George St. G1	36	W12
George St., Barr.	59	L18
George St., John.	43	D14
George St., Pais.	46	J14
Gertrude Pl., Barr.	59	L19
Gibb St. G21	36	X11
Royston Rd.		
Gibson Cres., John.	43	D15
Gibson Rd., Renf.	31	L11
Gibson St. G12	35	U11
Gibson St. G40	36	X13
Giffnock Pk. Av., Giff.	62	T18
Gifford Dr. G52	32	P13
Gilbert St. G3	34	T12
Gilbertfield Pl. G33	38	BB11
Gilbertfield Rd. G72	67	CC18
Gilbertfield St. G33	38	BB11
Gilfillan Way, Pais.	45	G16
Ashton Way		
Gilhill St. G20	20	T8
Gilia St. G72	66	AA17
Gillies La., Bail.	56	FF14
Bredisholm Rd.		
Gills St. G31	37	Y13
Gilmerton St. G32	54	BB14
Gilmour Av., Clyde.	5	L5
Gilmour Cres. G73	52	X16
Gilmour Pl. G5	52	W14
Gilmour St., Clyde.	5	M6
Gilmour St., Pais.	30	K13
Girthon St. G32	55	CC14
Girvan St. G33	37	Z11
Gladney Av. G13	18	N8
Gladsmuir Rd. G52	32	P13
Gladstone Av., Barr.	59	L19
Gladstone St. G4	35	V11
Gladstone St., Dalm.	4	K7
Glaive Rd. G13	7	Q7
Glamis Av., John.	44	E15
Glamis Gdns., Bish.	11	Y6
Glamis Pl. G31	53	Z14
Glamis Rd.		
Glamis Rd. G31	53	Z14
Glanderston Av., Barr.	60	N19
Glanderston Dr. G13	18	P8
Glaselune St. G34	40	FF12
Lochdochart Rd.		
Glasgow Rd. G72	66	AA17
Glasgow Rd. G72	66	AA19
Glasgow Rd. G73	52	X15
Glasgow Rd., Bail.	55	DD14
Glasgow Rd., Barr.	59	M18
Glasgow Rd., Blan.	68	FF19
Glasgow Rd., Clyde.	5	L5
Glasgow Rd., Clyde.	17	L8
Glasgow Rd., Cumb.	71	PP2
Glasgow Rd., Cumb.	70	MM4
Glasgow Rd., E.K.	66	AA19
Glasgow Rd., Pais.	31	L13
Glasgow Rd., Renf.	18	N10
Glasgow Rd., Udd.	56	FF16
Glasgow St. G12	21	U10
Glassel Rd. G34	40	FF11
Glasserton Pl. G43	63	U17
Glasserton Rd. G43	63	U17
Glassford St. G1	36	W12
Glebe, The, Both.	69	HH19
Glebe Av. G71	69	HH19
Green St.		
Glebe Ct. G4	36	W12
Glebe Hollow G71	69	HH19
Glebe Wynd		
Glebe Pl. G72	66	BB17
Glebe Pl. G73	52	X16
Glebe St. G4	36	W11
Glebe St., Renf.	17	M10
Glebe Wynd G71	69	HH19
Gleddoch Rd. G52	32	N13
Glen Affric Av. G53	61	Q18
Glen Affric Dr. G53	61	Q18
Glen Affric Pl. G53	61	Q18
Glen Alby Pl. G53	61	Q18
Glen Av. G32	38	BB13
Glen Av., Chr.	15	GG7
Glen Clunie Av. G53	61	Q18
Glen Clunie Dr. G53	61	Q18
Glen Clunie Pl. G53	61	Q18
Glen Cona Dr. G53	61	Q17
Glen Cres. G13	18	N8

Glen Esk Dr. G53	61	Q18
Glen Fyne Rd., Cumb.	70	MM2
Glen Gdns., John.	44	F14
Glen La., Pais.	30	K13
Glen Lednock Dr., Cumb.	70	MM2
Glen Fyne Rd.		
Glen Livet Pl. G53	61	Q18
Glen Loy Pl. G53	61	Q18
Glen Mallie Dr. G53	61	Q18
Glen Markie Dr. G53	61	Q18
Glen Moriston Rd.,	61	Q18
Thorn.		
Glen Nevis Pl. G73	65	Z19
Glen Ogle St. G32	55	CC14
Glen Orchy Dr. G53	61	Q18
Glen Orchy Pl. G53	61	Q18
Glen Pk. Av., Thorn.	61	R19
Glen Rd. G32	38	BB12
Glen Sax Dr., Renf.	32	N11
Glen Sq. G33	24	BB10
Glen St. G72	67	CC18
Glen St., Barr.	59	M18
Glen St., Pais.	30	K13
Glen Vw., Cumb.	71	QQ2
Glenacre Cres., Udd.	57	GG16
Glenacre Dr. G45	64	W18
Glenacre Quad. G45	64	W18
Glenacre Rd., Cumb.	70	NN4
Glenacre St. G45	64	W18
Glenacre Ter. G45	64	W18
Glenallan Way, Pais.	45	G16
Glenalmond Rd. G73	65	Z18
Glenalmond St. G32	54	BB14
Glenapp Av., Pais.	47	L15
Glenapp Rd., Pais.	47	L15
Glenapp St. G41	51	U14
Glenarklet Dr., Pais.	47	L15
Glenartney Row, Chr.	14	FF7
Glenashdale Way, Pais.	47	L15
Glenbrittle Dr.		
Glenavon Av. G73	65	Z18
Glenavon Rd. G20	20	T8
Thornton St.		
Glenavon Ter. G11	34	S11
Crow Rd.		
Glenbank Av., Lenz.	13	CC6
Glenbank Dr., Thorn.	61	R19
Glenbank Rd., Lenz.	13	CC6
Glenbarr St. G21	36	X11
Glenbervie Pl. G23	8	T7
Glenbrittle Dr., Pais.	47	L15
Glenbrittle Way, Pais.	46	K15
Glenbuck Av. G33	24	AA9
Glenbuck Dr. G33	24	AA9
Glenburn Av. G73	65	Z17
Glenburn Av., Bail.	40	FF13
Glenburn Av., Chr.	15	GG7
Glenburn Cres., Pais.	46	J16
Glenburn Gdns., Bish.	10	X7
Glenburn Rd., Bear.	7	Q5
Glenburn Rd., Giff.	62	S19
Glenburn Rd., Pais.	45	H16
Glenburn St. G20	21	U8
Glenburnie Pl. G34	40	EE12
Glencairn Dr. G41	50	T15
Glencairn Dr. G73	52	X16
Glencairn Dr., Chr.	15	GG7
Glencairn Gdns. G41	51	U15
Glencairn Dr.		
Glencairn Rd., Cumb.	71	QQ3
Glencairn Rd., Pais.	31	L12
Glencally Av., Pais.	47	L15
Glencart Gro., John.	43	C15
Milliken Pk. Rd.		
Glenclora Dr., Pais.	47	L15
Glencloy St. G20	20	T8
Glencoats Cres., Pais.	29	H13
Glencoats Dr., Pais.	29	H13
Glencoe Pl. G13	19	R8
Glencoe Rd. G73	65	Z18
Glencoe St. G13	19	R8
Glencorse Rd., Pais.	46	J15
Glencorse St. G32	38	AA12
Glencroft Av., Udd.	57	GG16
Glencroft Rd. G44	64	W17
Glencryan Rd., Cumb.	71	PP4
Glendale Cres., Bish.	23	Z8
Glendale Dr., Bish.	23	Z8
Glendale Pl. G31	37	Y13
Glendale St.		
Glendale Pl. G64	23	Z8
Glendale St. G31	37	Y13
Glendaruel Av., Bear.	8	S6
Glendaruel Rd. G73	66	AA19
Glendee Gdns., Renf.	31	M11
Glendee Rd., Renf.	31	M11
Glendenning Rd. G13	7	R7
Glendevon Pl., Dalm.	4	K6
Glendevon Sq. G33	38	BB11
Glendore St. G14	33	R11
Glendower Way, Pais.	45	G16
Spencer Dr.		
Glendufhill Rd., Bail.	39	DD13
Gleneagles Av., Cumb.	71	PP1
Muirfield Rd.		
Gleneagles Cotts. G14	19	Q10
Dumbarton Rd.		
Gleneagles Dr., Bish.	11	Y6
Gleneagles Gdns., Bish.	11	Y6
Gleneagles La. N. G14	19	Q10
Dunglass Av.		
Gleneagles Pk., Both.	69	GG19
Gleneagles Ter. G14	19	Q10
Dumbarton Rd.		
Glenelg Quad. G34	40	FF11
Glenetive Pl. G73	66	AA19
Glenfarg Cres., Bear.	8	S6
Glenfarg Rd. G73	65	Y18
Glenfarg St. G20	35	V11
Glenfield Cres., Pais.	58	J17
Glenfield Rd., Pais.	58	J17
Glenfinnan Dr. G20	20	T9
Glenfinnan Dr., Bear.	8	T6
Glenfinnan Pl. G20	20	T9
Glenfinnan Rd. G20	20	T9
Glenfruin Dr., Pais.	47	L15
Glengarry Dr. G52	33	Q13
Glengavel Cres. G33	24	AA9
Glengyre St. G34	40	FF11
Glenhead Cres. G22	22	W9
Glenhead Rd., Dalm.	5	L5
Glenhead Rd., Lenz.	13	CC6
Glenhead St. G22	22	W9
Glenholme, Pais.	45	H15
Glenhove Rd., Cumb.	71	PP3
Gleniffer Av. G13	18	P9
Gleniffer Cres., John.	44	F15
Gleniffer Dr., Barr.	59	L17
Gleniffer Rd., Pais.	45	H16
Gleniffer Rd., Renf.	31	L11
Gleniffer Vw., Clyde.	5	M6
Kirkoswald Dr.		
Glenisa Av., Chr.	15	HH6
Glenisla St. G31	53	Z14
Glenkirk Dr. G15	6	P7
Glenlee Cres. G52	48	N14
Glenlora Dr. G53	48	P16
Glenlora Ter. G53	48	P16
Glenluce Dr. G32	55	CC14
Glenlui Av. G73	65	Y17
Glenlyon Pl. G73	65	Z18
Glenmalloch Pl., John.	44	F14
Glenmanor Av., Chr.	15	GG7
Glenmore Av. G42	52	X16
Glenmuir Dr. G53	60	P17
Glenpark Rd. G31	37	Y13
Glenpark St. G31	37	Y13
Glenpark Ter. G72	54	AA16
Glenpatrick Bldgs.,	44	F15
John.		
Glenpatrick Rd., John.	44	F15
Glenraith Rd. G33	24	BB10
Glenraith Sq. G33	24	BB10
Glenraith Wk. G33	25	CC10
Glenshee St. G31	53	Z14
Glenshiel Av., Pais.	47	L15
Glenside Av. G53	48	P15
Glenside Dr. G73	65	Z17
Glenspean Pl. G43	62	T17
Glenspean St.		
Glenspean St. G43	62	T17
Glentanar Pl. G22	21	V8
Glentarbert Rd. G73	65	Z18
Glenturret St. G32	54	BB14
Glentyan Av., Kilb.	42	B14
Glentyan Dr. G53	60	P17
Glentyan Ter. G53	48	P16
Glenview Cres., Chr.	15	HH6
Glenview Pl., Blan.	68	FF19
Glenville Av., Giff.	62	S18
Glenwood Ct., Kirk.	12	BB5
Glenwood Dr., Thorn.	61	R19
Glenwood Gdns., Kirk.	12	BB5
Glenwood Pl., Kirk.	12	BB5
Glenwood Rd., Kirk.	12	BB5
Gloucester Av. G73	65	Z17
Gloucester St. G5	35	V13
Gockston Rd., Pais.	30	J12
Gogar Pl. G33	38	AA12
Gogar St. G33	38	AA12
Goldberry Av. G14	18	P9
Goldie Rd., Udd.	69	HH18
Golf Ct. G44	63	U19
Golf Dr. G15	6	N7
Golf Dr., Pais.	47	M14
Golf Rd. G73	65	Y18
Golf Vw., Bear.	6	P5
Golf Vw., Dalm.	4	K6
Golfhill Dr. G31	37	Y12
Golfhill La. G31	37	Y12
Whitehill St.		
Golfhill Ter. G31	36	X12
Firpark St.		
Golspie St. G51	34	S12
Goosedubbs G1	36	W13
Stockwell St.		
Gopher Av., Udd.	57	HH16
Myrtle Rd.		
Gorbals Cross G5	36	W13
Gorbals La. G5	35	V13
Oxford St.		
Gorbals St. G5	35	V13
Gordon Av. G44	63	U19
Gordon Av., Bail.	39	DD13
Gordon Dr. G44	63	U18
Gordon La. G1	35	V12
Gordon St.		
Gordon Rd. G44	63	U19
Gordon St. G1	35	V12
Gordon St., Pais.	46	K14
Gordon Ter., Blan.	68	FF19
Gorebridge St. G32	38	AA12
Gorget Av. G13	7	Q7
Gorget Pl. G13	7	Q7
Gorget Quad. G15	6	P7
Gorget Av.		
Gorse Dr., Barr.	59	L18
Gorse Pl., Udd.	57	HH16
Myrtle Rd.		
Gorsewood, Bish.	10	X7
Gorstan Pl. G20	20	T9
Wyndford Rd.		
Gorstan St. G23	20	T8
Gosford La. G14	18	N9
Dumbarton Rd.		
Goudie St., Pais.	30	J12
Gough St. G33	37	Z12
Gourlay Path G21	22	W10
Endrick St.		
Gourlay St. G21	22	W10
Gourock St. G5	51	V14
Govan Cross G51	34	S12
Govan Rd. G51	33	R12
Govanhill St. G42	51	V15
Gowanbank Gdns., John.	43	D15
Floors St.		
Gowanbrae, Lenz.	13	CC5
Gallowhill Rd.		
Gowanlea Av. G15	6	P7
Gowanlea Dr., Giff.	62	T18
Gowanlea Ter., Udd.	57	HH16
Gower La. G51	34	T13
Gower St.		
Gower St. G41	50	T14
Gower Ter. G41	34	T13

Name	Page	Grid
Goyle Av. G15	7	Q6
Grace Av., Bail.	41	GG13
Grace St. G3	35	U12
Graffham Av., Giff.	62	T18
Grafton Pl. G4	36	W12
Graham Av. G72	67	CC17
Graham Av., Clyde.	5	L6
Graham Sq. G31	36	X13
Graham St., Barr.	59	L18
Graham St., John.	43	D15
Graham Ter., Bish.	23	Y8
Grahamston Ct., Pais.	47	M16
Grahamston Cres., Pais.	47	M16
Grahamston Pk., Barr.	59	L17
Grahamston Pl., Pais.	47	M16
Grahamston Rd.		
Grahamston Rd., Barr.	59	L17
Graighead Av. G33	23	Z10
Graignestock Pl. G40	36	X13
London Rd.		
Grainger Rd., Bish.	11	Z7
Grampian Av., Pais.	46	J16
Grampian Cres. G32	54	BB14
Grampian Pl. G32	54	BB14
Grampian St. G32	54	BB14
Grampian Way, Barr.	59	M19
Gran St., Clyde.	18	N8
Granby La. G12	20	T10
Great George St.		
Granby Pl. G12	20	T10
Great George St.		
Grandtully Dr. G12	20	T9
Grange Gdns. G71	69	HH19
Blairston Av.		
Grange Rd. G42	51	V16
Grange Rd., Bear.	7	R5
Grangeneuk Gdns., Cumb.	70	MM3
Grant St. G3	35	U11
Grantlea Gro. G32	55	CC14
Grantlea Ter. G32	55	CC14
Grantley Gdns. G41	50	T16
Grantley St. G41	50	T16
Granton St. G5	52	X15
Granville St. G3	35	U12
Granville St., Clyde.	5	L6
Gray Dr., Bear.	7	R6
Gray St. G3	34	T11
Great Dovehill G1	36	W13
Great George La. G12	20	T10
Great George St.		
Great George St. G12	20	T10
Great Hamilton St., Pais.	46	K15
Great Kelvin La. G12	21	U10
Glasgow St.		
Great Western Rd. G12	20	T10
Great Western Ter. G12	20	T10
Green, The G40	36	X13
Green Fm. Rd., Linw.	28	E13
Green Lo. Ter. G40	52	X14
Greenhead St.		
Green Pk., Both.	69	HH19
Green St.		
Green Rd. G73	53	Y16
Green Rd., Pais.	45	H14
Green St. G40	36	X13
Green St., Both.	69	HH19
Green St., Clyde.	5	L6
Greenan Av. G42	52	X16
Greenbank Dr., Pais.	46	J16
Greenbank Rd., Cumb.	70	MM3
Greenbank St. G43	62	S17
Harriet St.		
Greenbank St. G73	53	Y16
Greendyke St. G1	36	W13
Greenend Av., John.	43	C15
Greenend Pl. G32	39	CC12
Greenfaulds Cres., Cumb.	71	PP4
Greenfaulds Rd., Cumb.	70	NN4
Greenfield Av. G32	38	BB12
Greenfield Pl. G32	38	BB13
Budhill Av.		
Greenfield Rd. G32	39	CC13
Greenfield St. G51	33	R12
Greengairs Av. G51	33	Q12
Greenhaugh St. G51	34	S12
Greenhead Rd., Bear.	7	R6
Greenhead Rd., Renf.	16	J8
Greenhead St. G40	52	X14
Greenhill, Bish.	11	Y7
Greenhill Av., Gart.	27	GG8
Greenhill Av., Giff.	62	S19
Greenhill Ct. G73	53	Y16
Greenhill Cres., John.	44	F15
Greenhill Cres., Linw.	28	F13
Greenhill Dr., Linw.	28	F13
Greenhill Rd. G73	53	Y16
Greenhill Rd., Pais.	30	J13
Greenhill St. G73	53	Y16
Greenholm Av., Udd.	57	GG16
Greenholme St. G40	63	V17
Holmlea Rd.		
Greenknowe Rd. G43	62	S17
Greenlaw Av., Pais.	31	L13
Greenlaw Cres., Pais.	31	L13
Greenlaw Dr.		
Greenlaw Dr., Pais.	31	L13
Greenlaw Rd. G14	18	N9
Greenlaw Ter., Pais.	31	L13
Greenlaw Av.		
Greenlea Rd., Chr.	26	EE8
Greenlea St. G13	19	R9
Greenlees Gdns. G72	66	AA18
Greenlees Pk. G72	66	BB18
Greenlees Rd. G72	66	BB17
Greenloan Av. G51	33	Q12
Greenmount G22	21	V8
Greenock Av. G44	63	V17
Greenock Rd., Pais.	30	J12
Greenock Rd., Renf.	16	J9
Greenrig St. G33	23	Z10
Greenrig St., Udd.	69	GG17
Greenrigg Rd., Cumb.	71	PP3
Greenshields Rd., Bail.	40	EE13
Greenside Cres. G33	24	AA10
Greenside St. G33	24	AA10
Greentree Dr., Bail.	55	DD14
Greenview St. G43	50	T16
Greenways Av., Pais.	45	H15
Greenways Ct., John.	45	H15
Greenwell Pl. G51	34	S12
Greenwell St. G51	34	S12
Govan Rd.		
Greenwood Av. G72	67	DD17
Greenwood Av., Chr.	15	GG7
Greenwood Dr., Bear.	8	S6
Greenwood Quad., Clyde.	5	M7
Greer Quad., Clyde.	5	L6
Grenville Dr. G72	66	AA18
Greran Dr., Renf.	17	L10
Gretna St. G40	53	Y14
Greyfriars St. G32	38	AA12
Greystone Av. G73	65	Z17
Greywood St. G13	19	R8
Grier Path G31	37	Z13
Grierson La. G33	37	Z12
Lomax St.		
Grierson St. G33	37	Z12
Grieve Rd., Cumb.	71	PP2
Griqua Ter. G71	69	HH19
Grogarry Rd. G15	6	P6
Springside Pl.		
Grosvenor Cres. G12	20	T10
Observatory Rd.		
Grosvenor Cres. La. G12	20	T10
Byres Rd.		
Grosvenor La. G12	20	T10
Byres Rd.		
Grosvenor Mans. G12	20	T10
Observatory Rd.		
Grosvenor Ter. G12	20	T10
Grove, The, Kilb.	42	B14
Grove Pk., Lenz.	13	CC6
Groveburn Av., Thorn.	62	S18
Grovepark Gdns. G20	35	V11
Grovepark Pl. G20	21	V10
Grovepark St. G20	21	V10
Groves, The, Bish.	23	Z8
Woodhill Rd.		
Grudie St. G34	40	EE12
Gryffe Av., Renf.	17	L10
Gryffe Cres., Pais.	45	G15
Gryffe St. G44	63	V17
Guildford St. G33	39	CC11
Gullane Cres., Cumb.	70	NN1
Gullane St. G11	34	S11
Purdon St.		
Guthrie St. G20	20	T9
Haberlea Av. G53	61	Q18
Haberlea Gdns. G53	61	Q19
Hagg Cres., John.	43	D14
Hagg Pl., John.	43	D14
Hagg Rd., John.	43	D15
Haggs Rd. G41	50	T15
Haggs Wd. Av. G41	50	T15
Haghill Rd. G31	37	Z12
Haig Dr., Bail.	55	DD14
Haig St. G21	23	Y10
Hailes Av. G32	39	CC13
Haining Rd., Renf.	17	M10
Hairmyres St. G42	51	V15
Govanhill St.		
Hairst St., Renf.	17	M10
Halbeath Av. G15	6	N6
Halbert St. G41	51	U15
Haldane La. G14	19	Q10
Haldane St.		
Haldane St. G14	19	Q10
Halgreen Av. G15	6	N6
Halifax Way, Renf.	31	M11
Britannia Way		
Hall St., Clyde.	5	L7
Hallbrae St. G33	38	AA11
Halley Dr. G13	18	N8
Halley Pl. G13	18	N9
Halley Sq. G13	18	N8
Halley St. G13	18	N8
Hallhill Cres. G33	39	DD13
Hallhill Rd. G32	38	BB13
Hallhill Rd., John.	43	C16
Hallidale Cres., Renf.	32	N11
Hallrule Dr. G52	33	Q13
Hallside Av. G72	67	DD17
Hallside Cres. G72	67	DD17
Hallside Dr. G72	67	DD17
Hallside Rd. G72	67	DD18
Hallside St. G5	52	W14
Hallydown Dr. G13	19	Q9
Halton Gdns., Bail.	55	DD14
Hamilton Av. G41	50	S14
Hamilton Cres. G72	67	CC18
Hamilton Cres., Renf.	17	M9
Hamilton Dr. G12	21	U10
Hamilton Dr. G72	66	BB17
Hamilton Dr., Both.	69	HH19
Hamilton Dr., Giff.	62	T19
Hamilton Pk. Av. G12	21	U10
Hamilton Rd. G32	55	DD15
Hamilton Rd. G72	66	BB17
Hamilton Rd. G73	53	Y16
Hamilton Rd., Blan.	67	DD18
Hamilton Rd., Both.	69	HH19
Hamilton St. G42	52	W15
Hamilton St., Clyde.	17	M8
Hamilton St., Pais.	30	K13
Hamilton Ter., Clyde.	17	M8
Hamilton Vw., Udd.	57	HH16
Hamiltonhill Cres. G22	21	V10
Hamiltonhill Rd.		
Hamiltonhill Rd. G22	21	V10
Hampden Dr. G42	51	V16
Cathcart Rd.		
Hampden La. G42	51	V16
Cathcart Rd.		
Hampden Ter. G42	51	V16
Cathcart Rd.		
Hampden Way, Renf.	31	M11
Lewis Av.		
Hangingshaw Pl. G42	52	W16
Haning, The, Renf.	31	M11
Hanover St. G1	36	W12
Hanson St. G31	36	X12

Name	Page	Grid
Hapland Av. G53	49	Q15
Hapland Rd. G53	49	Q15
Harbour La., Pais.	30	K13
Harbour Rd., Pais.	30	K12
Harburn Pl. G23	9	U7
Harbury Pl. G14	18	N9
Harcourt Dr. G31	37	Y12
Hardgate Dr. G51	33	Q12
Hardgate Gdns. G51	33	Q12
Hardgate Pl. G51	33	Q12
Hardgate Rd. G51	33	Q12
Hardie Av. G73	53	Z16
Hardridge Av. G52	49	Q15
Hardridge Rd.		
Hardridge Pl. G52	49	R15
Hardridge Rd. G52	49	Q15
Harefield Dr. G14	18	P9
Harelaw Av. G44	63	U18
Harelaw Av., Barr.	59	M19
Harelaw Cres., Pais.	46	J16
Harhill St. G51	33	R12
Harland Cotts. G14	33	Q11
South St.		
Harland St. G14	19	Q10
Harlaw Gdns. G64	11	Z7
Harley St. G51	34	T13
Harmetray St. G22	22	W9
Harmony Pl. G51	34	S12
Harmony Row G51	34	S12
Harmony Sq. G51	34	S12
Harmsworth St. G11	33	R11
Harport St. G46	61	R18
Harriet St. G73	53	Y16
Harris Rd. G23	9	U7
Harris Rd., Old K.	4	J5
Harrison Dr. G51	34	S13
Harrow Ct. G15	6	N6
Linkwood Dr.		
Harrow Pl. G15	6	N6
Hart St. G31	38	AA13
Hart St., Linw.	28	E13
Hartfield Ter., Pais.	47	L15
Hartlaw Cres. G52	32	P13
Hartree Av. G13	18	N8
Hartstone Pl. G53	48	P16
Hartstone Rd. G53	48	P16
Hartstone Ter. G53	48	P16
Harvey St. G4	36	W11
Harvie St. G51	34	T13
Harwood St. G32	38	AA12
Hastie St. G3	34	T11
Old Dumbarton Rd.		
Hatfield Dr. G12	19	R9
Hathaway Dr., Giff.	62	S19
Hathaway La. G20	21	U9
Avenuepark St.		
Hathaway St. G20	21	U9
Hathersage Av., Bail.	40	EE13
Hathersage Dr., Bail.	40	EE13
Hathersage Gdns., Bail.	40	EE13
Hatters Row G40	52	X14
Dalmarnock Rd.		
Hatton Dr. G52	48	P14
Hatton Gdns. G52	48	P14
Haugh Rd. G3	34	T12
Haughburn Pl. G53	48	P16
Haughburn Rd. G53	48	P16
Haughburn Ter. G53	49	Q16
Havelock La. G11	34	T11
Dowanhill St.		
Havelock St. G11	34	T11
Hawick Av. G78	45	H15
Hawick St. G13	18	N8
Hawkhead Av., Pais.	47	L15
Hawkhead Rd., Pais.	47	L14
Hawthorn Av., Bish.	23	Y8
Hawthorn Av., Lenz.	13	CC5
Hawthorn Av., Renf.	16	K8
Hawthorn Cres., Renf.	4	K7
Hawthorn Quad. G22	22	W9
Hawthorn Rd., Renf.	16	K8
Hawthorn St. G22	22	W9
Hawthorn St., Clyde.	5	L6
Hawthorn Ter., Udd.	57	HH16
Douglas St.		
Hawthorn Wk. G72	65	Z17
Hawthorn Wk., Bish.	23	Z8
Letham Dr.		
Hawthornden Gdns. G23	9	U7
Hawthorne Av., John.	44	E15
Hay Dr., John.	44	E14
Hayburn Ct. G11	34	S11
Hayburn Cres. G11	20	S10
Hayburn La. G12	20	S10
Queensborough Gdns.		
Hayburn St. G11	34	S11
Hayfield St. G5	52	W14
Hayhill Cotts., Gart.	27	HH9
Hayle Gdns., Chr.	15	GG6
Haylynn St. G14	33	R11
Haymarket St. G32	38	AA12
Haystack Pl., Lenz.	13	CC6
Hayston Cres. G22	21	V9
Hayston St. G22	21	V9
Haywood St. G22	21	V9
Hazel Av. G44	63	U18
Clarkston Rd.		
Hazel Av., John.	44	E15
Hazel Av., Lenz.	13	CC5
Hazel Dene, Bish.	11	Y7
Hazel Gro., Lenz.	13	CC5
Hazel Rd., Cumb.	71	QQ2
Hazel Ter., Udd.	57	HH16
Douglas St.		
Hazelden Gdns. G44	63	U18
Hazellea Dr., Giff.	62	T18
Hazelwood Av. G78	45	G16
Hazelwood Gdns. G73	65	Z18
Hazelwood Rd. G41	50	T14
Hazlitt St. G20	21	V9
Heath Av., Bish.	23	Y8
Heath Av., Lenz.	13	CC6
Heathcliffe Av., Blan.	68	FF19
Heathcot Av. G15	6	N7
Heathcot Pl. G15	6	N7
Heathcot Av.		
Heather Av., Barr.	59	L17
Heather Dr., Lenz.	12	BB6
Heather Gdns., Lenz.	12	BB6
Heather Pl., John.	44	E15
Heather Pl., Lenz.	12	BB5
Heather St. G41	35	U13
Scotland St.		
Heatherbrae, Bish.	10	X7
Heatheryknowe Rd.,	41	GG12
Bail.		
Heathfield Av., Chr.	15	GG7
Heathfield St. G33	39	CC12
Heathfield Ter. G21	22	X9
Broomfield Rd.		
Heathside Rd., Giff.	62	T18
Heathwood Dr., Thorn.	62	S18
Hecla Av. G15	6	N6
Hecla Pl. G15	6	N6
Hector Rd. G41	50	T16
Heddle Pl. G2	35	V12
Cadogan St.		
Heggie Ter. G14	19	Q10
Dumbarton Rd.		
Helen St. G52	33	R13
Helensburgh Dr. G13	19	Q9
Helenslea G72	67	CC18
Helenvale Ct. G31	37	Z13
Helenvale St.		
Helenvale St. G31	53	Z14
Helmsdale Av., Blan.	68	FF18
Helmsdale Ct. G72	67	CC17
Hemlock St. G13	19	R8
Henderland Rd., Bear.	7	R7
Henderson Av. G72	67	CC17
Henderson St. G20	21	U10
Henderson St., Clyde.	18	N8
Henderson St., Pais.	30	J13
Henrietta St. G14	19	Q10
Henry St., Barr.	59	L18
Hepburn Rd. G52	32	P12
Herald Av. G13	7	Q7
Herald Way, Renf.	31	M11
Viscount Av.		
Herbert St. G20	21	U10
Herbertson St. G5	35	V13
Eglinton St.		
Hercla Av. G15	6	N6
Hercla Pl. G15	6	N6
Hercla Sq. G15	6	N7
Hercules Way, Renf.	31	M11
Friendship Way		
Herichell St. G13	19	R9
Foulis La.		
Heriot Av., Pais.	45	G16
Heriot Cres., Bish.	11	Y6
Heriot Rd., Lenz.	13	CC6
Herma St. G23	21	U8
Hermiston Av. G32	39	CC13
Hermiston Pl. G32	39	CC13
Hermiston Rd. G32	38	BB12
Hermitage Av. G13	19	Q9
Heron Ct., Clyde.	5	L5
Heron Pl., John.	43	C16
Heron St. G40	52	X14
Heron Way, Renf.	31	M11
Britannia Way		
Herries Rd. G41	50	T15
Herriet St. G41	51	U14
Herschell St. G13	19	R9
Foulis La.		
Hertford Av. G12	20	S9
Hexham Gdns. G41	50	T15
Heys St., Barr.	59	M19
Hickman St. G42	51	V15
Hickory St. G22	22	X9
High Barholm, Kilb.	42	B14
High Calside, Pais.	46	J14
High Craighall Rd. G4	35	V11
High Parksail, Renf.	16	J8
High Rd., Pais.	46	J14
High St. G1	36	W13
High St. G73	53	Y16
High St., John.	43	D14
High St., Pais.	46	J14
High St., Renf.	17	M10
Highburgh Dr. G73	65	Y17
Highburgh Rd. G12	34	T11
Highburgh Ter. G12	34	T11
Highburgh Rd.		
Highcraig Av., John.	43	C15
Highcroft Av. G44	64	W17
Highfield Av., Pais.	46	J16
Highfield Cres., Pais.	46	J16
Highfield Dr. G12	20	S9
Highfield Dr. G73	65	Z18
Highfield Pl. G12	20	S9
Highkirk Vw., John.	43	D15
Highland La. G51	34	T12
Hilary Av. G73	65	Z17
Hilary Dr., Bail.	39	DD13
Hilda Cres. G33	24	AA10
Hill Pk., Clyde.	5	L5
Hill Path G52	32	P13
Hill Pl. G52	32	P13
Hill Rd., Cumb.	70	NN3
Hill St. G3	35	V11
Hillcrest, Chr.	26	FF8
Hillcrest Av. G32	54	BB16
Hillcrest Av. G44	63	U18
Hillcrest Av., Cumb.	70	NN3
Hillcrest Av., Pais.	58	J17
Hillcrest Ct., Cumb.	70	NN3
Hillcrest Rd. G32	55	CC16
Hillcrest Rd., Bear.	7	R6
Hillcrest Rd., Udd.	57	HH16
Hillcrest Ter., Both.	69	HH18
Churchill Cres.		
Hillcroft Ter., Bish.	22	X8
Hillend Cres., Clyde.	4	K5
Hillend Rd. G22	21	V8
Hillend Rd. G73	65	Y17
Hillfoot Av. G73	53	Y16
Hillfoot Av., Bear.	7	R5
Hillfoot Dr., Bear.	7	R5
Hillfoot Gdns., Udd.	57	GG16
Hillfoot St. G31	37	Y12
Hillfoot Ter., Bear.	8	S5
Milngavie Rd.		
Hillhead Av. G73	65	Y18

Name	Map	Grid
Hillhead Av., Chr.	15	GG7
Hillhead Gdns. G12	34	T11
Hillhead St.		
Hillhead Pl. G12	35	U11
Bank St.		
Hillhead St. G12	34	T11
Hillhouse St. G21	23	Y10
Hillington Gdns. G52	49	Q14
Hillington Ind. Est. G52	32	N12
Hillington Pk. Cres. G52	33	Q13
Hillington Quad. G52	32	P13
Hillington Rd. G52	32	N11
Hillington Rd. S., Renf.	32	P13
Hillington Ter. G52	32	P13
Hillkirk Pl. G21	22	X10
Hillkirk St. G21	22	X10
Hillkirk St. La. G21	22	X10
Hillkirk St.		
Hillneuk Av., Bear.	7	R5
Hillneuk Dr., Bear.	8	S5
Hillpark Av., Pais.	46	J15
Hillpark Dr. G43	62	T17
Hillsborough Rd., Bail.	39	DD13
Hillsborough Sq. G12	34	T11
Hillhead St.		
Hillsborough Ter. G12	21	U10
Bower St.		
Hillside Av., Bear.	7	R5
Hillside Ct., Thorn.	61	R18
Hillside Dr., Barr.	59	L18
Hillside Dr., Bear.	8	S5
Hillside Dr., Bish.	11	Y7
Hillside Gdns. G11	20	S10
Turnberry Rd.		
Hillside Gdns. La. G11	20	S10
North Gardner St.		
Hillside Gro., Barr.	59	L18
Hillside Quad. G43	62	S17
Hillside Rd. G43	62	S17
Hillside Rd., Barr.	59	L18
Hillside Rd., Pais.	47	L15
Hillswick Cres. G22	21	V8
Hilltop Rd., Chr.	15	GG7
Eastwood Rd.		
Hillview Cres., Udd.	57	GG16
Hillview Dr., Blan.	68	FF19
Hillview Rd., John.	44	F15
Hillview St. G32	38	AA13
Hilton Gdns. G13	19	R8
Hilton Gdns. La. G13	19	R8
Fulton St.		
Hilton Pk., Bish.	10	X6
Hilton Rd., Bish.	10	X6
Hilton Ter. G13	19	R8
Hilton Ter. G72	66	AA18
Hilton Ter., Bish.	10	X6
Hinshaw St. G20	21	V10
Hinshelwood Dr. G51	34	S13
Hinshelwood Pl. G51	34	S13
Edmiston Dr.		
Hirsel Pl., Udd.	69	HH18
Lomond Dr.		
Hobart Cres., Dalm.	4	J5
Hobart St. G22	21	V10
Hobden St. G21	23	Y10
Hoddam Av. G45	64	X18
Hoddam Ter. G45	65	Y18
Hoey St. G51	34	T12
Hogan Ct., Clyde.	4	K5
Dalgleish Av.		
Hogarth Av. G32	37	Z12
Hogarth Cres. G32	37	Z12
Hogarth Dr. G32	37	Z12
Hogarth Gdns. G32	37	Z12
Hogg Av., John.	43	D15
Hogganfield St. G33	37	Z11
Holburn Av., Pais.	29	H13
Hole Brae, Cumb.	71	PP2
Holeburn Rd. G43	62	T17
Holehouse Dr. G13	18	P9
Holland St. G2	35	V12
Hollinwell Rd. G23	21	U8
Hollowglen Rd. G32	38	BB13
Hollows Av., Pais.	45	G16
Hollows Cres., Pais.	45	G16
Holly Dr. G21	23	Y10
Holly Pl., John.	44	E16
Holly St., Clyde.	5	L6
Hollybank Pl. G72	66	BB18
Hollybank St. G21	37	Y11
Hollybrook St. G42	51	V15
Hollybush Av., Pais.	45	H16
Hollybush Rd. G52	32	N13
Hollymount, Bear.	7	R7
Holm Av., Pais.	46	K15
Holm Av., Udd.	57	GG16
Holm Pl., Linw.	28	E12
Holm St. G2	35	V12
Holmbank Av. G41	50	T16
Holmbrae Av., Udd.	57	GG16
Holmbrae Rd., Udd.	57	GG16
Holmbyre Rd. G45	64	W19
Holmbyre Ter. G45	64	W19
Holmes Av., Renf.	31	M11
Holmfauldhead Dr. G51	33	R12
Holmfauldhead Pl. G51	33	R12
Govan Rd.		
Holmhead Cres. G44	63	V17
Holmhead Pl. G44	63	V17
Holmhead Rd. G44	63	V17
Holmhill Av. G72	66	BB18
Holmhills Dr. G72	66	AA18
Holmhills Gdns. G72	66	AA18
Holmhills Gro. G72	66	AA18
Holmhills Pl. G72	66	AA18
Holmhills Rd. G72	66	AA18
Holmhills Ter. G72	66	AA18
Holmlea Rd. G44	51	V16
Holms Pl., Gart.	27	GG8
Holmswood Av., Blan.	68	FF19
Holmwood Av., Udd.	57	GG16
Holmwood Gdns., Udd.	69	GG17
Holyrood Cres. G20	35	U11
Holyrood Quad. G20	35	U11
Holywell St. G31	37	Y13
Homeston Av., Udd.	69	HH18
Honeybog Rd. G52	32	N13
Hood St., Clyde.	5	M7
Hope St. G2	35	V12
Hopefield Av. G12	20	T9
Hopehill Pl. G20	21	V10
Hopehill Rd.		
Hopehill Rd. G20	21	V10
Hopeman Av. G46	61	R18
Hopeman Dr. G46	61	R18
Hopeman Path, Thorn.	61	R18
Kennishead Pl.		
Hopeman Rd. G46	61	R18
Hopeman St. G46	61	R18
Hopetoun Pl. G23	9	U7
Hopetoun Ter. G21	23	Y10
Foresthall Dr.		
Hornal Rd., Udd.	69	HH18
Hornbeam Dr., Dalm.	5	L6
Hornbeam Rd., Udd.	57	HH16
Myrtle Rd.		
Horndean Ct., Bish.	11	Y6
Horndean Cres. G33	39	CC11
Horne St. G22	22	X9
Hawthorn St.		
Hornshill Rd. G33	25	DD8
Hornshill St. G21	23	Y10
Horsburgh St. G33	39	CC11
Horse Shoe La., Bear.	7	R6
Horse Shoe Rd., Bear.	7	R5
Horslethill Rd. G12	20	T10
Hospital St. G5	51	V14
Hotspur St. G20	21	U10
Houldsworth La. G3	35	U12
Finnieston St.		
Houldsworth St. G3	35	U12
Househillmuir Cres. G53	49	Q16
Househillmuir La. G53	49	Q16
Househillmuir Pl. G53	49	Q16
Househillmuir Rd. G53	60	P17
Househillwood Cres. G53	48	P16
Househillwood Rd. G53	60	P17
Housel Av. G13	18	P8
Houston Pl. G5	35	U13
Houston Pl., John.	44	F15
Houston Sq., John.	43	D14
Houston St. G5	35	U13
Houston St., Renf.	17	M10
Howard St. G1	35	V13
Howard St., Pais.	47	L14
Howat St. G51	34	S12
Howden Dr., Linw.	28	E13
Howe St., Pais.	45	G14
Howford Rd. G52	48	P14
Howgate Av. G15	6	N6
Howieshill Av. G72	66	BB17
Howieshill Rd. G72	66	BB18
Howth Dr. G13	19	R8
Howth Ter. G13	19	R8
Howwood St. G41	35	U13
Hoylake Pk., Both.	69	GG19
Hoylake Pl. G23	9	U7
Hozier Cres., Udd.	57	GG16
Hozier St. G40	52	X14
Hubbard Dr. G11	33	R11
Hugh Murray Gro. G72	67	CC17
Hughenden Dr. G12	20	S10
Hughenden Gdns. G12	20	S10
Hughenden La. G12	20	S10
Hughenden Rd. G12	20	S10
Hughenden Ter. G12	20	S10
Hughenden Rd.		
Hugo St. G20	21	U9
Hume St., Both.	69	HH18
Hume Dr., Udd.	57	GG16
Hume Rd., Cumb.	71	PP2
Hume St., Clyde.	5	L7
Hunter Pl. G78	42	B15
Hunter Rd. G73	53	Z15
Hunter St. G4	36	X13
Hunter St., Pais.	30	K13
Hunterfield Dr. G72	66	AA17
Hunterhill Av., Pais.	46	K14
Hunterhill Rd.		
Hunterhill Rd., Pais.	46	K14
Huntersfield Rd., John.	43	C15
Huntershill Rd., Bish.	22	X8
Huntershill St. G21	22	X9
Huntershill Way, Bish.	22	X8
Crowhill Rd.		
Huntingdon Sq. G21	36	X11
Huntingdon Rd.		
Huntington Rd. G21	36	X11
Huntingtower Rd., Bail.	56	EE14
Huntley Rd. G52	32	N12
Huntly Av., Giff.	62	T19
Huntly Dr. G72	66	BB18
Huntly Gdns. G12	20	T10
Huntly Path, Chr.	15	HH7
Burnbrae Av.		
Huntly Rd. G12	20	T10
Huntly Ter., Pais.	47	L15
Hurlet Rd., Pais.	47	M15
Hurley Hawkin, Bish.	23	Z8
Hurlford Av. G13	18	N8
Hutcheson Rd., Thorn.	62	S19
Hutcheson St. G1	36	W12
Hutchinson Ct. G2	35	V12
Hope St.		
Hutchinson Pl. G72	67	DD18
Hutchison Ct., Giff.	62	S18
Berryhill Rd.		
Hutchison Dr., Bear.	8	S7
Hutton Dr. G51	33	R12
Huxley St. G20	21	U9
Hydepark Pl. G21	22	X9
Springburn Rd.		
Hydepark St. G3	35	U12
Hyndal Av. G53	49	Q15
Hyndford St. G51	34	S12
Hyndland Av. G11	34	S11
Hyndland Rd. G12	20	S10
Hyndland St. G11	34	T11
Hyndlee Dr. G52	33	Q13
Hyslop Pl., Clyde.	5	L6
Albert Rd.		

Iain Dr., Bear. 7 Q5
Iain Rd., Bear. 7 Q5
Ibrox St. G51 34 T13
Ibrox Ter. G51 34 S13
Ibrox Ter. La. G51 34 S13
Ibroxholm La. G51 34 T13
  Paisley Rd. W.
Ibroxholm Oval G51 34 S13
Ibroxholm Pl. G51 34 T13
Ilay Av., Bear. 19 R8
Ilay Ct., Bear. 20 S8
Ilay Rd., Bear. 20 S8
Inchbrae Rd. G52 49 Q14
Inchfad Dr. G15 6 N6
Inchholm St. G11 33 R11
Inchinnan Rd., Pais. 30 K12
Inchinnan Rd., Renf. 17 L10
Inchkeith Pl. G32 38 BB12
Inchlee St. G14 33 R11
Inchmurrin Dr. G73 65 Z19
Inchmurrin Gdns. G73 65 Z19
Inchmurrin Pl. G73 65 Z19
Inchoch St. G33 39 DD11
Inchrory Pl. G15 6 N6
Incle St., Pais. 30 K13
India Dr., Renf. 16 J9
India St. G2 35 V12
Inga St. G20 21 U8
Ingerbreck Av. G73 65 Z18
Ingleby Dr. G31 37 Y12
Inglefield St. G42 51 V15
Ingleneuk Av. G33 24 BB9
Inglestone Av., Thorn. 62 S19
Inglis St. G31 37 Y13
Ingram St. G1 36 W12
Inishail Rd. G33 39 CC11
Inkerman Rd. G52 32 N13
Innerwick Dr. G52 32 P13
Inver Rd. G33 39 DD12
Inveraray Dr., Bish. 11 Y6
Invercanny Dr. G15 6 N6
Invercanny Pl. G15 6 P6
Inverclyde Gdns. G11 19 R10
  Broomhill Dr.
Inverclyde Gdns. G73 66 AA18
Inveresk Cres. G32 38 BB13
Inveresk St. G32 38 BB13
Inverewe Av. G46 61 Q18
Inverewe Dr. G46 61 Q19
Inverewe Gdns. G46 61 Q19
Inverewe Pl. G46 61 Q18
Invergarry Av. G46 61 Q19
Invergarry Ct. G46 61 Q19
Invergarry Dr. G46 61 Q19
Invergarry Gdns. G46 61 Q19
Invergarry Gro. G46 61 Q19
Invergarry Pl. G46 61 Q19
Invergarry Quad. G46 61 R19
Invergarry Vw. G46 61 R19
Inverglas Av., Renf. 32 N11
  Morriston Cres.
Invergordon Av. G43 51 U16
Invergyle Dr. G52 32 P13
Inverkar Dr., Pais. 45 H15
Inverkip St. G5 36 W13
Inverlair Av. G43 63 U17
Inverleith St. G32 37 Z13
Inverlochy St. G33 39 CC11
Inverness St. G51 33 Q13
Inveroran Dr., Bear. 8 S6
Invershiel Rd. G23 8 T7
Invershin Dr. G20 20 T9
  Wyndford Rd.
Inverurie St. G21 22 W10
Inzievar Ter. G32 54 BB15
Iona Ct. G51 34 S12
Iona Cres., Old K. 4 J5
Iona Dr., Old K. 4 J5
Iona Dr., Pais. 46 J16
Iona Gdns., Old K. 4 J5
Iona La., Chr. 15 HH7
  Heathfield Av.
Iona Pl., Old K. 4 J5
Iona Rd. G73 66 AA18
Iona Rd., Renf. 31 M11

Iona St. G51 34 S12
Iris Av. G45 65 Y18
Irongray St. G31 37 Z12
Irvine Dr., Linw. 28 E13
Irvine St. G40 53 Y14
Irving Av., Clyde. 5 L5
  Stewart Dr.
Irving Quad., Clyde. 5 L5
  Stewart Dr.
Iser La. G41 51 U16
Island Rd., Cumb. 70 MM4
Islay Av. G73 66 AA18
Islay Cres., Old K. 4 J5
Islay Cres., Pais. 46 J16
Islay Dr., Old K. 4 J5
Ivanhoe Rd. G13 19 Q8
Ivanhoe Rd., Cumb. 70 NN4
Ivanhoe Rd., Pais. 45 G15
Ivanhoe Way, Pais. 45 G15
  Ivanhoe Rd.
Ivybank Av. G72 67 CC18

Jacks Rd., Udd. 69 HH17
Jagger Gdns., Bail. 55 DD14
Jamaica St. G1 35 V13
James Dunlop Gdns., 23 Y8
  Bish.
  Graham Ter.
James Gray St. G41 51 U16
James Morrison St. G1 36 W13
  St. Andrews Sq.
James Nisbet St. G21 36 X12
James St. G40 52 X14
James Watt La. G2 35 V12
  James Watt St.
James Watt St. G2 35 V12
Jamieson Ct. G42 51 V15
Jamieson Path G42 51 V15
  Jamieson St.
Jamieson St. G42 51 V15
Janebank Av. G72 67 CC18
Janefield Av., John. 43 D15
Janefield St. G31 37 Y13
Janes Brae, Cumb. 70 NN4
Janetta St., Clyde. 5 L6
Jardine St. G20 21 U10
Jardine Ter., Gart. 27 GG9
Jasgray St. G42 51 U15
Jean Armour Dr., Clyde. 5 M6
Jedburgh Av. G73 53 Y16
Jedburgh Dr., Pais. 45 H15
Jedburgh Gdns. G20 21 U10
Jedworth Av. G15 6 P6
Jellicoe St., Dalm. 4 K6
Jennys Well Rd., Pais. 47 L15
Jerviston Rd. G33 39 CC11
Jessie St. G42 52 W15
Jessiman Sq., Renf. 31 L11
John Brown Pl., Chr. 26 FF8
John Knox La. G4 36 X12
  Drygate
John Knox St. G4 36 X12
John Knox St., Clyde. 17 M8
John Lang St., John. 44 E14
John St. G1 36 W12
John St., Barr. 59 L18
John St., Pais. 46 J14
Johnshaven St. G43 50 T16
  Bengal St.
Johnston Rd., Gart. 27 HH9
Johnston St., Pais. 46 K14
  Gordon St.
Johnstone Av. G52 32 P13
Johnstone Av., Clyde. 17 M8
Johnstone Dr. G72 66 BB17
Johnstone Dr. G73 53 Y16
Joppa St. G33 38 AA12
Jordan St. G14 33 Q11
Jordanhill Cres. G13 19 Q9
Jordanhill Dr. G13 19 Q9
Jordanhill La. G13 19 R9
  Austen Rd.
Jordanvale Av. G14 33 Q11
Jowitt Av., Clyde. 5 M7

Joycelyn Sq. G1 36 W13
Jubilee Bk., Lenz. 13 CC6
  Heriot Rd.
Jubilee Path, Bear. 7 R6
Jubilee Ter., John. 43 C15
Julian Av. G12 20 T10
Julian La. G12 20 T10
  Julian Av.
Juniper Ct., Lenz. 12 BB5
Juniper Pl. G32 55 DD14
Juniper Pl., John. 44 E16
Juniper Ter. G32 55 DD14
Jura Av., Renf. 31 M11
Jura Ct. G52 33 R13
Jura Dr., Blan. 68 FF18
Jura Dr., Old K. 4 J5
  Jura Rd.
Jura Gdns., Old K. 4 J5
  Jura Rd.
Jura Pl., Old K. 4 J5
  Jura Rd.
Jura Rd., Old K. 4 J5
Jura Rd., Pais. 46 J16
Jura St. G52 33 R13

Kaim Dr. G53 61 Q17
Kames St. G5 51 V14
Karol Path G4 35 V11
  St. Peters St.
Katewell Av. G15 6 N6
Katrine Av., Bish. 11 Y7
Katrine Dr., Pais. 45 G15
Katrine Pl. G72 66 BB17
Kay St. G21 22 X10
Kaystone Rd. G15 6 P7
Keal Av. G15 18 P8
Keal Cres. G15 18 P8
Keal Dr. G15 18 P8
Keal Pl. G15 18 P8
Kearn Av. G15 6 P7
Kearn Pl. G15 6 P7
Keats Pk., Udd. 69 HH18
Keir Dr., Bish. 10 X7
Keir St. G41 51 U14
Keirhill Rd., Cumb. 70 MM3
  Woodburn Rd.
Keirs Wk. G72 66 BB17
Keith Av., Giff. 62 T18
Keith Ct. G11 34 T11
  Keith St.
Keith St. G11 34 T11
Kelbourne St. G20 21 U10
Kelburn St., Barr. 59 L19
Kelburne Dr., Pais. 31 L13
Kelburne Gdns., Bail. 56 EE14
Kelburne Gdns., Pais. 31 L13
Kelburne Oval, Pais. 31 L13
Kelhead Av. G52 32 N13
Kelhead Dr. G52 32 N13
Kelhead Path G52 32 P13
Kelhead Pl. G52 32 N13
Kellas St. G51 34 S13
Kells Pl. G15 6 N6
Kelso Av. G73 53 Y16
Kelso Av., Pais. 45 H15
Kelso Pl. G14 18 N9
Kelso St. G13 18 N9
Kelton St. G32 54 BB14
Kelty Pl. G5 35 V13
  Bedford St.
Kelty St. G5 51 V14
  Eglinton St.
Kelvin Av. G52 32 N11
Kelvin Ct. G12 19 R9
Kelvin Cres., Bear. 7 R7
Kelvin Dr. G20 20 T10
Kelvin Dr., Barr. 59 M19
Kelvin Dr., Bish. 11 Y7
Kelvin Dr., Chr. 15 GG7
Kelvin Rd., Cumb. 71 PP4
Kelvin Rd., Udd. 57 GG16
Kelvin Way G3 34 T11
Kelvin Way, Udd. 69 HH18
  Bracken Ter.

Kelvindale Bldgs. G12	20	T9
Kelvindale Rd.		
Kelvindale Cotts. G12	20	T9
Kelvindale Rd.		
Kelvindale Gdns. G20	20	T9
Kelvindale Glen G12	20	T9
Kelvindale Rd.		
Kelvindale Pl. G20	20	T9
Kelvindale Rd. G12	20	T9
Kelvingrove St. G3	35	U12
Kelvingrove St.		
Kelvingrove Ter. G3	35	U12
Kelvingrove St.		
Kelvinhaugh Pl. G3	34	T12
Kelvinhaugh St.		
Kelvinhaugh St. G3	34	T12
Kelvinside Av. G20	21	U10
Queen Margaret Dr.		
Kelvinside Dr. G20	21	U10
Kelvinside Gdns. G20	21	U10
Kelvinside Gdns. E. G20	21	U10
Kelvinside Ter. S. G20	21	U10
Kelvinside Ter. W. G20	21	U10
Kemp Av., Renf.	31	L11
Kemp St. G21	22	X10
Kempock St. G31	53	Z14
Kempsthorn Cres. G53	48	P15
Kempsthorn Path G53	48	P15
Kempsthorn Rd. G53	48	P15
Kendal Av., Giff.	62	T18
Kendal Dr. G12	20	S9
Kendal Ter. G12	20	S9
Kendon Av. G15	6	N6
Kenilworth Av. G41	50	T16
Kenilworth Cres., Bear.	7	Q5
Kenilworth Way, Pais.	45	G16
Kenmar Gdns., Udd.	56	FF16
Kenmore Gdns., Bear.	8	S5
Kenmore Rd., Cumb.	71	PP3
Kenmore St. G32	38	BB13
Kenmuir Av. G32	55	DD14
Kenmuir Rd. G32	55	CC16
Kenmuirhill Rd. G32	55	CC15
Kenmure Av., Bish.	10	X7
Kenmure Cres., Bish.	10	X7
Kenmure Dr., Bish.	10	X7
Kenmure Gdns., Bish.	10	X7
Kenmure Row G22	9	V7
Kenmure St. G41	51	U14
Kenmure Way G73	65	Y18
Kennedar Dr. G51	33	R12
Kennedy Ct., Giff.	62	T18
Braidholm Cres.		
Kennedy St. G4	36	W12
Kennet St. G21	37	Y11
Kennishead Av. G46	61	R17
Kennishead Path, Thorn.	61	R17
Kennishead Pl.		
Kennishead Pl. G46	61	R17
Kennishead Rd. G46	61	R17
Kennishead Rd. G53	61	Q18
Kennisholm Av. G46	61	R17
Kennisholm Path, Thorn.	61	R18
Kennisholm Av.		
Kennisholm Pl. G46	61	R17
Kennoway Dr. G11	33	R11
Kennoway La. G11	33	R11
Thornwood Dr.		
Kennyhill Sq. G31	37	Y12
Kensington Dr., Giff.	62	T19
Kensington Gate G12	20	T10
Kensington Rd.		
Kensington Rd. G12	20	T10
Kent Dr. G73	65	Z17
Kent Rd. G3	35	U12
Kent St. G40	36	X13
Kentallen Rd. G33	39	DD13
Kentigern Ter., Bish.	23	Y8
Keppel Dr. G44	52	X16
Keppoch St. G21	22	W10
Keppochhill Rd. G22	22	W10
Kerfield Pl. G15	6	N6
Kerr St. G40	36	X13
Kerr St., Barr.	59	L19
Kerr St., Pais.	30	J13
Kerrera Pl. G33	39	CC13

Kerrera Rd. G33	39	CC13
Kerry Pl. G15	6	N6
Kerrycroy Av. G42	52	W16
Kerrycroy Pl. G42	52	W16
Kerrycroy Av.		
Kerrycroy St. G42	52	W16
Kerrydale St. G40	53	Y14
Kerrylamont Av. G42	52	X16
Kersland La. G12	20	T10
Kersland St.		
Kersland St. G12	20	T10
Kessington Dr., Bear.	8	S6
Kessington Rd., Bear.	8	S6
Kestral Ct., Clyde.	5	L5
Kestrel Pl., John.	43	C16
Kestrel Rd. G13	19	Q9
Kew Gdns. G12	20	T10
Ruthven St.		
Kew Gdns., Udd.	57	HH16
Kew La. G12	20	T10
Saltoun St.		
Kew Ter. G12	20	T10
Keyden St. G41	35	U13
Kibbleston Rd., Kilb.	42	B14
Kidston Dr. G5	52	W14
Kierhill Rd., Cumb.	70	MM3
Kilbarchan Rd., John.	43	C15
Kilbarchan St. G5	35	V13
Bedford St.		
Kilbeg Ter. G46	61	Q18
Kilberry St. G21	37	Y11
Kilbirnie St. G5	51	V14
Kilbowie Ct., Clyde.	5	L6
Crown Av.		
Kilbowie Rd., Clyde.	5	L5
Kilbowie Rd., Cumb.	71	PP3
Kilbrennan Rd., Linw.	28	E13
Kilbride St. G5	52	W15
Kilbride Vw., Udd.	57	HH16
Hamilton Vw.		
Kilburn Gro., Blan.	68	FF19
Kilburn Pl. G13	18	P9
Kilchattan Dr. G44	52	W16
Kilchoan Rd. G33	39	CC11
Kilcloy Av. G15	6	P6
Kildale St. G73	52	X16
Kildale Way G73	52	X16
Kildary Av. G44	63	V17
Kildary Rd. G44	63	V17
Kildermorie Rd. G34	40	EE12
Kildonan Dr. G11	34	S11
Kildonan Ter. G51	34	S13
Copland Rd.		
Kildrostan St. G41	51	U15
Terregles Av.		
Kildrum Rd., Cumb.	71	PP2
Kilearn Rd., Pais.	31	L12
Kilfinan St. G22	21	V8
Kilkerran Dr. G33	24	AA9
Killarn Way, Pais.	31	L12
Killearn Dr., Pais.	48	N14
Killearn St. G22	21	V10
Killermont Av., Bear.	8	S7
Killermont Ct., Bear.	8	S6
Killermont Meadows, Both.	69	GG19
Killermont Rd., Bear.	8	S6
Killermont St. G1	36	W12
Killermont Vw. G20	8	S7
Killiegrew Rd. G41	50	T15
Killin St. G32	54	BB14
Killoch Av., Pais.	29	H13
Killoch Dr. G13	18	P8
Killoch Dr., Barr.	59	M19
Killoch Rd., Pais.	29	H13
Kilmailing Rd. G44	63	V17
Kilmair Pl. G20	20	T9
Wyndford Rd.		
Kilmaluag Ter. G46	61	Q18
Kilmany Dr. G32	38	AA13
Kilmany Gdns. G32	38	AA13
St. Mark St.		
Kilmardinny Av., Bear.	7	R5
Kilmardinny Cres., Bear.	7	R5
Kilmardinny Dr., Bear.	7	R5

Kilmardinny Gate, Bear.	7	R5
Kilmardinny Av.		
Kilmardinny Gro., Bear.	7	R5
Kilmarnock Rd. G43	62	T17
Kilmartin Pl., Thorn.	61	R18
Kilmaurs Dr., Giff.	63	U18
Kilmaurs St. G51	33	R13
Kilmorie Dr. G73	52	X16
Kilmory Av., Udd.	57	HH16
Spindlehowe Rd.		
Kilmuir Cres. G46	61	Q18
Kilmuir Dr. G46	61	R18
Kilmuir Rd. G46	61	R18
Kilmuir Rd., Udd.	57	GG15
Kilmun La. G20	20	T8
Kilmun St.		
Kilmun Pl. G20	20	T8
Kilmun St.		
Kilmun St. G20	20	T8
Kilnside Rd., Pais.	30	K13
Kiloran St. G46	61	R18
Kilpatrick Av., Pais.	45	H15
Kilpatrick Cres., Pais.	46	J15
Kiltearn Rd. G33	39	DD12
Kilvaxter Dr. G46	61	R18
Kilwynet Way, Pais.	31	L12
Kimberley St., Dalm.	4	J5
Kinalty Rd. G44	63	V17
Kinarvie Cres. G53	48	N16
Kinarvie Gdns. G53	48	N16
Kinarvie Rd.		
Kinarvie Pl. G53	48	N16
Kinarvie Rd. G53	48	N16
Kinarvie Ter. G53	48	N16
Kinbuck St. G22	22	W10
Kincaid Gdns. G72	66	BB17
Kincardine Cres., Bish.	23	Y8
Graham Ter.		
Kincardine Dr., Bish.	23	Y8
Kincardine Pl., Bish.	23	Z8
Kincardine Sq. G33	39	CC11
Kincath Av. G73	65	Z18
Kinclaven Av. G15	6	P6
Kincraig St. G51	33	Q13
Kinellan Rd., Bear.	7	R7
Kinellar Dr. G14	18	P9
Kinfauns Dr. G15	6	N6
Kinfauns Ter. G51	34	S13
Copland Rd.		
King Edward Rd. G13	19	R9
King George V Bri. G5	35	V13
King St. G1	36	W13
King St. G73	53	Y16
King St., Clyde.	17	M8
King St., Pais.	30	J13
Kingarth St. G42	51	V15
Kinghorn Dr. G44	52	W16
Kinglas Rd., Bear.	7	Q7
Kings Cres. G72	66	BB17
Kings Cres., John.	44	F14
Kings Cross G31	36	X12
Kings Dr. G40	52	X14
Kings Dr., Cumb.	70	NN1
Kings Inch Rd., Renf.	17	M9
Kings La. W., Renf.	17	M10
Bell St.		
Kings Pk. Av. G44	64	W17
Kings Pk. Rd. G44	51	V16
Kings Pl. G22	21	V8
Kings Rd., John.	44	E15
Kingsacre Rd. G44	52	W16
Kingsbarns Dr. G44	51	V16
Kingsborough Gdns. G12	20	S10
Kingsborough Gate G12	20	S10
Prince Albert Rd.		
Kingsborough Ter. G12	20	S10
Hyndland Rd.		
Kingsbrae Dr. G44	52	W16
Kingsbridge Cres. G44	64	W17
Kingsbridge Dr. G44	64	W17
Kingsburgh Dr., Pais.	31	L13
Kingsburn Dr. G73	65	Y17
Kingsburn Gro. G73	65	Y17
Kingscliffe Av. G44	64	W17
Kingscourt Av. G44	64	W17

Street	Page	Grid
Kingsdale Av. G44	52	W16
Kingsdyke Av. G44	52	W16
Kingsford Av. G44	63	U18
Kingsheath Av. G73	64	X17
Kingshill Dr. G44	64	W17
Kingshouse Av. G44	64	W17
Kingshurst Av. G44	52	W16
Kingsknowe Dr. G73	64	X17
Kingsland Cres. G52	32	P13
Kingsland Dr. G52	32	P13
Kingsley Av. G42	51	V15
Kingsley Ct., Udd.	57	HH16
Kingslynn Dr. G44	64	W17
Kingslynn La. G44	64	W17
Kingslynn Dr.		
Kingsmuir Dr. G73	64	X17
Kingston Bri. G3	35	U13
Kingston Pl., Dalm.	4	J6
Kingston St. G5	35	V13
Kingsway G14	18	P9
Kingsway Ct. G14	18	P9
Kingswood Dr. G44	64	W17
Kingussie Dr. G44	64	W17
Kiniver Dr. G15	6	P7
Kinloch Av. G72	66	BB18
Kinloch Av., Linw.	28	E13
Pentland Dr.		
Kinloch Rd., Renf.	31	L11
Kinloch St. G40	53	Z14
Kinmount Av. G44	51	V16
Kinmount La. G44	51	V16
Kinmount Av.		
Kinnaird Cres., Bear.	8	S6
Kinnaird Dr., Linw.	28	E13
Kinnaird Pl. G64	23	Y8
Kinnear Rd. G40	53	Y14
Kinnell Av. G52	49	Q14
Kinnell Cres. G52	49	Q14
Kinnell Path G52	49	Q14
Kinnell Cres.		
Kinnell Pl. G52	49	R15
Mosspark Dr.		
Kinnell Sq. G52	49	Q14
Kinning St. G5	35	U13
Kinnoul La. G12	20	T10
Dowanhill St.		
Kinpurnie Rd., Pais.	31	M13
Kinross Av. G52	48	P14
Kinsail Dr. G52	32	N13
Kinstone Av. G14	18	P9
Kintessack Pl., Bish.	11	Z7
Kintillo Dr. G13	18	P9
Kintore Rd. G43	63	U17
Kintra St. G51	34	S13
Kintyre Av., Linw.	28	E13
Kintyre St. G21	37	Y11
Kippen St. G22	22	W9
Kippford St. G32	55	CC14
Kirk La. G43	50	T16
Riverbank St.		
Kirk Pl., Udd.	69	GG17
Kirk Rd., Bear.	7	R5
Kirkaig Av., Renf.	32	N11
Kirkbean Av. G73	65	Y18
Kirkburn Av. G72	66	BB18
Kirkcaldy Rd. G41	50	T15
Kirkconnel Av. G13	18	N9
Kirkconnel Dr. G73	64	X17
Kirkdale Dr. G52	49	R14
Kirkfield Rd., Udd.	69	HH18
Kirkford Rd., Chr.	15	GG7
Bridgeburn Dr.		
Kirkhill Av. G72	66	BB18
Kirkhill Dr. G20	20	T9
Kirkhill Gdns. G72	66	BB18
Kirkhill Gro. G72	66	BB18
Kirkhill Pl. G20	20	T9
Kirkhill Rd., Gart.	27	GG9
Kirkhill Rd., Udd.	57	GG16
Kirkhill Ter. G72	66	BB18
Kirkhope Dr. G15	6	P7
Kirkinner Rd. G32	55	CC14
Kirkintilloch Rd., Bish.	22	X8
Kirkintilloch Rd., Lenz.	13	CC5
Kirkland St. G20	21	U10
Kirklandneuk Rd., Renf.	17	L10
Kirklands Cres., Udd.	69	HH18
Kirklea Av., Pais.	29	H13
Kirklee Circ. G12	20	T10
Kirklee Gdns. G12	20	T9
Bellshaugh Rd.		
Kirklee Gdns. La. G12	20	T9
Bellshaugh Rd.		
Kirklee Pl. G12	20	T10
Kirklee Quad. G12	20	T10
Kirklee Quad. La. G12	20	T10
Kirklee Quad.		
Kirklee Rd. G12	20	T10
Kirklee Ter. G12	20	T10
Kirklee Ter. La. G12	20	T10
Kirklee Ter.		
Kirkliston St. G32	38	AA13
Kirkmuir Av., Renf.	31	L11
Kirkmuir Dr. G73	65	Y18
Kirknewton St. G32	38	BB13
Kirkoswald Dr., Clyde.	5	M6
Kirkoswald Rd. G43	62	T17
Kirkpatrick St. G40	37	Y13
Kirkriggs Av. G73	65	Y17
Kirkriggs Gdns. G73	65	Y17
Kirkriggs Way, Ruth.	65	Y17
Kirkstall Gdns., Bish.	11	Y6
Kirkstonside, Barr.	59	L19
Kirkton Av. G13	18	P9
Kirkton Cres. G13	18	P9
Kirkton Rd. G72	66	BB17
Kirkview Gdns., Udd.	57	GG16
Glencroft Av.		
Kirkville Pl. G15	6	P7
Kirkwall, Cumb.	71	PP1
Kirkwall Av., Blan.	68	FF18
Kirkwell Rd. G44	63	V17
Kirkwood Av., Clyde.	5	M7
Kirkwood Quad., Clyde.	5	M7
Kirkwood Av.		
Kirkwood Rd., Udd.	57	GG15
Newlands Rd.		
Kirkwood St. G51	34	T13
Kirkwood St. G73	53	Y16
Kirn St. G20	20	T8
Kilmun St.		
Kirriemuir Av. G52	49	Q14
Kirriemuir Gdns., Bish.	11	Z7
Kirriemuir Rd., Bish.	11	Z7
Kirtle Dr., Renf.	32	N11
Kirton Av., Barr.	59	L19
Kishorn Pl. G33	39	CC11
Knapdale St. G22	21	V8
Knightsbridge Rd. G13	19	Q9
Knightscliffe Av. G13	19	Q8
Knightswood Cross G13	19	Q8
Knightswood Rd. G13	7	Q7
Knightswood Ter., Blan.	69	GG19
Knock Way, Pais.	31	L12
Knockburnie Rd., Udd.	69	HH18
Knockhall St. G33	39	CC11
Knockhill Dr. G44	51	V16
Knockhill La. G44	51	V16
Mount Annan Dr.		
Knockhill Rd., Renf.	31	L11
Knockside Av., Pais.	46	J16
Knowe Rd., Chr.	26	FF8
Knowe Rd., Pais.	31	L12
Knowe Ter. G22	21	V8
Hillend Rd.		
Knowehead Dr., Udd.	69	GG17
Knowehead Gdns. G41	51	U14
Knowehead Ter.		
Knowehead Gdns., Udd.	69	GG17
Knowehead Ter. G41	51	U14
Knowetap St. G20	21	U8
Knox St., Pais.	45	H14
Kyle Dr., Giff.	62	T18
Kyle Pl., Cumb.	71	PP2
Kyle Sq. G73	65	Y17
Kyle St. G4	36	W11
Kyleakin Gdns., Blan.	68	EE19
Kyleakin Rd. G46	61	Q18
Kyleakin Ter. G46	61	Q18
Kylepark Av., Udd.	68	FF17
Kylepark Cres., Udd.	56	FF16
Kylepark Dr., Udd.	56	FF16
Kylerhea Rd. G46	61	Q18
La Belle Pl. G3	35	U11
Laburnum Gdns., Lenz.	12	BB5
Laburnum Gro.		
Laburnum Gro., Lenz.	12	BB5
Laburnum Pl., John.	44	E16
Laburnum Rd. G41	50	T14
Laburnum Rd., Cumb.	71	QQ3
Lacrosse Ter. G12	21	U10
Lacy St., Pais.	31	L13
Lade Ter. G52	48	P14
Ladeside Dr., John.	43	C15
Ladhope Pl. G13	18	N8
Lady Anne St. G14	18	N9
Lady Isle Cres., Udd.	69	GG17
Lady Jane Gate, Both.	69	GG18
Lady La., Pais.	46	J14
Ladybank Dr. G52	49	R14
Ladyburn St., Pais.	47	L14
Ladyhill Dr., Bail.	56	EE14
Ladykirk Cres. G52	32	P13
Ladykirk Cres., Pais.	46	K14
Ladykirk Dr. G52	32	P13
Ladyloan Av. G15	6	N6
Ladyloan Pl. G15	6	N6
Ladymuir Cres. G53	49	Q15
Ladysmith Av., Kilb.	43	C15
Ladywell St. G4	36	X12
Laggan Rd. G43	63	U17
Laggan Rd., Bish.	11	Y7
Laggan Ter., Renf.	17	L10
Laidlaw Gdns., Udd.	57	GG15
Laidlaw St. G5	35	V13
Laigh Kirk La., Pais.	46	K14
Causeyside St.		
Laigh Possil Rd. G23	21	V8
Balmore Rd.		
Laighcartside St., John.	44	E14
Laighlands Rd. G71	69	HH19
Laighmuir St., Udd.	69	GG17
Laighpark Harbour, Pais.	30	K12
Lainshaw Dr. G45	63	V19
Laird Pl. G40	52	X14
Lairds Gate, Both.	69	GG17
Lairds Hill, Cumb.	70	NN3
Lairg Dr., Blan.	68	FF19
Lamb St. G22	21	V9
Lambhill St. G41	34	T13
Lamerton Dr. G52	32	P13
Lamerton Rd., Cumb.	71	QQ3
Lamington Rd. G52	48	P14
Lamlash Cres. G33	38	BB12
Lammermoor Av. G52	49	Q14
Lammermoor Dr., Cumb.	70	NN4
Lammermuir Dr., Pais.	46	K16
Lamont Rd. G21	23	Y9
Lanark St. G1	36	W13
Lancaster Cres. G12	20	T10
Lancaster Cres. La. G12	20	S9
Clevedon Rd.		
Lancaster Rd., Bish.	11	Y6
Lancaster Ter. G12	20	T10
Westbourne Gdns. W.		
Lancaster Ter. La. G12	20	T10
Westbourne Gdns. W.		
Lancefield Quay G3	35	U12
Lancefield St. G3	35	U12
Landemer Dr. G73	64	X17
Landressy St. G40	52	X14
Lanfine Rd., Pais.	47	L14
Lang Av., Renf.	31	M11
Lang St., Pais.	47	L14
Langa St. G20	21	U8
Langbank St. G5	51	V14
Eglinton St.		
Langbar Cres. G33	39	DD12
Langbar Path G33	39	CC12
Langcraigs Dr., Pais.	58	J17
Langcraigs Ter., Pais.	58	J17
Langcroft Dr. G72	67	CC18
Langcroft Pl. G51	33	Q12

Street	Page	Grid
Langcroft Rd. G51	33	Q12
Langcroft Ter. G51	33	Q12
Langdale Av. G33	24	AA10
Langdale Av., Cumb.	70	MM3
Langdale St. G33	24	AA10
Langford Av. G53	60	P18
Langford Dr. G53	60	P18
Langford Pl. G53	60	P18
Langford Dr.		
Langhill Dr., Cumb.	70	MM2
Langholm Ct., Chr.	15	HH7
Heathfield Av.		
Langholm Dr., Linw.	28	F13
Langlands Av. G51	33	Q12
Langlands Dr. G51	33	Q12
Langlands Path G51	33	R12
Langlands Rd. G51	33	Q12
Langlands Rd. G51	34	S12
Langlea Av. G72	65	Z18
Langlea Gro. G72	66	AA18
Langlea Rd. G72	66	AA18
Langley Av. G13	18	P8
Langmuir Rd., Bail.	41	HH13
Langmuir Way, Bail.	41	HH13
Langmuirhead Rd., Lenz.	24	BB8
Langness Rd. G33	38	BB12
Langrig Rd. G21	23	Y10
Langshot St. G51	34	T13
Langside Av. G41	51	U15
Langside Dr. G43	63	U17
Langside Dr. G78	42	B15
Langside Gdns. G42	51	V16
Langside La. G42	51	V15
Langside Pk. G78	42	B15
Langside Pl. G41	51	U16
Langside Rd. G42	51	V16
Langside Rd., Both.	69	HH19
Langside St., Clyde.	6	N5
Langstile Pl. G52	32	N13
Langstile Rd. G52	32	N13
Langton Cres. G53	49	Q15
Langton Cres., Barr.	59	M19
Langton Gdns., Bail.	55	DD14
Langton Rd. G53	49	Q15
Langtree Av., Giff.	62	S19
Lanrig Pl., Chr.	26	FF8
Lanrig Rd., Chr.	26	FF8
Lansbury Gdns., Pais.	30	J12
Cowdie St.		
Lansdowne Cres. G20	35	U11
Lansdowne Cres. La. G12	21	U10
Great Western Rd.		
Lansdowne Dr., Cumb.	70	NN2
Lanton Dr. G52	32	P13
Lanton Rd. G43	63	U17
Lappin St., Clyde.	17	M8
Larch Av., Bish.	23	Y8
Larch Av., Lenz.	13	CC5
Larch Ct., Cumb.	71	QQ2
Larch Cres., Lenz.	13	CC5
Larch Gro. G67	71	RR2
Larch Pl., John.	44	E16
Larch Rd. G41	50	S14
Larch Rd., Cumb.	71	QQ2
Larches, The, Chr.	15	HH6
Larchfield Av. G14	18	P10
Larchfield Dr. G73	65	Y18
Larchfield Pl. G14	18	P10
Larchfield Rd. G69	15	GG7
Larchfield Rd., Bear.	7	R7
Larchgrove Av. G32	39	CC13
Larchgrove Pl. G32	39	CC12
Larchgrove Rd.		
Larchgrove Rd. G32	39	CC12
Larchwood Ter., Barr.	60	N19
Largie Rd. G43	63	U17
Largo Pl. G51	33	R12
Largs St. G31	37	Y12
Larkfield Rd., Lenz.	13	DD5
Larkfield St. G42	51	V15
Cathcart Rd.		
Larkin Gdns., Pais.	30	J12
Lasswade St. G14	18	N9
Latherton Dr. G20	20	T9
Latherton Pl. G20	20	T9
Latherton Dr.		
Latimer Gdns. G52	48	P14
Lauder Dr. G73	65	Z17
Lauder Dr., Linw.	28	E13
Lauder Gdns., Blan.	68	FF19
Lauder St. G5	51	V14
Eglinton St.		
Lauderdale Gdns. G12	20	S10
Laundry La. G33	25	CC9
Laurel Av., Dalm.	4	J6
Laurel Av., Lenz.	13	CC5
Laurel Bk. Rd., Chr.	26	EE8
Laurel Gdns., Udd.	57	GG16
Laurel Pl. G11	34	S11
Laurel St. G11	34	S11
Laurel Wk. G73	65	Z18
Laurel Way, Barr.	59	L18
Graham St.		
Laurence Dr., Bear.	7	Q5
Laurie Ct., Udd.	57	HH16
Hillcrest Rd.		
Laurieston La. G51	34	T13
Paisley Rd.		
Laurieston Rd. G5	36	W13
Laurieston Way G73	65	Y18
Laverock Ter., Chr.	15	GG7
Laverockhall St. G21	22	X10
Law St. G40	37	Y13
Lawers Rd. G43	62	S17
Lawers Rd., Bear.	7	Q5
Lawers Rd., Renf.	31	M11
Lawhill Av. G44	64	W18
Lawmoor Av. G5	52	W14
Lawmoor La. G5	36	W13
Ballater St.		
Lawmoor Pl. G5	52	W15
Lawmoor Av.		
Lawmoor Rd. G5	52	W14
Lawmoor St. G5	52	W14
Lawn St., Pais.	30	K13
Lawrence Av., Giff.	62	T19
Lawrence St. G11	34	T11
Lawrie St. G11	34	S11
Lawside Dr. G53	49	Q16
Laxford Av. G44	63	V18
Laxton Dr., Lenz.	13	DD6
Leabank Av., Pais.	46	K16
Leadburn Rd. G21	23	Z10
Rye Rd.		
Leadburn St. G32	38	AA12
Leader St. G33	37	Z11
Leander Cres., Renf.	32	N11
Leckethill St. G21	22	X10
Springburn Rd.		
Leckie St. G43	50	T16
Ledaig Pl. G31	37	Z12
Ledaig St. G31	37	Z12
Ledard Rd. G42	51	U16
Ledcameroch Cres., Bear.	7	Q6
Ledcameroch Pk., Bear.	7	Q6
Ledcameroch Rd.		
Ledcameroch Rd., Bear.	7	Q6
Ledgowan Pl. G20	20	T8
Ledi Dr., Bear.	7	Q5
Ledi Rd. G43	62	T17
Ledmore Dr. G15	6	N6
Lednock Rd. G33	25	CC9
Lednock Rd. G52	32	P13
Lee Av. G33	38	AA11
Lee Cres., Bish.	22	X8
Leebank Dr. G44	63	U19
Leefield Av. G44	63	U19
Leehill Rd. G21	22	X8
Leeside Rd. G21	22	X8
Leewood Dr. G44	63	U19
Leicester Av. G12	20	S9
Leighton St. G20	21	U9
Leitchland Rd. G78	44	F16
Leitchs Ct. G1	36	W13
Trongate		
Leith St. G33	37	Z12
Leithland Av. G53	48	P16
Leithland Rd. G53	48	P15
Lendale La., Bish.	11	Y6
Lendel Pl. G51	35	U13
Paisley Rd. W.		
Lenhall Dr. G45	64	X19
Lenhall Ter. G45	64	X19
Lennox Av. G14	19	Q10
Lennox Cres., Bish.	22	X8
Lennox Dr., Bear.	7	R5
Lennox La. W. G14	19	Q10
Lennox Av.		
Lennox Pl. G14	19	Q10
Scotstoun St.		
Lennox Pl., Dalm.	4	K6
Swindon St.		
Lennox Rd., Cumb.	70	NN3
Lennox St. G20	20	T8
Maryhill Rd.		
Lennox Ter., Pais.	31	L12
Lennox Vw., Clyde.	5	L6
Granville St.		
Lentran St. G34	40	FF12
Leny St. G20	21	V10
Lenzie Dr. G21	22	X9
Lenzie Rd. G33	25	CC9
Lenzie St. G21	22	X9
Lenziemill Rd., Cumb.	71	PP4
Lerwick St. G4	35	V11
Dobbies Ln.		
Leslie Rd. G41	51	U15
Leslie St. G41	51	U14
Lesmuir Dr. G14	18	P9
Lesmuir Pl. G14	18	N9
Letham Ct. G43	63	U17
Letham Dr. G43	63	U17
Letham Dr. G64	23	Z8
Letham Gra., Cumb.	70	NN2
Lethamhill Cres. G33	38	AA11
Lethamhill Pl. G33	38	AA11
Lethamhill Rd. G33	38	AA11
Letherby Dr. G44	51	V16
Lethington Av. G41	51	U16
Letterfearn Dr. G23	9	U7
Letterickhills Cres. G72	67	DD18
Lettoch St. G51	34	S13
Leven Av., Bish.	11	Y7
Leven Ct., Barr.	59	L17
Leven Dr., Bear.	7	R6
Leven Sq., Renf.	17	L10
Leven St. G41	51	U14
Leven Vw., Clyde.	5	L6
Radnor St.		
Leven Way, Pais.	45	G15
Levern Cres., Barr.	59	L19
Levern Gdns., Barr.	59	L18
Chappel St.		
Levernside Av., Barr.	59	L19
Levernside Cres. G53	48	P15
Levernside Rd. G53	48	P15
Lewis Av., Renf.	31	M11
Lewis Ct., Kilb.	42	B15
Lewis Cres., Old K.	4	J5
Lewis Gdns., Bear.	6	P5
Lewis Gdns., Old K.	4	J5
Lewis Cres.		
Lewis Gro., Old K.	4	J5
Lewiston Dr. G23	8	T7
Lewiston Rd.		
Lewiston Pl. G23	8	T7
Lewiston Rd.		
Lewiston Rd. G23	8	T7
Lexwell Av., John.	44	F14
Lexwell Rd., Pais.	45	G15
Leyden Ct. G20	21	U9
Leyden St.		
Leyden Gdns. G20	21	U9
Leyden St.		
Leyden St. G20	21	U9
Leys, The, Bish.	11	Y7
Liberton St. G33	37	Z12
Liberty Av., Bail.	41	HH13
Libo Av. G53	49	Q15
Liddale Way G73	52	X16
Liddel Rd., Cumb.	70	NN3
Liddell St. G32	55	CC15
Liddesdale Av., Pais.	44	F16

Name	Pg	Grid
Liddesdale Pl. G22	22	W8
Liddesdale Sq.		
Liddesdale Rd. G22	22	W8
Liddesdale Sq. G22	22	W8
Liddesdale Ter. G22	22	X8
Liff Gdns., Bish.	23	Z8
Liff Pl. G34	40	FF11
Lightburn Pl. G32	38	BB12
Lightburn Rd. G72	67	CC18
Lilac Av., Dalm.	4	K6
Lilac Gdns., Bish.	23	Y8
Lilac Pl., John.	44	E15
Lily St. G40	53	Y14
Lilybank Av. G72	67	CC18
Lilybank Av., Chr.	26	FF8
Lilybank Gdns. G12	34	T11
Lilybank Gdns. La. G12	20	T10
Great George St.		
Lilybank Ter. G12	20	T10
Great George St.		
Lilybank Ter. La. G12	20	T10
Great George St.		
Lilyburn Pl. G15	6	N5
Lime Gro., Blan.	68	FF19
Lime Gro., Lenz.	13	CC5
Lime St. G14	19	Q10
Limecraigs Cres., Pais.	46	J16
Limecraigs Rd., Pais.	46	J16
Limeside Av. G73	53	Y16
Limeside Gdns. G73	53	Z16
Calderwood Rd.		
Limetree Av., Udd.	57	HH16
Limetree Dr., Dalm.	5	L6
Limeview Av., Pais.	45	H16
Limeview Cres., Pais.	45	H16
Limeview Rd., Pais.	45	H16
Limeview Av.		
Limeview Way, Pais.	45	H16
Limeview Av.		
Linacre Dr. G32	39	CC13
Linacre Gdns. G32	39	CC13
Linbank Av. G53	49	Q16
Linburn Pl. G52	32	P13
Linburn Rd. G52	32	N12
Linclive Link Rd., Linw.	29	G13
Linclive Ter., Linw.	28	F13
Lincoln Av. G13	18	P9
Lincoln Av., Udd.	57	GG15
Lindams, Udd.	69	GG17
Linden Dr., Clyde.	5	L5
Linden St. G13	19	R8
Lindores Av. G73	53	Y16
Lindores St. G42	51	V16
Somerville Dr.		
Lindrick Dr. G23	9	U7
Lindsay Dr. G12	20	S9
Lindsay Pl. G12	20	S9
Lindsay Pl., Lenz.	13	CC6
Lindsaybeg Rd., Lenz.	13	DD6
Linfern Rd. G12	20	T10
Links Rd. G32	55	CC14
Links Rd. G44	64	W18
Linkwood Av. G15	6	N6
Kinfauns Dr.		
Linkwood Cres. G15	6	N6
Linkwood Dr. G15	6	N6
Linkwood Pl. G15	6	N6
Kinfauns Dr.		
Linlithgow Gdns. G32	39	CC13
Linn Cres., Pais.	46	J16
Linn Dr. G44	63	U18
Linnet Av., John.	43	C16
Linnhe Av. G44	63	V18
Linnhe Av., Bish.	11	Y7
Linnhe Dr., Barr.	59	L17
Linnhe Pl., Blan.	68	FF19
Linnhead Dr. G53	60	P17
Linnhead Pl. G14	18	P10
Linnpark Av. G44	63	U19
Linnpark Ct. G44	63	U19
Linnpark Gdns., John.	44	E15
Lunn Brae		
Linside Av., Pais.	47	L14
Lintfield Ln., Udd.	69	HH17
Myers Cres.		
Linthaugh Rd. G53	48	P15
Linthouse Bldgs. G51	33	R12
Lintlaw, Blan.	68	FF19
Lintlaw Dr. G52	33	Q13
Linton St. G33	38	AA12
Linwell Cres., Pais.	46	J16
Linwood Ct. G44	63	V17
Bowling Grn. Rd.		
Linwood Moss Rd., Linw.	28	F13
Linwood Rd., John.	28	F13
Linwood Ter. G12	21	U10
Glasgow St.		
Lismore Av., Renf.	31	M11
Lismore Dr., Pais.	46	J16
Lismore Gdns., John.	43	C15
Lismore Pl., Chr.	15	HH6
Altnacreag Gdns.		
Lismore Rd. G12	20	S10
Lister Rd. G52	32	P12
Lister St. G4	36	W11
Lithgow Cres., Pais.	47	L15
Little Dovehill G1	36	W13
Little Holm, Dalm.	4	K6
Little St. G3	35	U12
Littlehill St. G21	22	X10
Edgefauld Rd.		
Littleton Dr. G23	8	T7
Rothes Dr.		
Livingstone Av. G52	32	P12
Livingstone Cres., Blan.	68	FF19
Livingstone St. G21	22	W10
Keppochhill Rd.		
Livingstone St., Clyde.	5	M7
Lloyd Av. G32	54	BB15
Lloyd St. G31	37	Y12
Lloyd St. G73	53	Y15
Loanbank Quad. G51	34	S12
Loancroft Av., Bail.	56	FF14
Loancroft Gdns., Udd.	69	GG17
Loancroft Pl., Bail.	56	EE14
Loanend Cotts. G72	67	DD19
Loanfoot Av. G13	18	P8
Loanhead Av., Linw.	28	E13
Loanhead Av., Renf.	17	M10
Loanhead La., Linw.	28	E13
Loanhead Rd.		
Loanhead Rd., Linw.	28	E13
Loanhead St. G32	38	AA12
Lobnitz Av., Renf.	17	M10
Loch Achray St. G32	55	CC14
Loch Katrine St. G32	55	CC14
Loch Laidon St. G32	55	CC14
Loch Voil St. G32	55	CC14
Lochaber Dr. G73	65	Z18
Lochaber Rd., Bear.	8	S7
Lochaline Av. G78	45	H15
Lochaline Dr. G44	63	V18
Lochalsh Dr., Pais.	45	H15
Lochalsh Pl., Blan.	68	EE19
Lochar Cres. G53	49	Q15
Lochard Dr., Pais.	45	H15
Lochay St. G32	55	CC14
Lochbrae Dr. G73	65	Z18
Lochbridge Rd. G33	40	EE12
Lochburn Dr., Pais.	45	H15
Lochburn Cres. G20	21	U8
Lochburn Gro. G20	21	U8
Cadder Rd.		
Lochburn Pas. G20	21	U8
Lochburn Rd. G20	20	T9
Lochdochart Path G34	40	FF12
Lochdochart Rd.		
Lochdochart Rd. G34	40	FF12
Lochearn Cres., Pais.	45	H15
Lochearnhead Rd. G33	25	CC9
Lochend Av., Gart.	27	GG8
Lochend Cres., Bear.	7	Q6
Lochend Dr., Bear.	7	Q6
Lochend Rd. G34	40	EE11
Lochend Rd., Bear.	7	R6
Lochend Rd., Gart.	27	GG8
Locher Rd., Kilb.	42	A14
Lochfauld Rd. G23	9	V7
Lochfield Cres., Pais.	46	K15
Lochfield Dr., Pais.	47	L15
Lochfield Rd., Pais.	46	K15
Lochgilp St. G20	20	T8
Lochgoin Av. G15	6	N6
Lochgreen St. G33	24	AA10
Lochhead Av., Linw.	28	E13
Lochiel La. G73	65	Z18
Lochiel Rd., Thorn.	61	R18
Lochinver Cres., Pais.	45	H15
Lochinver Dr. G44	63	V18
Lochinver Gro. G72	67	CC17
Andrew Sillars Av.		
Lochlea Av., Clyde.	5	M6
Lochlea Rd. G43	62	T17
Lochlea Rd., Cumb.	71	QQ2
Lochleven La. G42	51	V16
Battlefield Rd.		
Lochleven Rd. G42	51	V16
Lochlibo Av. G13	18	N9
Lochlibo Cres., Barr.	59	L19
Lochlibo Rd., Barr.	59	L19
Lochlibo Ter., Barr.	59	L19
Lochmaben Rd. G52	48	N14
Lochmaddy Av. G44	63	V18
Lochside, Bear.	7	R6
Drymen Rd.		
Lochside, Gart.	27	GG9
Lochside St. G41	51	U15
Minard Rd.		
Lochview Cotts., Gart.	27	GG10
Lochview Cres. G33	24	AA10
Lochview Dr. G33	24	AA10
Lochview Gdns. G33	24	AA10
Lochview Pl. G33	24	AA10
Lochview Rd., Bear.	7	R6
Lochview Ter., Gart.	27	GG9
Lochwood St. G33	38	AA11
Lochy Av., Renf.	32	N11
Lochy Gdns., Bish.	11	Y7
Lockerbie Av. G43	63	U17
Lockhart Av. G72	67	CC17
Lockhart Dr. G72	67	CC17
Lockhart St. G21	37	Y11
Locksley Av. G13	19	Q8
Locksley Rd., Pais.	45	G15
Logan Av., Cumb.	70	MM2
Logan Dr., Pais.	30	J13
Logan St. G5	52	W15
Logan Twr. G72	67	DD18
Claude Av.		
Loganswell Dr. G46	61	Q19
Loganswell Gdns. G46	61	R19
Loganswell Pl. G46	61	R19
Loganswell Rd. G46	61	R19
Logie St. G51	34	S12
Lomax St. G33	37	Z12
Lomond Av., Renf.	31	L11
Lomond Ct., Barr.	59	M19
Lomond Cres., Pais.	46	J16
Lomond Dr., Barr.	59	L18
Lomond Dr., Udd.	69	HH18
Lomond Gdns., John.	44	F15
Lomond Pl. G33	25	CC10
Lomond Rd., Bear.	7	R7
Lomond Rd., Bish.	10	X6
Lomond Rd., Lenz.	13	CC5
Lomond Rd., Udd.	57	GG15
Lomond St. G22	21	V9
Lomond Vw., Clyde.	5	L6
Granville St.		
London Arc. G1	36	W13
London Rd.		
London La. G1	36	W13
London Rd.		
London Rd. G1	36	W13
London St., Renf.	17	M9
Long Row, Bail.	40	FF13
Longay Pl. G22	22	W8
Longay St. G22	22	W8
Longcroft Dr., Renf.	17	M10
Longdale Rd., Chr.	15	GG7
Longden St., Clyde.	17	M8
Longford St. G33	37	Z12
Longlee, Bail.	56	EE14
Longmeadow, John.	43	C15
Longstone Rd. G33	38	BB12

Name	No.	Ref.
Longwill Ter., Cumb.	71	PP2
Lonmay Rd. G33	39	CC12
Lonsdale Av., Giff.	62	T18
Loom St. G40	36	X13
Stevenson St.		
Loom Wk., Kilb.	42	B14
Shuttle St.		
Lora Dr. G52	49	R14
Loretto Pl. G33	38	AA12
Loretto St. G33	38	AA12
Lorne Av., Chr.	26	FF8
Lorne Cres., Bish.	11	Z7
Lorne Dr., Linw.	28	E13
Lorne Rd. G52	32	N12
Lorne St. G51	34	T13
Lorne Ter. G72	66	AA18
Lorraine Gdns. G12	20	T10
Kensington Rd.		
Lorraine Rd. G12	20	T10
Loskin Dr. G22	21	V8
Lossie Cres., Renf.	32	N11
Lossie St. G33	37	Z11
Lothian Cres., Pais.	46	J15
Lothian Gdns. G20	21	U10
Lothian St. G52	32	N12
Loudon Gdns., John.	44	E14
Loudon Rd. G33	24	BB9
Loudon Ter. G12	20	T10
Observatory Rd.		
Lounsdale Cres., Pais.	45	H15
Lounsdale Dr., Pais.	45	H15
Lounsdale Pl. G14	18	P10
Lounsdale Rd., Pais.	45	H15
Lourdes Av. G52	49	Q14
Lovat Pl. G73	65	Z18
Lovat St. G4	36	W11
Love St., Pais.	30	K13
Low Barholm, Kilb.	42	B15
Low Cres., Clyde.	18	N8
Low Parksail, Renf.	16	J8
Low Rd., Pais.	46	J14
Lower Bourtree Dr. G73	65	Z18
Lower English Bldgs.	51	V14
G42		
Lower Millgate, Udd.	57	GG16
Lowndes La., Pais.	30	K13
New Sneddon St.		
Lowndes St., Barr.	59	M19
Lowther Ter. G12	20	T10
Loyne Dr., Renf.	32	N11
Morriston Cres.		
Luath St. G51	34	S12
Lubas Av. G42	52	W16
Lubas Pl. G42	52	W16
Lubnaig Rd. G43	63	U17
Luckingsford Av., Renf.	16	J8
Luckingsford Dr., Renf.	16	J8
Luckingsford Rd., Renf.	16	J8
Lucy Brae, Udd.	57	GG16
Ludovic Sq., John.	43	D14
Luffness Gdns. G32	54	BB15
Lugar Dr. G52	49	R14
Lugar Pl. G44	64	X17
Luggiebank Pl., Bail.	57	HH14
Luing Rd. G52	33	R13
Lumloch St. G21	23	Y10
Lumsden La. G3	34	T12
Lumsden St.		
Lumsden St. G3	34	T12
Lunan Dr., Bish.	23	Z8
Lunan Pl. G51	33	R12
Luncarty Pl. G32	54	BB14
Luncarty St. G32	54	BB14
Lunderston Dr. G53	48	P16
Lundie Gdns., Bish.	23	Z8
Lundie St. G32	54	AA14
Lunn Brae, John.	43	D15
Luss Rd. G51	33	R12
Lusset Vw., Clyde.	5	L6
Radnor St.		
Lusshill Ter., Udd.	56	EE15
Lyall Pl. G21	22	W10
Keppochhill Rd.		
Lyall St. G21	22	W10
Lybster Cres. G73	65	Z18
Lye Brae, Cumb.	71	PP3
Lyle Ter., Pais.	46	K15
Lymburn St. G3	34	T12
Lyndale Pl. G20	20	T8
Lyndale Rd. G20	20	T8
Lyndhurst Gdns. G20	21	U10
Lyne Cft., Bish.	11	Y6
Lyne Dr. G23	9	U7
Lynedoch Cres. G3	35	U11
Lynedoch Pl. G3	35	U11
Lynedoch St. G3	35	U11
Lynedoch Ter. G3	35	U11
Lynn Gdns. G12	20	T10
Great George St.		
Lynn Wk., Udd.	69	HH17
Flax Rd.		
Lynnhurst, Udd.	57	GG16
Lynton Av., Giff.	62	S19
Lyon Cross Av., Barr.	59	M19
Lyon Rd., Pais.	45	G15
Lyoncross Cres., Barr.	59	M18
Lyoncross Rd. G53	48	P15
Lytham Dr. G23	9	U7
Lytham Meadows, Both.	69	GG19
Macbeth Pl. G31	53	Z14
Macbeth St.		
Macbeth St. G31	53	Z14
Macdonald St. G73	53	Y16
Greenhill Rd.		
Macdougal St. G43	50	T16
Macdowall St., John.	43	D14
Macdowall St., Pais.	30	J13
Macduff Pl. G31	53	Z14
Macduff St. G31	53	Z14
Mace Rd. G13	7	Q7
Macfarlane Rd., Bear.	7	R7
Machrie Dr. G45	64	X18
Machrie Rd. G45	64	X18
Machrie St. G45	64	X18
Mackean St., Pais.	30	J13
Mackeith St. G40	52	X14
Mackenchnie St. G51	34	S12
Mackenzie Dr., John.	42	B16
Mackie St. G4	22	W10
Borron St.		
Mackiesmill Rd., John.	44	F16
Mackinlay St. G5	51	V14
Maclay Av., Kilb.	42	B15
Maclean St. G41	35	U13
Maclean St. G51	34	T13
Maclean St., Clyde.	18	N8
Wood Quad.		
Maclehose Rd., Cumb.	71	QQ2
Maclellan St. G41	34	T13
Madison Av. G44	63	V17
Madison La. G44	63	V17
Carmunnock Rd.		
Madras Pl. G40	52	X14
Madras St.		
Madras St. G40	52	X14
Mafeking St. G51	34	S13
Magdalen Way, Pais.	44	F16
Magnus Cres. G44	63	V18
Mahon Ct., Chr.	15	GG7
Maida St. G43	50	S16
Maidland Rd. G53	49	Q16
Mailerbeg Gdns., Chr.	15	GG6
Mailing Av., Bish.	11	Y7
Main Rd., John.	44	F14
Main Rd., Pais.	46	J14
Main St. G40	52	X14
Main St. G72	66	BB17
Main St. G73	53	Y16
Main St., Bail.	56	EE14
Main St., Barr.	59	L19
Main St., Both.	69	HH19
Main St., Chr.	14	FF7
Main St., Cumb.	71	PP1
Main St., Thorn.	61	R18
Main St., Udd.	69	GG17
Mainhead Ter., Cumb.	71	PP1
Roadside		
Mainhill Av., Bail.	40	FF13
Mainhill Dr., Bail.	40	FF13
Mainhill Pl., Bail.	40	FF13
Mainhill Rd., Bail.	41	GG13
Mains Av., Giff.	62	S19
Mains Dr., Renf.	4	J7
Mains Hill, Renf.	4	J7
Mains Holm, Renf.	4	J7
Mains River, Renf.	4	J7
Mains Wd., Renf.	4	J7
Mainscroft, Renf.	4	J7
Mair St. G51	35	U13
Maitland Pl., Renf.	31	L11
Maitland St. G4	35	V11
Malcolm St. G31	37	Z13
Malin Pl. G33	38	AA12
Mallaig Path G51	33	Q12
Mallaig Pl. G51	33	Q12
Mallaig Rd. G51	33	Q12
Mallard Rd., Clyde.	5	L5
Malloch Cres., John.	44	E15
Malloch St. G20	21	U9
Malta St., Clyde.	17	M8
Maltbarns St. G20	21	V10
Malvern Ct. G31	37	Y13
Malvern Way, Pais.	30	J12
Mambeg Dr. G51	33	R12
Mamore Pl. G43	62	T17
Mamore St. G43	62	T17
Manchester Dr. G12	20	S9
Manitoba Pl. G31	37	Y13
Janefield St.		
Mannering Ct. G41	50	T16
Pollokshaws Rd.		
Mannering Rd. G41	50	T16
Mannering Rd., Pais.	45	G16
Mannofield, Bear.	7	Q6
Chesters Rd.		
Manor Rd. G14	19	R10
Manor Rd. G15	6	N7
Manor Rd., Gart.	27	GG9
Manor Rd., Pais.	45	G15
Manor Way G73	65	Y18
Manse Av., Bear.	7	R5
Manse Av., Both.	69	HH19
Manse Brae G44	63	V17
Manse Ct., Barr.	59	M18
Manse Rd. G32	55	CC14
Manse Rd., Bail.	41	GG13
Manse Rd., Bear.	7	R5
Manse St., Renf.	17	M10
Mansefield Av. G72	66	BB18
Mansefield Dr., Udd.	69	HH17
Mansefield St. G11	34	T11
Mansel St. G21	22	X9
Mansewood Rd. G43	62	S17
Mansfield Rd. G52	32	N12
Mansion Ct. G72	66	BB17
Mansion St. G22	22	W9
Mansion St. G72	66	BB17
Mansionhouse Av. G32	55	CC16
Mansionhouse Dr. G32	39	CC13
Mansionhouse Gdns.	51	U16
G41		
Mansionhouse Rd.		
Mansionhouse Gro. G32	55	DD14
Mansionhouse Rd. G32	55	DD14
Mansionhouse Rd. G41	51	U16
Mansionhouse Rd. G42	51	U16
Mansionhouse Rd., Pais.	31	L13
Maple Dr., Dalm.	4	K5
Maple Dr., John.	44	E16
Maple Dr., Lenz.	12	BB5
Maple Rd. G41	50	S14
Mar Gdns. G73	65	Z18
March La. G41	51	U15
Nithsdale Dr.		
March St. G41	51	U15
Marchfield, Bish.	10	X6
Marchfield Av., Pais.	30	J12
Marchglen Pl. G51	33	Q12
Mallaig Rd.		
Marchmont Gdns., Bish.	10	X6
Marchmont Ter. G12	20	T10
Observatory Rd.		
Maree Dr. G52	49	R14

109

Name	Page	Grid
Maree Gdns., Bish.	11	Y7
Maree Rd., Pais.	45	H15
Marfield St. G32	38	AA13
Margaret St. G1	36	W12
Martha St.		
Margarette Bldgs. G44	63	V17
Clarkston Rd.		
Marguerite Av., Lenz.	13	CC5
Marguerite Dr., Lenz.	13	CC5
Marguerite Gdns., Lenz.	13	CC5
Marguerite Gdns., Udd.	69	HH18
Marguerite Gro., Lenz.	13	CC5
Marine Cres. G51	35	U13
Marine Gdns. G51	35	U13
Mariscat Rd. G41	51	U15
Marjory Dr., Pais.	31	L12
Marjory Rd., Renf.	31	L11
Market St. G40	36	X13
Markinch St. G5	35	V13
West St.		
Marlborough Av. G11	19	R10
Marlinford Rd., Renf.	18	P10
Marlow St. G41	51	U14
Marlow Ter. G41	35	U13
Seaward St.		
Marmion Pl., Cumb.	70	NN4
Marmion Rd., Cumb.	70	NN4
Marmion Rd., Pais.	45	G16
Marmion St. G20	21	U10
Marne St. G31	37	Y12
Marnock Ter., Pais.	47	L15
Marnock Way, Chr.	15	GG7
Braeside Av.		
Marr St. G51	34	S12
Marshalls La., Pais.	46	K14
Mart St. G1	36	W13
Martha St. G1	36	W12
Martin Cres., Bail.	40	FF13
Martin St. G40	52	X14
Martlet Dr., John.	43	C16
Martyr St. G4	36	X12
Martyrs Pl. G64	23	Y8
Marwick St. G31	37	Y12
Marwood Av., Chr.	14	EE5
Mary St. G4	35	V11
Mary St., John.	44	E14
Mary St., Pais.	46	K15
Maryhill Rd., Bear.	8	S7
Maryland Dr. G52	33	R13
Maryland Gdns. G52	33	R13
Marys La., Renf.	17	M10
Maryston Pl. G33	37	Z11
Maryston St. G33	37	Z11
Maryview Gdns., Udd.	56	FF15
Edinburgh Rd.		
Maryville Av., Giff.	62	T19
Maryville Vw., Udd.	56	FF15
Marywood Sq. G41	51	U15
Masonfield Av., Cumb.	70	MM3
Masterton St. G21	22	W10
Mathieson La. G5	52	W14
Mathieson St.		
Mathieson Rd. G73	53	Z15
Mathieson St. G5	52	W14
Mathieson St., Pais.	31	L13
Matilda Rd. G41	51	U14
Mauchline St. G5	51	V14
Maukinfauld Ct. G31	54	AA14
Maukinfauld Rd. G32	54	AA14
Mauldslie St. G40	53	Y14
Maule Dr. G11	34	S11
Mavis Bk., Bish.	22	X8
Mavisbank Gdns. G51	35	U13
Mavisbank Rd. G51	34	S12
Govan Rd.		
Mavisbank Ter., Pais.	46	K14
Maxton Av., Barr.	59	L18
Maxton Gro., Barr.	59	L18
Maxton Ter. G72	66	AA18
Maxwell Av. G41	51	U14
Maxwell Av., Bail.	56	EE14
Maxwell Av., Bear.	7	R7
Maxwell Dr. G41	50	T14
Maxwell Dr., Bail.	40	EE13
Maxwell Gdns. G41	50	T14
Maxwell Gro. G41	50	T14
Maxwell Oval G41	51	U14
Maxwell Pl. G41	51	V14
Maxwell Rd. G41	51	U14
Maxwell Sq. G41	51	U14
Maxwell St. G1	36	W13
Maxwell St., Bail.	56	EE14
Maxwell St., Dalm.	4	K6
Maxwell St., Pais.	30	K13
Maxwellton Rd. G78	45	H14
Maxwellton St., Pais.	46	J14
Maxwelton Rd. G33	37	Z11
May Rd., Pais.	46	K16
May Ter. G42	51	V16
Prospecthill Rd.		
May Ter., Giff.	62	T18
Maybank La. G42	51	V15
Victoria Rd.		
Maybank St. G42	51	V15
Mayberry Cres. G32	39	CC13
Mayberry Gdns. G32	39	CC13
Maybole St. G53	60	N17
Mayfield St. G20	21	U9
McAlpine St. G2	35	V13
McArthur St. G43	50	T16
Pleasance St.		
McArthur St., Clyde.	17	M9
McAslin Ct. G4	36	W12
McAslin St. G4	36	X12
McCallum Av. G73	53	Y16
McClue Av., Renf.	17	L10
McClue Rd., Renf.	17	L10
McCracken Av., Renf.	31	L11
McCreery St., Clyde.	17	M8
McCulloch St. G41	51	U14
McDonald Av., John.	43	D15
McDonald Cres., Clyde.	17	M8
McEwan St. G31	37	Z13
McFarlane St. G4	36	X13
McFarlane St., Pais.	30	J12
McGhee St., Clyde.	5	L6
McGown St., Pais.	30	J13
McGregor Av., Renf.	31	L11
Porterfield Rd.		
McGregor Rd., Cumb.	70	NN3
McGregor St. G51	33	R13
McGregor St., Clyde.	17	M8
McIntosh Ct. G31	36	X12
McIntosh St.		
McIntosh St. G31	36	X12
McIntyre Pl., Pais.	46	J15
McIntyre St. G3	35	U12
McIntyre Ter. G72	66	BB17
McIver St. G72	67	CC17
McKay Cres., John.	44	E15
McKenzie Av., Clyde.	5	L6
McKenzie St., Pais.	30	J13
McKerrel St., Pais.	31	L13
McLaren Av., Renf.	31	M11
Newmains Rd.		
McLaurin Cres., John.	43	C15
McLean Pl., Pais.	30	J12
McLean Sq. G51	34	T13
McLean St., Clyde.	18	N8
Wood Quad.		
McLennan St. G42	51	V16
McLeod St. G4	36	X12
McNair St. G32	38	BB13
McNeil St. G5	52	W14
McNeill Av., Clyde.	6	N7
McPhail St. G40	52	X14
McPhater St. G4	35	V11
Dunblane St.		
McPherson Dr., Udd.	69	HH18
Wordsworth Way		
McPherson St. G1	36	W13
High St.		
McTaggart Rd., Cumb.	70	NN4
Meadow La., Renf.	17	M9
Meadow Rd. G11	34	S11
Meadow Vw., Cumb.	71	QQ2
Meadowbank La., Udd.	69	GG17
Meadowburn, Bish.	11	Y6
Meadowburn Av. G66	13	DD5
Meadowhead Av., Chr.	15	GG7
Meadowpark St. G31	37	Y12
Meadowside Av., John.	44	F15
Meadowside St. G11	34	S11
Meadowside St., Renf.	17	M9
Meadowwell St. G32	38	BB13
Meadside Av. G78	42	B14
Meadside Rd., Kilb.	42	B14
Mears Way, Bish.	11	Z7
Medlar Rd., Cumb.	71	QQ3
Medwin St. G72	67	DD17
Mill Rd.		
Medwyn St. G14	19	Q10
Meek Pl. G72	66	BB17
Meetinghouse La., Pais.	30	K13
Moss St.		
Megan Gate G40	52	X14
Megan St.		
Megan St. G40	52	X14
Meikle Av., Renf.	31	M11
Meikle Rd. G53	49	Q16
Meiklerig Cres. G53	49	Q15
Meikleriggs Dr., Pais.	45	H15
Meiklewood Rd. G51	33	Q13
Melbourne Av., Dalm.	4	J5
Melbourne Ct., Giff.	62	T18
Melbourne St. G31	36	X13
Meldon Pl. G51	33	R12
Meldrum Gdns. G41	50	T15
Meldrum St., Clyde.	18	N8
Melford Av., Giff.	62	T19
Melford Way, Pais.	31	L12
Knock Way		
Melfort Av. G41	50	S14
Melfort Av., Clyde.	5	L6
Melfort Gdns., John.	43	C15
Milliken Pk. Rd.		
Mellerstain Dr. G14	18	N9
Melness Pl. G51	33	Q12
Mallaig Rd.		
Melrose Av. G73	53	Y16
Melrose Av., Bail.	41	GG13
Melrose Av., Linw.	28	E13
Melrose Av., Pais.	45	H15
Melrose Ct. G73	53	Y16
Dunard Rd.		
Melrose Gdns. G20	21	U10
Melrose Gdns., Udd.	57	GG15
Lincoln Av.		
Melrose Pl., Blan.	68	FF19
Melrose St. G4	35	V11
Queens Cres.		
Melvaig Pl. G20	20	T9
Melvick Pl. G51	33	Q12
Mallaig Rd.		
Melville Ct. G1	36	W12
Brunswick St.		
Melville Gdns., Bish.	11	Y7
Melville St. G41	51	U14
Memel St. G21	22	X9
Memus Av. G52	49	Q14
Mennock Dr., Bish.	11	Y6
Menock Rd. G44	63	V17
Menteith Av., Bish.	11	Y7
Menteith Dr. G73	65	Z19
Menteith Pl. G73	65	Z19
Menzies Dr. G21	23	Y9
Menzies Pl. G21	23	Y9
Menzies Rd. G21	23	Y9
Merchant La. G1	36	W13
Clyde St.		
Merchants Clo., Pais.	42	B14
Church St.		
Merchiston St. G32	38	AA12
Merkland Ct. G11	34	S11
Vine St.		
Merkland St. G11	34	S11
Merksworth Way, Pais.	30	J12
Mosslands Rd.		
Merlewood Av. G71	69	HH18
Merlin Way, Pais.	31	L12
Merlinford Av., Renf.	18	N10
Merlinford Cres., Renf.	18	N10
Merlinford Dr., Renf.	18	N10
Merlinford Way, Renf.	18	N10
Merrick Gdns. G51	34	S13

Street	Page	Grid
Merrick Ter., Udd.	57	HH16
Merrick Way G73	65	Y18
Merryburn Av., Giff.	62	T17
Merrycrest Av., Giff.	62	T18
Merrycroft Av., Giff.	62	T18
Merryland Pl. G51	34	T12
Merryland St. G51	34	S12
Merrylee Cres., Giff.	62	T17
Merrylee Pk. Av., Giff.	62	T18
Merrylee Pk. La., Giff.	62	T18
Merrylee Pk. Ms., Giff.	62	T18
Merrylee Rd. G43	62	T17
Merryton Av. G15	6	P6
Merryton Av., Giff.	62	T18
Merryton Pl. G15	6	P6
Merryvale Av., Giff.	62	T18
Merryvale Pl., Giff.	62	T17
Merton Dr. G52	32	P13
Meryon Gdns. G32	55	CC15
Meryon Rd. G32	55	CC15
Methil St. G14	19	Q10
Methuen Rd., Renf.	31	L11
Methven Av., Bear.	8	S5
Methven St. G31	53	Z14
Methven St., Dalm.	4	K6
Metropole La. G1	35	V13
Howard St.		
Michillen Rd., Bear.	8	T5
Micklehouse Oval, Bail.	40	EE13
Micklehouse Rd.		
Micklehouse Pl., Bail.	40	EE13
Micklehouse Rd.		
Micklehouse Rd., Bail.	40	EE13
Micklehouse Wynd, Bail.	40	EE13
Micklehouse Rd.		
Mid Cotts., Gart.	26	FF10
Midcroft, Bish.	10	X6
Midcroft Av. G44	64	W17
Middlemuir Av., Lenz.	13	CC5
Middlemuir Rd., Lenz.	13	CC5
Middlerigg Rd., Cumb.	70	MM3
Middlesex St. G41	35	U13
Middleton Cres., Pais.	30	J13
Middleton Rd., Linw.	28	F12
Middleton St. G51	34	T13
Midland St. G1	35	V13
Midlem Dr. G52	33	Q13
Midlem Oval G52	33	Q13
Midlock St. G51	34	T13
Midlothian Dr. G41	50	T15
Midton Cotts., Chr.	15	HH7
Midton St. G21	22	X10
Midwharf St. G4	36	W11
Migvie Pl. G20	20	T9
Wyndford Rd.		
Milan St. G41	51	V14
Milford St. G33	38	BB12
Mill Ct. G73	53	Y16
Mill Cres. G40	52	X14
Mill Pl., Linw.	28	E13
Mill River, Lenz.	13	CC6
Mill Rd. G72	67	CC18
Mill Rd., Barr.	59	L18
Mill Rd., Both.	69	HH19
Mill Rd., Clyde.	17	M8
Mill Rd. Gdns. G40	36	X13
Mill St. G40	52	X14
Mill St. G73	53	Y16
Mill St., Pais.	46	K14
Mill Vennel, Renf.	18	N10
High St.		
Millands Av., Blan.	68	FF19
Millar St., Pais.	30	K13
Millar Ter. G73	53	Y15
Millarbank St. G21	22	X10
Millarston Av., Pais.	45	H14
Millarston Dr., Pais.	45	H14
Millbeg Cres. G33	39	DD13
Millbeg Pl. G33	39	DD13
Millbrae Ct. G42	51	U16
Millbrae Rd.		
Millbrae Cres. G13	17	M8
Millbrae Cres. G42	51	U16
Millbrae Rd. G42	51	U16
Millbrix Av. G14	18	P9
Millburn Av. G73	65	Y17
Millburn Av., Clyde.	18	N8
Millburn Av., Renf.	18	N10
Millburn Dr., Renf.	17	M10
Millburn Rd., Renf.	17	M10
Millburn St. G21	37	Y11
Millburn Way, Renf.	18	N10
Millcroft Rd. G73	52	X15
Millcroft Rd., Cumb.	71	PP3
Miller St. G1	36	W12
Miller St., Bail.	56	EE14
Miller St., Clyde.	5	L7
Miller St., John.	44	E14
Millerfield Pl. G40	53	Y14
Millerfield Rd. G40	53	Y14
Millers Pl., Lenz.	13	CC6
Millersneuk Av., Lenz.	13	CC6
Millersneuk Cres. G33	24	BB9
Millersneuk Dr., Lenz.	13	CC6
Millerston St. G31	37	Y13
Milford Dr., Linw.	28	E13
Millgate, Udd.	57	GG16
Millgate Av., Udd.	57	GG16
Millholm Rd. G44	63	V18
Millhouse Cres. G20	20	T8
Millhouse Dr. G20	20	T8
Milliken Dr., Kilb.	43	C15
Milliken Pk. Rd., Kilb.	43	C15
Millpond Dr. G40	36	X13
Millport Av. G44	52	W16
Millroad Dr. G40	36	X13
Millroad St. G40	36	X13
Millview Pl. G53	60	P18
Millwood St. G41	51	U16
Milnbank St. G31	37	Y12
Milncroft Rd. G33	38	BB11
Milner Rd. G13	19	R9
Milngavie Rd., Bear.	7	R6
Milnpark Gdns. G41	35	U13
Milnpark St. G41	35	U13
Milovaig St. G23	8	T7
Milrig Rd. G73	52	X16
Milton Av. G72	66	AA17
Milton Douglas Rd., Clyde.	5	L5
Milton Dr., Bish.	22	X8
Milton Gdns., Udd.	57	GG16
Milton Mains Rd., Dalm.	5	L5
Milton St. G4	35	V11
Milverton Av., Bear.	7	Q5
Milverton Rd., Giff.	62	S19
Minard Rd. G41	51	U15
Minard Way, Udd.	57	HH16
Newton Dr.		
Minerva St. G3	35	U12
Minerva Way G3	35	U12
Mingarry La. G20	20	T10
Clouston St.		
Mingary St. G20	21	U10
Mingulay Cres. G22	22	W8
Mingulay Pl. G22	22	X8
Mingulay St. G22	22	W8
Minmoir Rd. G53	48	N16
Minstrel Rd. G13	7	Q7
Minto Av. G73	65	Z18
Minto Cres. G52	33	R13
Minto St. G52	33	R13
Mireton St. G22	21	V9
Mirrlees Dr. G12	20	T10
Mirrlees La. G12	20	T10
Redlands Rd.		
Mitchell Av. G72	67	DD17
Mitchell Av., Renf.	31	L11
Mitchell Dr. G73	65	Y17
Mitchell La. G1	35	V12
Buchanan St.		
Mitchell Rd., Cumb.	71	PP3
Mitchell St. G1	35	V12
Mitchell St., Coat.	57	HH14
Mitchellhill Rd. G45	64	X19
Mitchison Rd., Cumb.	71	PP2
Mitre Ct. G14	19	Q10
Mitre Rd.		
Mitre La. G14	19	R10
Mitre La. W. G14	19	R10
Mitre La.		
Mitre Rd. G14	19	R10
Moat Av. G13	19	Q8
Mochrum Rd. G43	63	U17
Moffat Pl., Blan.	68	FF19
Moffat St. G5	52	W14
Mogarth Av., Pais.	45	H16
Amochrie Rd.		
Moidart Av., Renf.	17	L10
Moidart Ct., Barr.	59	M17
Moidart Cres. G52	33	R13
Moidart Rd.		
Moidart Pl. G52	33	R13
Moidart Rd.		
Moidart Rd. G52	33	R13
Moir La. G1	36	W13
Moir St.		
Moir St. G1	36	W13
Molendinar St. G1	36	W13
Mollinsburn St. G21	22	X10
Monach Rd. G33	39	CC12
Monachie Gdns., Bish.	11	Z7
Muirhead Way		
Monart Pl. G20	21	U10
Caithness St.		
Moncrieff Av., Lenz.	13	CC5
Moncrieff Gdns., Lenz.	13	CC5
Moncrieff Pl. G4	35	V11
North Woodside Rd.		
Moncrieff St. G4	35	V11
Braid Sq.		
Moncur St. G40	36	X13
Moness Dr. G52	49	R14
Monica Gdns. G53	61	Q19
Monifieth Av. G52	49	Q14
Monikie Gdns., Bish.	11	Z7
Muirhead Way		
Monkcastle Dr. G73	66	BB17
Monkland Av., Lenz.	13	CC5
Monkland Vw., Udd.	57	HH15
Lincoln Av.		
Monkland Vw. Cres., Bail.	41	HH13
Monksbridge Av. G13	7	Q7
Monkscroft Av. G11	20	S10
Monkscroft Ct. G11	34	S11
Monkscroft Gdns. G11	20	S10
Monkscroft Av.		
Monkton Dr. G15	6	P7
Monmouth Av. G12	20	S9
Monreith Av., Bear.	7	Q7
Monreith Rd. G43	62	T17
Monreith Rd. E. G44	63	V17
Monroe Dr., Udd.	57	GG15
Monroe Pl., Udd.	57	GG15
Montague La. G12	20	S10
Montague St. G4	35	U11
Montague Ter. G12	20	S10
Hyndland Rd.		
Montclair Pl., Linw.	28	E13
Monteith Dr., Clark.	63	V19
Monteith Pl. G40	36	X13
Monteith Row G40	36	X13
Monteith Row La. G40	36	X13
Monteith Pl.		
Montford Av. G44	52	W16
Montgomerie Gdns. G14	19	Q10
Lennox Av.		
Montgomery Av., Pais.	31	L12
Montgomery Dr., Giff.	62	T19
Montgomery Dr., Kilb.	42	B14
Meadside Av.		
Montgomery La. G42	51	V16
Somerville Dr.		
Montgomery Rd., Pais.	31	L12
Montgomery St. G42	52	X14
London Rd.		
Montgomery St. G72	67	DD17
Mill Rd.		
Montrave St. G52	49	Q14
Montrave St. G73	53	Y15
Montreal Ho., Dalm.	4	J5
Perth Cres.		
Montron Dr. G15	6	P7
Moraine Av.		

Name	Page	Grid
Montrose Av. G32	54	BB15
Montrose Av. G52	32	N12
Montrose Gdns., Blan.	68	FF19
Montrose Pl., Linw.	28	E13
Montrose Rd., Pais.	45	G16
Montrose St. G4	36	W12
Montrose St., Clyde.	5	L7
Montrose Ter., Bish.	23	Z8
Monymusk Gdns., Bish.	11	Z7
Monymusk Pl. G15	6	N5
Moodies Ct. G2	35	V12
Argyle St.		
Moodiesburn St. G33	37	Z11
Moorburn Av., Giff.	62	S18
Moore Dr., Bear.	7	R6
Moore St. G31	37	Y13
Gallowgate		
Moorehouse Av. G13	18	N9
Moorehouse Av., Pais.	45	H15
Moorfoot, Bish.	11	Z7
Moorfoot Av. G46	62	S18
Moorfoot Av., Pais.	46	J15
Moorfoot St. G32	38	AA13
Moorhouse Av. G13	18	N9
Moorhouse St., Barr.	59	M19
Moorpark Av. G52	32	N13
Moorpark Av., Chr.	26	FF8
Moorpark Dr. G52	32	P13
Moorpark Pl. G52	32	N13
Moorpark Sq., Renf.	31	L11
Morag Av., Blan.	68	FF19
Moraine Av. G15	6	P7
Moraine Circ. G15	6	P7
Moraine Dr. G15	6	P7
Moraine Pl. G15	6	P7
Moraine Dr.		
Morar Av., Clyde.	5	L6
Morar Ct., Clyde.	5	L6
Morar Ct., Cumb.	70	LL4
Morar Cres., Bish.	10	X7
Morar Cres., Clyde.	5	L6
Morar Dr. G73	65	Y18
Morar Dr., Bear.	8	S6
Morar Dr., Clyde.	5	L6
Morar Dr., Cumb.	70	LL4
Morar Dr., Linw.	28	E13
Morar Dr., Pais.	45	H15
Morar Pl., Clyde.	5	L6
Morar Pl., Renf.	17	L10
Morar Rd. G52	33	R13
Morar Rd., Clyde.	5	L6
Morar Ter., Udd.	57	HH16
Moravia Av., Both.	69	HH18
Moray Gdns., Cumb.	71	PP1
Moray Gdns., Udd.	57	GG16
Moray Gate, Both.	69	GG18
Moray Pl. G41	51	U15
Moray Pl., Bish.	11	Z7
Moray Pl., Linw.	28	E13
Mordaunt St. G40	53	Y14
Moredun Cres. G32	39	CC12
Moredun Dr., Pais.	45	H15
Moredun Rd., Pais.	45	H15
Moredun St. G32	39	CC12
Morefield Rd. G51	33	Q12
Morgan Ms. G42	51	V14
Morion Rd. G13	19	Q8
Morley St. G42	51	V16
Morna Pl. G14	33	R11
Victoria Pk. Dr. S.		
Morningside St. G33	37	Z12
Morrin Path G21	22	X10
Crichton St.		
Morrin Sq. G4	36	X12
Collins St.		
Morrin St. G21	22	X10
Morris Pl. G40	36	X13
Morrison Quad., Clyde.	6	N7
Morrison St. G5	35	V13
Morrison St., Clyde.	4	K5
Morrisons Ct. G2	35	V12
Argyle St.		
Morriston Cres., Renf.	32	N11
Morriston Pk. Dr. G72	54	BB16
Morriston St. G72	66	BB17
Mortimer St. G20	21	U10
Hotspur St.		
Morton Gdns. G41	50	T15
Morven Av., Bish.	11	Z7
Morven Av., Blan.	68	FF19
Morven Av., Pais.	46	J16
Morven Dr., Linw.	28	E13
Morven Gdns., Udd.	57	GG16
Morven Rd. G72	66	AA18
Morven Rd., Bear.	7	R5
Morven St. G52	33	R13
Mosesfield St. G21	22	X9
Mosesfield Ter. G21	22	X9
Balgrayhill Rd.		
Moss Av., Linw.	28	E13
Moss Dr., Barr.	59	L17
Moss Heights Av. G52	33	Q13
Moss Knowe, Cumb.	71	QQ3
Moss Path, Bail.	55	DD14
Castle St.		
Moss Rd. G51	33	Q12
Moss Rd., Chr.	26	FF8
Moss Rd., Cumb.	71	QQ2
Moss Rd., Lenz.	13	CC5
Moss Sq. G33	38	BB11
Moss St., Pais.	30	K13
Moss-side Rd. G41	51	U15
Mossbank Dr. G33	24	AA10
Mosscastle Rd. G33	39	CC11
Mossend La. G33	39	CC12
Mossend Rd., Pais.	30	J12
Mosslands Rd.		
Mossend St. G33	39	CC12
Mossgiel Av. G73	65	Y17
Mossgiel Dr., Clyde.	5	M6
Mossgiel Gdns., Udd.	57	GG16
Mossgiel Pl. G73	65	Y17
Mossgiel Rd. G43	62	T17
Mossgiel Rd., Cumb.	71	PP3
Mossgiel Ter., Blan.	68	FF19
Mossland Rd. G52	32	N12
Mosslands Rd., Pais.	30	J12
Mossneuk Dr., Pais.	46	J16
Mosspark Av. G52	49	R14
Mosspark Boul. G52	49	R14
Mosspark Dr. G52	49	Q14
Mosspark La. G52	49	R15
Mosspark Dr.		
Mosspark Oval G52	49	R14
Mosspark Sq. G52	49	R14
Mossvale Cres. G33	39	CC11
Mossvale La., Pais.	30	J13
Mossvale Path G33	25	CC10
Mossvale Rd. G33	39	CC11
Mossvale Sq. G33	39	CC11
Mossvale St., Pais.	30	J12
Mossvale Ter., Chr.	15	HH6
Mossvale Wk. G33	39	CC11
Mossvale Way G33	39	CC11
Mossview Cotts., Chr.	26	FF9
Mossview Quad. G52	33	Q13
Mossview Rd. G33	25	DD9
Mote Hill Rd., Pais.	31	L13
Moulin Circ. G52	48	P14
Moulin Pl. G52	48	P14
Moulin Rd. G52	48	P14
Moulin Ter. G52	48	P14
Mount Annan Dr. G44	51	V16
Mount Harriet Av. G33	25	DD9
Mount Harriet Dr. G33	25	CC9
Mount St. G20	21	U10
Mount Stuart St. G41	51	U16
Mount Vernon Av. G32	55	DD14
Mountainblue St. G31	37	Y13
Mountblow Ho., Dalm.	4	J5
Melbourne Av.		
Mountblow Rd., Dalm.	4	K5
Mountgarrie Path G51	33	Q12
Mountgarrie Rd.		
Mountgarrie Rd. G51	33	Q12
Mowbray Av., Gart.	27	GG9
Mowcraigs Ct., Clyde.	17	M8
Yokerburn Ter.		
Moy St. G11	34	T11
Church St.		
Moyne Rd. G53	48	P15
Muckcroft Rd., Chr.	14	EE6
Muir Pk. Ter. G64	22	X8
Muir St. G21	22	X10
Muir St., Bish.	11	Y7
Muir St., Renf.	17	M10
Muir Ter., Pais.	31	L12
Muirbank Av. G73	52	X16
Muirbank Gdns. G73	52	X16
Muirbrae Rd. G73	65	Y18
Muirbrae Way G73	65	Y18
Muirburn Av. G44	63	U18
Muirdrum Av. G52	49	Q14
Muirdykes Av. G52	32	P13
Muirdykes Cres., Pais.	29	H13
Muirdykes Rd. G52	32	P13
Muirdykes Rd., Pais.	29	H13
Muiredge Ct., Udd.	69	GG17
Watson St.		
Muiredge Ter., Bail.	56	EE14
Muirend Av. G44	63	U18
Muirend Rd. G44	63	U18
Muirfield Cres. G23	9	U7
Muirfield Rd., Cumb.	71	PP1
Muirhead Ct., Bail.	56	FF14
Muirhead Dr., Linw.	28	E13
Muirhead Gdns., Bail.	56	FF14
Muirhead Rd., Udd.	56	EE14
Muirhead St. G11	34	S11
Purdon St.		
Muirhead Way, Bish.	11	Z7
Muirhill Av. G44	63	U18
Muirhill Cres. G13	18	P8
Muirhouse St. G41	51	U15
Pollokshaws Rd.		
Muirkirk Dr. G13	19	R8
Muirpark Av., Renf.	31	M11
Muirpark Dr., Bish.	23	Y8
Muirpark St. G11	34	S11
Muirpark Ter., Bish.	22	X8
Crowhill Rd.		
Muirshiel Av. G53	61	Q17
Muirshiel Cres. G53	61	Q17
Muirside Av. G32	55	DD14
Muirside Rd., Bail.	56	EE14
Muirside St., Bail.	56	EE14
Muirskeith Cres. G43	63	U17
Muirskeith Pl. G43	63	U17
Muirskeith Rd. G43	63	U17
Muirton Dr., Bish.	10	X6
Muirton Gdns., Bish.	10	X6
Muiryfauld Dr. G31	54	AA14
Mulben Cres. G53	48	N16
Mulben Pl. G53	48	N16
Mulben Ter. G53	48	N16
Mulberry Rd. G43	62	T17
Mull Av., Pais.	46	K16
Mull Av., Renf.	31	M11
Mull St. G21	37	Y11
Mullardoch St. G23	8	T7
Rothes Dr.		
Mungo Pl., Udd.	57	HH15
Lincoln Av.		
Munlochy Rd. G51	33	Q12
Munro Ct., Clyde.	4	K5
Gentle Row		
Munro La. G13	19	R9
Munro Pl. G13	19	R9
Munro Pl., Udd.	57	HH15
Kirkwood Rd.		
Munro Rd. G13	19	R9
Munro Vw., Udd.	57	HH15
Kirkwood Rd.		
Murano St. G20	21	U10
Murdoch St. G21	22	X9
Lenzie St.		
Muriel St., Barr.	59	M18
Murray Pl., Barr.	59	M18
Murray Rd., Both.	69	HH18
Murray St., Pais.	30	J13
Murray St., Renf.	17	M10
Murrayfield, Bish.	11	Y6
Ashfield		
Murrayfield Dr., Bear.	7	R7
Murrayfield St. G32	38	AA12

Name	No.	Ref.
Murrin Av., Bish.	11	Z7
Murroes Rd. G51	33	Q12
Muslin St. G40	52	X14
Mybster Pl. G51	33	Q12
Mybster Rd. G51	33	Q12
Myers Cres., Udd.	69	HH17
Myres Rd. G53	49	Q16
Myreside Pl. G32	37	Z13
Myreside St. G32	37	Z13
Myrie Gdns., Bish.	11	Y7
Myroch Pl. G34	40	FF11
Myrtle Av., Lenz.	13	CC5
Myrtle Hill La. G42	52	W16
Myrtle Hill Vw. G42	52	W16
Myrtle Pk. G42	52	W15
Myrtle Pl. G42	52	W16
Myrtle Rd., Dalm.	4	J6
Myrtle Rd., Udd.	57	HH16
Myrtle Sq., Bish.	23	Y8
Myrtle St., Blan.	68	FF19
Myrtle Wk. G72	66	AA17
Naburn St. G5	52	W14
Nairn Av., Blan.	68	FF19
Nairn Gdns., Bear.	7	Q6
Nairn Pl., Dalm.	4	K6
Dumbarton Rd.		
Nairn St. G3	34	T11
Nairn St., Dalm.	4	K6
Nairn Way, Cumb.	71	PP1
Nairnside Rd. G21	23	Z8
Naismith St. G32	55	CC16
Nansen St. G20	21	V10
Napier Ct., Old K.	4	J5
Freelands Rd.		
Napier Dr. G51	34	S12
Napier Gdns., Linw.	28	F13
Napier Pl. G51	34	S12
Napier Pl., Old K.	4	J5
Old Dalnottar Rd.		
Napier Rd. G51	34	S12
Napier Rd. G52	32	N11
Napier St. G51	34	T12
Napier St., Clyde.	17	M8
Napier St., Linw.	28	F13
Napier Ter. G51	34	S12
Napiershall La. G20	35	U11
Napiershall St.		
Napiershall Pl. G20	35	U11
Napiershall St.		
Napiershall St. G20	35	U11
Naseby Av. G11	19	R10
Nasmyth Rd. G52	32	P12
Nasmyth Rd. N. G52	32	P12
Nasmyth Rd. S. G52	32	P12
National Bk. La. G2	35	V12
St. Vincent St.		
Navar Pl., Pais.	47	L15
Naver St. G33	38	AA11
Neil St., Renf.	17	M9
Neilsland Oval G53	49	Q16
Neilsland Sq. G53	49	Q15
Neilston Av. G53	61	Q17
Neilston Rd., Barr.	59	L19
Neilston Rd., Pais.	46	K14
Neilvaig Dr. G73	65	Z18
Nelson Mandela Pl. G1	36	W12
Buchanan St.		
Nelson Pl., Bail.	56	EE14
Nelson St. G5	35	V13
Nelson St., Bail.	56	EE14
Nelson Ter. G12	21	U10
Glasgow St.		
Neptune St. G51	34	S12
Nerston Av. G53	49	Q16
Ness Av., John.	43	C16
Ness Dr., Blan.	69	GG19
Ness Gdns., Bish.	11	Y7
Ness Rd., Renf.	17	L10
Ness St. G33	38	AA11
Netham St. G51	34	S12
Nether Auldhouse Rd. G43	62	S17
Netherburn Av. G44	63	U19
Netherby Dr. G41	50	T14
Nethercairn Rd. G43	62	T18
Nethercliffe Av. G44	63	U19
Nethercommon Harbour, Pais.	30	K12
Nethercraig Cotts., Pais.	58	J17
Glenfield Rd.		
Nethercraigs Dr., Pais.	46	J16
Nethercraigs Rd., Pais.	45	H16
Netherdale Dr., Pais.	48	N14
Netherfield St. G31	37	Z13
Netherhill Av. G44	63	U19
Netherhill Cres., Pais.	31	L13
Netherhill Rd., Chr.	15	GG7
Netherhill Rd., Pais.	30	K13
Netherhouse Av., Lenz.	13	DD6
Netherhouse Pl., Bail.	41	GG12
Netherhouse Rd., Bail.	40	FF12
Netherlee Rd. G44	63	U18
Netherpark Av. G44	63	U19
Netherplace Cres. G53	48	P16
Netherplace Rd. G53	48	P16
Netherton Ct. G45	64	X19
Netherton Dr., Barr.	60	N19
Netherton Rd. G13	19	R8
Netherton St. G13	19	R8
Crow Rd.		
Nethervale Av. G44	63	U19
Netherview Rd. G44	63	V19
Netherway G44	63	U19
Nethy Way, Renf.	32	N11
Teith Av.		
Neuk Way G32	55	CC16
Nevis Rd. G43	62	S17
Nevis Rd., Bear.	6	P5
Nevis Rd., Renf.	31	L11
New City Rd. G4	35	V11
New Edinburgh Rd., Udd.	57	GG16
New Inchinnan Rd., Pais.	30	K12
New Kirk Pl., Bear.	7	R5
New Kirk Rd.		
New Kirk Rd., Bear.	7	R5
New Rd. G72	67	DD18
New Sneddon St., Pais.	30	K13
New St., Clyde.	5	L5
New St., Kilb.	42	B14
New St., Pais.	46	K14
New Wynd G1	36	W13
Newark Dr. G41	50	T14
Newark Dr., Pais.	46	J16
Newbattle Ct. G32	54	BB15
Newbattle Gdns. G32	54	BB15
Newbattle Pl. G32	54	BB15
Newbattle Rd. G32	54	BB15
Newbold Av. G21	22	X8
Newburgh St. G43	50	T16
Newcastleton Dr. G23	9	U7
Newcroft Dr. G44	64	W17
Newfield Pl. G73	52	X16
Newfield Pl., Thorn.	61	R19
Rouken Glen Rd.		
Newfield Sq. G53	60	P17
Newhall St. G40	52	X14
Newhaven Rd. G33	38	BB12
Newhaven St. G32	38	BB12
Newhills Rd. G33	39	DD12
Newington St. G32	38	AA13
Newlands Gdns., John.	44	F15
Renshaw Rd.		
Newlands Rd. G43	63	U17
Newlands Rd., Udd.	57	GG16
Newlandsfield Rd. G43	50	T16
Newluce Dr. G32	55	CC14
Newmains Rd., Renf.	31	L11
Newmill Rd. G21	23	Z9
Newnham Rd., Pais.	48	N14
Newpark Ct. G72	54	BB16
Newshot Ct., Clyde.	17	M8
Clydeholm Ter.		
Newshot Dr., Renf.	4	J7
Newstead Gdns. G23	9	U7
Newton Av. G72	67	CC17
Newton Av., Barr.	59	M19
Newton Av., John.	45	G14
Newton Av., Pais.	31	L12
Newton Brae G72	67	DD17
Newton Dr., John.	45	G14
Newton Dr., Udd.	57	HH16
Newton Fm. Rd. G72	55	DD16
Newton Pl. G3	35	U11
Newton Rd., Lenz.	13	DD6
Newton Sta. Rd. G72	67	DD17
Newton St., Pais.	46	J14
Newton Ter. G3	35	U12
Sauchiehall St.		
Newton Ter. La. G3	35	U11
Elderslie St.		
Newtongrange Av. G32	54	BB15
Newtongrange Gdns. G32	54	BB15
Newtyle Pl., Bish.	11	Z7
Newtyle Rd., Pais.	47	M14
Nicholas St. G1	36	W12
Nicholson Ct. G33	25	CC9
Nicholson La. G5	35	V13
Nicholson St.		
Nicholson St. G5	35	V13
Niddrie Rd. G42	51	U15
Niddrie Sq. G42	51	U15
Niddry St., Pais.	30	K13
Nigel Gdns. G41	50	T15
Nigg Pl. G34	40	EE12
Nightingale Pl., John.	43	C16
Nimmo Dr. G51	33	R12
Nisbet St. G31	37	Z13
Nith Av., Pais.	45	G15
Nith Dr., Renf.	32	N11
Nith Pl., John.	43	C16
Nith St. G33	37	Z11
Nithsdale Cres., Bear.	7	Q5
Nithsdale Dr. G41	51	U15
Nithsdale Pl. G41	51	U14
Shields Rd.		
Nithsdale Rd. G41	50	S14
Nithsdale St. G41	51	U15
Nitshill Rd. G53	60	N17
Niven St. G20	20	T9
Noldrum Av. G32	55	CC16
Noldrum Gdns. G32	55	CC16
Norbreck Dr., Giff.	62	T18
Norby Rd. G11	19	R10
Norfield Dr. G44	51	V16
Norfolk Ct. G5	35	V13
Norfolk Cres., Bish.	10	X6
Norfolk La. G5	35	V13
Norfolk St.		
Norfolk St. G5	35	V13
Norham St. G41	51	U15
Norman St. G40	52	X14
Norse La. N. G14	19	Q10
Ormiston Av.		
Norse La. S. G14	19	Q10
Verona Av.		
Norse Rd. G14	19	Q10
North Av. G72	66	AA17
North Av., Clyde.	5	L7
North Bk. Pl., Clyde.	17	M8
North Bk. St.		
North Bk. St., Clyde.	17	M8
North Brae Pl. G13	18	P8
North British Rd., Udd.	69	GG17
North Canalbank St. G4	36	W11
North Carbrain Rd., Cumb.	70	NN4
North Claremont St. G3	35	U11
North Corsebar Av., Pais.	46	J15
North Ct. La. G1	36	W12
Buchanan St.		
North Cft. St., Pais.	30	K13
North Deanpark Av., Udd.	69	HH18
North Douglas St., Clyde.	17	M8
North Dr. G1	36	W13
North Dr., Linw.	28	E13
North Elgin St., Clyde.	17	M8
North Erskine Pk., Bear.	7	Q5
North Frederick St. G1	36	W12

Name	Page	Grid
North Gardner St. G11	20	S10
North Gra. Rd., Bear.	7	R5
North Greenhill Rd., Pais.	30	J12
North Hanover Pl. G4	36	W11
North Hanover St. G1	36	W12
North Iverton Pk. Rd., John.	44	E14
North Lo. Rd., Renf.	17	M10
North Moraine La. G15	7	Q7
Moraine Av.		
North Pk. Av., Thorn.	61	R18
North Pl. G3	35	U12
North St.		
North Portland St. G1	36	W12
North Queen St. G2	36	W12
George Sq.		
North Rd., John.	43	D15
North Spiers Wf. G4	35	V11
North St. G3	35	U12
North St., Clyde.	5	L7
Dumbarton Rd.		
North St., Pais.	30	K13
North Vw., Bear.	7	Q7
North Wallace St. G4	36	W11
North Way, Blan.	68	FF19
North Woodside Rd. G20	21	U10
Northampton Dr. G12	20	S9
Northampton La. G12	20	S9
Northampton Dr.		
Northbank Av. G72	67	CC17
Northbank St. G72	67	CC17
Northcroft Rd. G21	22	X10
Northcroft Rd., Chr.	15	GG7
Northgate Quad. G21	23	Z8
Northgate Rd. G21	23	Z8
Northinch St. G14	33	Q11
Northland Dr. G14	19	Q9
Northland La. G14	19	Q10
Northland Dr.		
Northmuir Rd. G15	6	P6
Northpark St. G20	21	U10
Northpark Ter. G12	21	U10
Hamilton Dr.		
Northumberland St. G20	21	U10
Norval St. G11	34	S11
Norwich Dr. G12	20	S9
Norwood, Bear.	7	R6
Norwood Dr., Giff.	62	S19
Norwood Ter. G12	35	U11
Southpark Av.		
Norwood Ter., Udd.	57	HH16
Nottingham Av. G12	20	S9
Nottingham La. G12	20	S9
Northampton Dr.		
Novar Dr. G12	20	S10
Novar Gdns., Bish.	10	X7
Numrow Ct., Clyde.	4	K5
Nuneaton St. G40	53	Y14
Nurseries Rd., Bail.	39	DD13
Nursery La. G41	51	U15
Nursery St. G41	51	U15
Pollokshaws Rd.		
Nursery St. La. G41	51	U15
Nithsdale Dr.		
Nutberry Ct. G42	51	V15
Oak Cres., Bail.	56	EE14
Oak Dr. G72	67	CC18
Oak Dr., Lenz.	12	BB5
Oak Pl., Bish.	11	Y7
Oak Rd., Dalm.	4	K5
Oak Rd., Pais.	47	L15
Oak St. G2	35	V12
Cadogan St.		
Oakbank Dr., Barr.	60	N19
Oakbank La. G20	21	V10
Oakbank Ter. G20	21	V10
Oakdene Av., Udd.	57	HH16
Oakfield Av. G12	35	U11
Oakfield Ter. G12	35	U11
Oakfield Av.		
Oakhill Av., Bail.	55	DD14
Oakley Dr. G44	63	U18
Oakley Ter. G31	36	X12
Oaks, The, John.	43	C15
Oakshaw Sch. Brae. Pais.	30	J13
Oakshaw St., Pais.	30	J13
Oakshawhead, Pais.	30	J13
Oakwood Av., Pais.	45	H15
Oatfield St. G21	23	Y10
Oban Ct. G22	21	U10
Oban Dr. G20	21	U10
Observatory La. G12	20	T10
Observatory Rd.		
Observatory Rd. G12	20	T10
Ochil Dr., Barr.	59	M19
Ochil Dr., Pais.	46	K16
Ochil Pl. G32	54	BB14
Ochil Rd., Bish.	11	Z7
Ochil Rd., Renf.	31	L11
Ochil St. G32	54	BB14
Ochiltree Av. G13	19	R8
Ogilvie Pl. G31	54	AA14
Ogilvie St. G31	53	Z14
Old Bothwell Rd., Both.	69	HH19
Old Castle Rd. G44	63	V17
Old Dalmarnock Rd. G40	52	X14
Old Dalnottar Rd., Old K.	4	J5
Old Dumbarton Rd. G3	34	T11
Old Edinburgh Rd., Udd.	57	GG15
Old Gartcosh Rd., Gart.	27	GG9
Old Glasgow Rd., Udd.	56	FF16
Old Govan Rd., Renf.	18	N10
Old Greenock Rd., Renf.	16	J8
Old Manse Rd. G32	39	CC13
Old Mill Rd. G72	67	CC17
Old Mill Rd., Both.	69	HH19
Old Mill Rd., Clyde.	5	L5
Old Mill Rd., Udd.	69	GG17
Old Renfrew Rd., Renf.	32	P11
Old Rd., John.	44	F14
Old Roundknowe Rd., Udd.	56	FF15
Old Rutherglen Rd. G5	52	W14
Old Shettleston Rd. G32	38	AA13
Old Sneddon St., Pais.	30	K13
Old St., Clyde.	4	K5
Old Wd. Rd., Bail.	56	EE14
Old Wynd G1	36	W13
Oldhall Rd., Pais.	31	M13
Olifard Av., Both.	69	HH18
Oliphant Cres., Pais.	45	G16
Olive St. G33	23	Z10
Olrig Ter. G41	51	U14
Shields Rd.		
Olympia St. G40	36	X13
Onslow Dr. G31	37	Y12
Onslow Rd., Clyde.	5	M7
Onslow Sq. G31	37	Y12
Onslow Dr.		
Oran Gdns. G20	21	U9
Oran Gate G20	21	U10
Oran Pl. G20	21	U9
Oran St. G20	21	U9
Oransay Cres., Bear.	8	S6
Orbiston Gdns. G32	38	BB13
Balintore St.		
Orcades Dr. G44	63	V18
Orchard Av. G17	69	HH19
Orchard Ct. G32	54	BB16
Orchard Ct., Thorn.	62	S18
Orchard Dr. G73	52	X16
Orchard Dr., Giff.	62	S18
Orchard Gro., Giff.	62	S18
Orchard Pk., Giff.	62	T18
Orchard Pk. Av., Thorn.	62	S18
Orchard Sq., Pais.	46	K14
Orchard St., Pais.	46	K14
Orchard St., Renf.	17	M10
Orchardfield, Lenz.	13	CC6
Orchy Ct., Clyde.	5	M5
Orchy Cres., Bear.	7	Q7
Orchy Cres., Pais.	45	G15
Orchy Dr., Clark.	63	U19
Orchy Gdns., Clark.	63	U19
Orchy St. G44	63	V17
Oregon Pl. G5	52	W14
Orion Way G72	66	BB17
Orkney Pl. G51	34	S12
Orkney St.		
Orkney St. G51	34	S12
Orleans Av. G14	19	R10
Orleans La. G14	19	R10
Ormiston Av. G14	19	Q10
Ormiston La. G14	19	Q10
Ormiston Av.		
Ormiston La. S. G14	19	Q10
Ormiston Av.		
Ormonde Av. G44	63	U18
Ormonde Ct. G44	63	U18
Ormonde Cres. G44	63	U18
Ormonde Dr. G44	63	U18
Ornsay St. G22	22	W8
Orr Pl. G40	36	X13
Orr Sq., Pais.	30	K13
Orr St. G40	36	X13
Orr St., Pais.	30	K13
Orton St. G51	34	S13
Orwell St. G21	22	X10
Osborn Ter. G51	34	S13
Copland Rd.		
Osborne St. G1	36	W13
Osborne St., Clyde.	5	L6
Osborne Vill. G44	63	V17
Holmhead Rd.		
Osprey Dr., Udd.	57	HH16
Ossian Av., Pais.	32	N13
Auchmannoch Av.		
Ossian Rd. G43	63	U17
Oswald La. G1	35	V13
Oswald St.		
Oswald St. G1	35	V13
Otago La. G12	35	U11
Otago St.		
Otago La. N. G12	35	U11
Otago St.		
Otago St. G12	35	U11
Ottawa Cres., Dalm.	4	J6
Otter La. G11	34	S11
Castlebank St.		
Otterburn Dr., Giff.	62	T19
Otterswick Pl. G33	39	CC11
Oval, The, Clark.	63	U19
Overbrae Pl. G15	6	N5
Overdale Av. G42	51	U16
Overdale Gdns. G42	51	U16
Overdale St. G42	51	U16
Overdale Vills. G42	51	U16
Overdale St.		
Overlea Av. G73	65	Z17
Overnewton Pl. G3	34	T12
Kelvinhaugh St.		
Overnewton Sq. G3	34	T12
Overnewton St. G3	34	T11
Overton Cres., John.	44	E14
Overton Rd. G72	67	CC18
Overton Rd., John.	44	E15
Overton St. G72	67	CC18
Overtoun Ct., Dalm.	4	K6
Dunswin Av.		
Overtoun Dr. G73	53	Y16
Overtoun Dr., Dalm.	4	K6
Overtoun Dr., Dalm.	4	K6
Overtown Av. G53	60	P17
Overtown St. G31	37	Y13
Overwood Dr. G44	64	W17
Oxford Dr., Linw.	28	E13
Oxford La. G5	35	V13
Oxford Rd., Renf.	17	M10
Oxford St. G5	35	V13
Oxton Dr. G52	32	P13
Paisley Ct., Barr.	59	L18
Paisley Rd.		
Paisley Rd. G5	35	U13
Paisley Rd., Barr.	59	L18
Paisley Rd., Renf.	31	L11
Paisley Rd. W. G52	48	P14
Palace St. G31	53	Z14
Paladin Av. G13	19	Q8

Name	Page	Grid		Name	Page	Grid		Name	Page	Grid
Palermo St. G21	22	X10		Parkvale Cres., Renf.	16	J8		Percy Dr., Giff.	62	T19
Palmer Av. G13	7	Q7		*Parkvale Av.*				Percy Rd., Renf.	31	L12
Palmerston Pl. G3	34	T12		Parkvale Dr., Renf.	16	J8		Percy St. G51	34	T13
Kelvinhaugh St.				*Parkvale Av.*				Perran Gdns., Chr.	15	GG7
Palmerston Pl., John.	43	C16		Parkvale Gdns., Renf.	16	J8		Perth Cres., Dalm.	4	J5
Pandora Way, Udd.	57	HH16		*Parkvale Av.*				Perth St. G3	35	U12
Hillcrest Rd.				Parkvale Pl., Renf.	16	J8		*Argyle St.*		
Panmure St. G20	21	V10		*Parkvale Av.*				Peters Ct. G20	20	T8
Park Av. G3	35	U11		Parkvale Way, Renf.	16	J8		*Maryhill Rd.*		
Park Av., Barr.	59	L19		*Parkvale Av.*				Petershill Ct. G21	23	Y10
Park Av., Bish.	11	Y6		Parkview G78	42	B14		Petershill Dr. G21	23	Y10
Park Av., John.	44	F15		Parkview, Pais.	46	J15		Petershill Pl. G21	23	Y10
Park Av., Pais.	46	J15		Parkview Av., Lenz.	13	CC5		Petershill Rd. G21	22	X10
Park Brae, Renf.	16	J8		Parkview Ct., Lenz.	13	CC5		Petition Pl., Udd.	69	HH17
Park Dr.				Parkview Dr. G33	25	DD9		Pettigrew St. G32	38	BB13
Park Circ. G3	35	U11		Parliament Rd. G21	36	X12		Peveril Av. G41	50	T15
Park Circ. La. G3	35	U11		Parnie St. G1	36	W13		Peveril Av. G73	65	Z17
Lynedoch Pl.				Parson St. G4	36	X12		Pharonhill St. G31	38	AA13
Park Circ. Pl. G3	35	U11		Parsonage Row G1	36	W12		*Quarrybrae St.*		
Park Ct., Bish.	11	Y6		Parsonage Sq. G1	36	W12		Phoenix Pk. Ter. G4	35	V11
Park Ct., Dalm.	4	K6		Partick Bri. St. G11	34	T11		*Corn St.*		
Little Holm				Partickhill Av. G11	20	S10		Phoenix Pl., John.	44	F14
Park Ct., Giff.	62	S18		Partickhill Ct. G11	20	S10		Phoenix Rd. G4	35	V11
Belmont Dr.				*Partickhill Av.*				*Great Western Rd.*		
Park Cot., Giff.	62	S19		Partickhill Rd. G11	20	S10		Piccadilly St. G3	35	U12
Park Cres., Bear.	6	P5		Paterson St. G5	35	V13		Pikeman Av. G13	19	Q9
Park Cres., Bish.	11	Y6		Pathead Gdns. G33	24	AA9		Pikeman Rd. G13	19	Q9
Park Cres., Renf.	16	J8		Patna St. G40	53	Y14		Pilmuir Av. G44	63	U18
Park Dr. G3	35	U11		Paton St. G31	37	Y12		Pilrig St. G32	38	AA12
Park Dr. G73	53	Y16		Patrick St., Pais.	46	K14		Pilton Rd. G15	6	P6
Park Dr., Renf.	16	J8		Patterton Dr., Barr.	59	M19		Pine Cres., John.	44	E15
Park Gdns. G3	35	U11		Pattison St., Dalm.	4	K6		Pine Gro., Udd.	57	HH16
Park Gdns., Kilb.	42	B14		Payne St. G4	36	W11		*Douglas Cres.*		
Park Gdns. La. G3	35	U11		Peacock Av., Pais.	45	G15		Pine Pl. G5	52	W14
Clifton St.				*Peacock Dr.*				Pine Pl., Cumb.	71	RR2
Park Gate G3	35	U11		Peacock Dr., Pais.	45	G14		Pine Rd., Cumb.	71	RR2
Park Gro., Renf.	16	J8		Pearce St. G51	34	S12		Pine Rd., Dalm.	4	J6
Park La. G40	36	X13		Pearson Dr., Renf.	31	M11		Pine St., Pais.	47	L15
Park La., Pais.	30	K13		Pearson Pl., Linw.	28	E13		Pinelands, Bish.	11	Y6
Netherhill Rd.				Peat Pl. G53	60	P17		Pinewood Av., Lenz.	12	BB5
Park Pl. G20	20	T8		Peat Rd. G53	60	P17		Pinewood Ct., Lenz.	12	BB5
Fingal St.				Peathill Av., Chr.	26	EE8		Pinewood Pl., Kirk.	12	BB5
Park Quad. G3	35	U11		Peathill St. G21	22	W10		Pinewood Pl., Lenz.	12	BB5
Park Ridge, Renf.	16	J8		Peel Glen Rd., Bear.	6	P5		Pinewood Sq. G15	6	N6
Park Dr.				Peel La. G11	34	S11		Pinkerton Av. G73	52	X16
Park Rd. G4	35	U11		*Burgh Hall St.*				Pinkston Dr. G21	36	W11
Park Rd., Bail.	41	GG13		Peel Pl., Both.	69	HH18		Pinkston Rd. G21	22	W10
Park Rd., Bish.	11	Y7		Peel St. G11	34	S11		Pinmore Path G53	60	N17
Park Rd., Chr.	26	FF8		Peel Vw., Clyde.	5	M6		Pinmore Pl. G53	60	N17
Park Rd., Dalm.	4	K6		*Kirkoswald Dr.*				Pinmore St. G53	60	N17
Park Rd., Giff.	62	T19		Peirshill St. G32	38	AA12		Pinwherry Dr. G33	24	AA9
Park Rd., John.	43	D15		Pembroke St. G3	35	U12		Pinwherry Pl., Udd.	69	HH18
Park Rd., Pais.	46	J15		Pencaitland Dr. G32	54	BB14		*Hume Dr.*		
Park Rd., Renf.	16	J8		*Falside Rd.*				Pirn St. G40	52	X14
Park St. S. G3	35	U11		Pencaitland Gro. G32	54	BB14		Pitcairn St. G31	54	AA14
Park Ter. G3	35	U11		*Falside Rd.*				Pitcaple Dr. G43	62	S17
Park Ter. G42	51	U15		Pencaitland Pl. G23	9	U7		Pitlochry Dr. G52	48	P14
Queens Dr.				Pendeen Cres. G33	39	DD13		Pitmedden Rd., Bish.	11	Z7
Park Ter., Giff.	62	T19		Pendeen Pl. G33	39	DD13		Pitmilly Rd. G15	7	Q6
Park Top, Renf.	16	J8		Pendeen Rd. G33	39	DD13		Pitreavie Pl. G33	39	CC11
Park Way, Cumb.	71	PP2		Pendicle Cres., Bear.	7	Q6		Pitt St. G2	35	V12
Park Winding, Renf.	16	J8		Pendicle Rd., Bear.	7	Q6		Pladda Rd., Renf.	31	M11
Parkburn Av., Lenz.	13	CC5		Penicuik St. G32	37	Z13		Plane Tree Pl., John.	44	E15
Parker St. G14	33	R11		Penilee Rd., Pais.	32	N13		Planetree Rd., Dalm.	5	L5
Parkgrove Av., Giff.	62	T18		Penilee Ter. G52	32	N12		Planetrees Av., Pais.	46	K15
Parkgrove Ct., Giff.	62	T18		Peninver Dr. G51	33	R12		*Carriagehill Dr.*		
Parkgrove Ter. G3	35	U11		Penman Av. G73	52	X16		Plant St. G31	37	Z13
Parkgrove Ter. La. G3	35	U12		Pennan Pl. G14	18	P9		Plantation Pk. Gdns. G51	34	T13
Derby St.				Penneld Rd. G52	32	N13		Plantation Pl. G51	35	U13
Parkhall Rd., Dalm.	4	K6		Penrith Av., Giff.	62	T19		*Govan Rd.*		
Parkhall Ter., Dalm.	4	K5		Penrith Dr. G12	20	S9		Plantation Sq. G51	35	U13
Parkhead Cross G31	37	Z13		Penryn Gdns. G32	55	CC14		Playfair St. G40	53	Y14
Parkhill Dr. G73	53	Y16		Penston Rd. G33	39	CC12		Pleaknowe Cres., Chr.	15	GG7
Parkhill Rd. G43	50	T16		Pentland Ct., Barr.	59	L19		Pleamuir Pl., Cumb.	70	MM3
Parkholm La. G5	35	U13		Pentland Cres., Pais.	46	J16		Plean St. G14	18	P9
Paisley Rd.				Pentland Dr., Barr.	59	M19		Pleasance La. G43	50	T16
Parkhouse Path G53	60	P18		Pentland Dr., Bish.	11	Z7		Pleasance St. G43	50	T16
Parkhouse Rd. G53	60	N18		Pentland Dr., Linw.	28	E13		Plover Pl., John.	43	C16
Parklands Rd. G44	63	U18		Pentland Dr., Renf.	31	L12		Pollock Dr., Bish.	10	X7
Parklea, Bish.	10	X6		Pentland Pl. G40	52	X14		Pollock Rd., Bear.	8	S6
Midcroft				Pentland Rd. G43	62	T17		Pollokshaws Rd. G43	50	S16
Parkneuk Rd. G43	62	T18		Pentland Rd., Chr.	26	FF8		Polmadie Av. G42	52	W15
Parksail, Renf.	16	J8		Penzance Way, Chr.	15	GG6		Polmadie Rd. G5	52	W15
Parksail Dr., Renf.	16	J8		Peockland Gdns., John.	44	E14		Polmadie St. G42	52	W15
Parkvale Av., Renf.	16	J8		Peockland Pl., John.	44	E14				

Polnoon Av. G13	18	P9
Polson Cres., Pais.	46	J15
Polson Dr., John.	43	D15
Polwarth Gdns. G12	20	S10
Novar Dr.		
Polwarth La. G12	20	S10
Novar Dr.		
Polwarth St. G12	20	S10
Poplar Av. G11	19	R10
Poplar Av., John.	44	E15
Poplar Cotts. G14	18	N9
Dumbarton Rd.		
Poplar Dr., Dalm.	4	K5
Poplar Dr., Lenz.	12	BB5
Poplar Pl., Blan.	68	FF19
Poplar Rd. G41	34	S13
Urrdale Rd.		
Poplin St. G40	52	X14
Porchester St. G33	39	CC11
Port Dundas Pl. G2	36	W12
Port Dundas Rd. G4	36	W11
Port St. G3	35	U12
Portal Rd. G13	19	Q8
Porterfield Rd., Renf.	31	L11
Portman Pl. G12	35	U11
Cowan St.		
Portman St. G41	35	U13
Portmarnock Dr. G23	20	T8
Portreath Rd., Chr.	15	GG6
Portsoy Av. G13	18	N8
Portsoy Pl. G13	18	N8
Portugal La. G5	35	V13
Bedford St.		
Portugal St. G5	35	V13
Norfolk Ct.		
Possil Cross G22	21	V10
Possil Rd. G4	21	V10
Post La., Renf.	17	M10
Potassels Rd., Chr.	26	FF8
Potter Clo. G32	54	AA14
Potter Pl.		
Potter Gro. G32	54	AA14
Potter Pl.		
Potter Pl. G32	54	AA14
Potter St. G32	54	AA14
Potterhill Av., Pais.	46	K16
Potterhill Rd. G53	48	P15
Powburn Cres., Udd.	56	FF16
Powfoot St. G31	37	Z13
Powrie St. G33	25	CC10
Preston Pl. G42	51	V15
Prestwick St. G53	60	P17
Priesthill Av. G53	61	Q17
Priesthill Cres. G53	61	Q17
Priesthill Rd. G53	60	P17
Primrose Ct. G14	19	Q10
Primrose St. G14	19	Q10
Prince Albert Rd. G12	20	S10
Prince Edward St. G42	51	V15
Prince of Wales Gdns. G20	20	T8
Prince of Wales Ter. G12	20	T10
Byres Rd.		
Princes Gdns. G12	20	S10
Princes Gate G73	53	Y16
Greenbank St.		
Princes Pl. G12	20	T10
Princes Sq. G1	36	W12
Princes Sq., Barr.	59	M18
Princes St. G73	53	Y16
Princes Ter. G12	20	T10
Princess Cres., Pais.	31	L13
Priory Av., Pais.	31	L12
Priory Cotts., Blan.	68	FF19
Priory Dr., Udd.	56	FF16
Priory Pl. G13	19	Q8
Priory Rd. G13	19	Q8
Prosen St. G32	54	AA14
Prospect Av. G72	66	AA17
Prospect Av., Udd.	57	GG16
Prospect Rd. G43	50	T16
Prospecthill Circ. G42	52	W15
Prospecthill Cres. G42	52	X16
Prospecthill Dr. G42	52	W16
Prospecthill Pl. G42	52	X16
Prospecthill Rd. G42	51	V16
Prospecthill Sq. G42	52	W16
Provan Rd. G33	37	Z11
Provand Hall Cres., Bail.	56	EE14
Provanhill Pl. G21	36	X11
Provanmill Pl. G33	23	Z10
Provanmill Rd.		
Provanmill Rd. G33	23	Z10
Purdon St. G11	34	S11
Pykestone Rd. G33	39	CC11
Quadrant Rd. G43	63	U17
Quarrelton Rd., John.	43	D15
Quarry Av. G72	67	DD18
Quarry Pl. G72	66	AA17
Quarry Rd., Barr.	59	L18
Quarry Rd., Pais.	46	K15
Quarry St., John.	43	D14
Quarrybank, John.	43	C15
Quarrybrae St. G31	38	AA13
Quarryknowe G73	52	X16
Quarryknowe St. G31	38	AA13
Quarrywood Av. G21	23	Z10
Quarrywood Rd. G21	23	Z10
Quay Rd. G73	53	Y15
Quay Rd. N. G73	53	Y15
Quebec Ho., Dalm.	4	J5
Perth Cres.		
Queen Arc. G2	35	V12
Renfrew St.		
Queen Elizabeth Av. G52	32	N12
Queen Elizabeth Sq. G5	52	W14
Queen Margaret Ct. G20	21	U10
Queen Margaret Cres. G12	21	U10
Hamilton Dr.		
Queen Margaret Dr. G12	20	T10
Queen Margaret Dr. G20	21	U10
Queen Margaret Rd. G20	21	U10
Queen Mary Av. G42	51	V15
Queen Mary Av., Clyde.	5	M7
Queen Mary St. G40	52	X14
Queen Sq. G41	51	U15
Queen St. G1	36	W12
Queen St. G73	53	Y16
Queen St., Pais.	46	J14
Queen St., Renf.	17	M10
Queen Victoria Dr. G14	19	Q10
Queen Victoria Gate G13	19	Q9
Queenbank Av., Gart.	27	GG8
Queens Av. G72	66	BB17
Queens Cres. G4	35	V11
Queens Cres., Bail.	41	GG13
Queens Cross G20	21	U10
Queens Dr. G42	51	U15
Queens Dr., Cumb.	70	NN1
Queens Dr. La. G42	51	V15
Queens Gdns. G12	20	T10
Victoria Cres. Rd.		
Queens Pk. Av. G42	51	V15
Queens Pl. G12	20	T10
Queens Rd., John.	44	F15
Queensborough Gdns. G12	20	S10
Queensby Av., Bail.	40	EE13
Queensby Rd.		
Queensby Dr., Bail.	40	EE13
Queensby Rd.		
Queensby Pl., Bail.	40	EE13
Queensby Rd.		
Queensby Rd., Bail.	40	EE13
Queensferry St. G5	52	X15
Rosebery St.		
Queenshill St. G21	22	X10
Queensland Ct. G52	33	Q13
Queensland Dr. G52	33	Q13
Queensland Gdns. G52	33	Q13
Queensland La. E. G52	32	P13
Kingsland Dr.		
Queensland La. W. G52	33	Q13
Queensland Dr.		
Queenslie Ind. Est. G33	39	CC12
Queenslie St. G33	37	Z11
Quendale Dr. G32	54	AA14
Quentin St. G41	51	U15
Quinton Gdns., Bail.	40	EE13
Raasay Dr., Pais.	46	J16
Raasay Pl. G22	22	W8
Raasay St. G22	22	W8
Rachan St. G34	40	FF11
Radnor St. G3	35	U12
Argyle St.		
Radnor St., Clyde.	5	L6
Raeberry St. G20	21	U10
Raeswood Dr. G53	48	N16
Raeswood Gdns. G53	48	N16
Raeswood Pl. G53	48	N16
Raeswood Rd. G53	48	N16
Raglan St. G4	35	V11
Raith Av. G44	64	W18
Raithburn Av. G45	64	W18
Raithburn Rd. G45	64	W18
Ralston Av., Pais.	48	N14
Ralston Ct. G52	48	N14
Ralston Dr. G52	48	N14
Ralston Path G52	48	N14
Ralston Dr.		
Ralston Pl. G52	48	N14
Ralston Rd., Bear.	7	R5
Ralston St., Barr.	59	M19
Ralston St., Pais.	47	L14
Seedhill Rd.		
Ram St. G32	38	AA13
Rampart Av. G13	18	P8
Ramsay Av., John.	43	D15
Ramsay Cres., John.	42	B16
Ramsay Pl., John.	43	D15
Ramsay St., Dalm.	4	K6
Ranald Gdns. G73	65	Z18
Randolph Av., Clark.	63	U19
Randolph Dr., Clark.	63	U19
Randolph Gdns., Clark.	63	U19
Randolph Rd. G11	19	R10
Randolph Ter. G72	66	BB17
Hamilton Rd.		
Ranfurley Rd. G52	32	N13
Rankin Pl., John.	43	D14
Rankine St.		
Rankine St., John.	43	D14
Rankines La., Renf.	17	M10
Manse St.		
Rannoch Av., Bish.	11	Y7
Rannoch Dr., Bear.	8	S7
Rannoch Dr., Renf.	17	M10
Rannoch Gdns., Bish.	11	Y7
Rannoch Pl., Pais.	47	L14
Rannoch Rd., John.	43	D15
Rannoch Rd., Udd.	57	GG15
Rannoch St. G44	63	V17
Ranza Pl. G33	23	Z10
Raploch Av. G14	18	P10
Ratford St. G51	34	S12
Rathlin St. G51	34	S12
Ratho Dr. G21	22	X9
Rattray St. G32	54	AA14
Ravel Row G31	37	Z13
Ravelston Rd., Bear.	7	R7
Ravelston St. G32	37	Z13
Ravens Ct., Bish.	22	X8
Lennox Cres.		
Ravenscliffe Dr., Giff.	62	S18
Ravenscraig Av., Pais.	46	J15
Ravenscraig Dr. G53	60	P17
Ravenscraig Ter. G53	61	Q17
Ravenshall Rd. G41	50	T16
Ravenstone Rd., Giff.	62	T18
Ravenswood Av. G78	45	G16
Ravenswood Dr. G41	50	T15
Ravenswood Rd., Bail.	40	FF13
Rayne Pl. G15	6	P6
Red Rd. G21	23	Y10
Red Rd. Ct. G21	23	Y10
Redan St. G40	36	X13
Redcastle Sq. G33	39	CC11
Redford St. G33	37	Z12

Street	Page	Grid
Redgate Pl. G14	18	P10
Redhill Rd., Cumb.	70	MM2
Redhurst Cres., Pais.	45	H16
Redhurst Way, Pais.	45	H16
Redlands La. G12	20	T10
Kirklee Rd.		
Redlands Rd. G12	20	T10
Redlands Ter. G12	20	T10
Redlands Ter. La. G12	20	T10
Julian Av.		
Redlawood Pl. G72	68	EE17
Redlawood Rd.		
Redlawood Rd. G72	68	EE17
Redmoss St. G22	21	V9
Rednock St. G22	22	W10
Redpath Dr. G52	32	P13
Redwood Dr. G21	23	Y10
Foresthall Dr.		
Redwood Pl., Lenz.	12	BB5
Redwood Rd., Cumb.	71	QQ3
Reelick Av. G13	18	N8
Reelick Quad. G13	18	N8
Regent Moray St. G3	34	T11
Regent Pk. Sq. G41	51	U15
Regent Pk. Ter. G41	51	U15
Pollokshaws Rd.		
Regent Pl., Dalm.	4	K6
Regent Sq., Lenz.	13	CC6
Regent St., Dalm.	4	K6
Regent St., Pais.	31	L13
Regents Gate, Both.	69	GG18
Regwood St. G41	50	T16
Reid Av., Bear.	8	S5
Reid Av., Linw.	28	E13
Reid Pl. G40	52	X14
Muslin St.		
Reid St. G40	52	X14
Reid St. G73	53	Y16
Reidhouse St. G21	22	X10
Muir St.		
Reids Row, Bail.	56	FF14
Reidvale St. G31	36	X13
Renfield St. G2	35	V12
Renfield St., Renf.	17	M10
Renfrew Ct. G2	35	V12
Renfrew St.		
Renfrew La. G2	35	V12
Renfield St.		
Renfrew Rd. G51	32	P11
Renfrew Rd., Pais.	30	K13
Renfrew Rd., Renf.	32	P11
Renfrew St. G3	35	V11
Rennies Rd., Renf.	16	J8
Renshaw Dr. G52	32	P13
Renshaw Rd., John.	44	F15
Renton St. G4	36	W11
Renwick St. G41	35	U13
Scotland St.		
Residdl Rd. G33	25	DD9
Reston Dr. G52	32	P13
Reuther Av. G73	53	Y16
Revoch Dr. G13	18	P8
Rhannan Rd. G44	63	V17
Rhannan Ter. G44	63	V17
Rhindhouse Pl., Bail.	40	FF13
Rhindhouse Rd., Bail.	40	FF13
Swinton Rd.		
Rhindmuir Av., Bail.	40	FF13
Rhindmuir Dr., Bail.	40	FF13
Rhindmuir Gro., Bail.	40	FF13
Rhindmuir Rd., Bail.	40	FF13
Rhindmuir Vw., Bail.	40	FF13
Rhinds St., Coat.	57	HH14
Rhinsdale Cres., Bail.	40	FF13
Rhumhor Gdns., John.	43	C15
Rhymer St. G21	36	X11
Rhymie Rd. G32	55	CC14
Rhynie Dr. G51	34	S13
Riccarton St. G42	52	W15
Riccartsbar Av., Pais.	46	J14
Richard St. G2	35	V12
Cadogan St.		
Richard St., Renf.	17	M10
Richmond Ct. G73	53	Z16
Richmond Dr. G72	66	AA17
Richmond Dr. G73	53	Z16
Richmond Dr., Bish.	11	Y6
Richmond Dr., Linw.	28	E12
Richmond Gdns., Chr.	14	EE7
Richmond Gro. G73	53	Z16
Richmond Pl. G73	53	Z16
Richmond St. G1	36	W12
Richmond St., Clyde.	5	M7
Riddell St., Clyde.	5	M6
Riddon Av. G13	18	N8
Riddrie Cres. G33	38	AA12
Riddrie Knowes G33	38	AA12
Riddrie Ter. G33	23	Z10
Provanmill Rd.		
Riddrievale Ct. G33	38	AA11
Riddrievale St. G33	38	AA11
Rigby St. G32	37	Z13
Rigg Pl. G33	39	DD12
Rigghead Av., Cumb.	71	PP1
Riggside Rd. G33	39	CC11
Riggside St. G33	39	CC11
Riglands Way, Renf.	17	M10
Riglaw Pl. G13	18	P8
Rigmuir Rd. G51	33	Q13
Rimsdale St. G40	37	Y13
Ringford St. G21	22	X10
Ripon Dr. G12	20	S9
Risk St. G40	36	X13
Risk St., Dalm.	4	K6
Ristol Rd. G13	19	Q9
Anniesland Rd.		
Ritchie Cres., John.	44	F14
Ritchie Pk., John.	44	E14
Ritchie St. G5	51	V14
River Rd. G32	54	BB16
River Rd. G41	51	U16
Mansionhouse Rd.		
Riverbank St. G43	50	T16
Riverford Rd. G43	50	T16
Riverford Rd. G73	53	Z15
Riversdale Cotts. G14	18	N9
Dumbarton Rd.		
Riversdale La. G14	18	N9
Dumbarton Rd.		
Riverside Ct. G44	63	V19
Riverside Pk. G44	63	V19
Linnpark Av.		
Riverside Pl. G72	67	DD17
Riverside Rd. G43	51	U16
Riverview Av. G5	35	V13
West St.		
Riverview Dr. G5	35	V13
Riverview Gdns. G5	35	V13
Riverview Pl. G5	35	V13
Roaden Av., Pais.	45	G16
Roaden Rd., Pais.	45	G16
Roadside, Cumb.	71	PP1
Robb St. G21	22	X10
Robert Burns Av., Clyde.	5	M6
Robert St. G51	34	S12
Robert Templeton Dr. G72	67	CC17
Roberton Av. G41	50	T15
Roberts St., Dalm.	4	K6
Robertson La. G2	35	V12
Robertson St.		
Robertson St. G2	35	V12
Robertson St., Barr.	59	L18
Robertson Ter., Bail.	40	FF13
Edinburgh Rd.		
Robin Way G32	55	CC16
Robroyston Av. G33	24	AA10
Robroyston Rd. G33	24	AA9
Roblee Cres., Thorn.	62	S18
Roblee Dr., Giff.	62	S18
Roblee Rd., Thorn.	62	S19
Robson Gro. G42	51	V15
Rock Dr. G78	42	B15
Rock St. G4	21	V10
Rockall Dr. G44	64	W18
Rockbank Pl. G40	37	Y13
Broad St.		
Rockbank Pl., Clyde.	5	L5
Glasgow Rd.		
Rockbank St. G40	37	Y13
Rockcliffe St. G40	52	X14
Rockfield Pl. G21	23	Z9
Rockfield Rd. G21	23	Z9
Rockmount Av., Barr.	59	M19
Rockmount Av., Thorn.	62	S18
Rockwell Av., Pais.	46	J16
Rodger Dr. G73	65	Y17
Rodger Pl., Ruth.	65	Y17
Rodil Av. G44	64	W18
Rodney St. G4	35	V11
Roebank Dr., Barr.	59	M19
Roebank St. G31	37	Y12
Roffey Pk. Rd., Pais.	31	M13
Rogart St. G40	36	X13
Rogerfield Rd., Bail.	40	FF12
Rokeby Ter. G12	20	T10
Great Western Rd.		
Roman Av. G15	6	P7
Roman Av., Bear.	7	R5
Roman Ct., Bear.	7	R5
Roman Dr., Bear.	7	R5
Roman Gdns., Bear.	7	R5
Roman Rd., Bear.	7	R5
Roman Rd., Clyde.	5	L5
Romney Av. G44	64	W17
Rona St. G21	37	Y11
Rona Ter. G72	66	AA18
Ronaldsay Dr., Bish.	11	Z7
Ronaldsay Pl., Cumb.	70	MM4
Ronaldsay St. G22	22	W8
Ronay St. G22	22	W8
Rooksdell Av., Pais.	46	J15
Rose Cotts. G13	19	R9
Crow Rd.		
Rose Dale, Bish.	23	Y8
Rose Knowe G73	52	X15
Rose St. G3	35	V12
Rosebank Av., Blan.	69	GG19
Rosebank Dr. G72	67	CC18
Rosebank Ter., Bail.	57	GG14
Roseberg Pl., Clyde.	5	L7
Kilbowie Rd.		
Rosebery Pl., Clyde.	5	L7
Miller St.		
Rosebery St. G5	52	X15
Rosedale Av. G78	44	F16
Rosedale Dr., Bail.	56	EE14
Rosedale Gdns. G20	20	T8
Rosefield Gdns., Udd.	57	GG16
Roselea Gdns. G13	19	R8
Roselea Pl., Blan.	68	FF19
Rosemont Meadows, Both.	69	GG19
Rosemount, Cumb.	70	NN1
Rosemount Cres. G21	37	Y11
Rosemount St. G21	36	X11
Rosemount Ter. G51	35	U13
Paisley Rd. W.		
Rosevale Rd., Bear.	7	R6
Rosevale St. G11	34	S11
Rosewood Av., Pais.	45	H15
Rosewood St. G13	19	R8
Roslea Dr. G31	37	Y12
Roslyn Dr., Bail.	41	GG13
Rosneath St. G51	34	S12
Ross Av., Renf.	31	L11
Ross St. G40	36	W13
Ross St., Pais.	47	L14
Rossendale Rd. G43	50	T16
Rosshall Av., Pais.	47	M14
Rosshill Av. G52	32	N13
Rosshill Rd. G52	32	N13
Rossie Cres., Bish.	23	Z8
Rosslea Dr., Giff.	62	T19
Rosslyn Av. G73	53	Y16
Rosslyn Rd., Bear.	6	P5
Rosslyn Ter. G12	20	T10
Horslethill Rd.		
Rostan Rd. G43	62	T17
Rosyth Rd. G5	52	X15
Rosyth St. G5	52	X15
Rotherwick Dr., Pais.	48	N14
Rotherwood Av. G13	7	Q7

Name	Page	Grid
Rotherwood Av., Pais.	45	G16
Rotherwood La. G13	7	Q7
Rotherwood Av.		
Rotherwood Pl. G13	19	Q8
Rothes Dr. G23	8	T7
Rothes Pl. G23	8	T7
Rottenrow G4	36	W12
Rottenrow E. G4	36	W12
Roual Ter., Pais.	31	L13
Greenlaw Av.		
Rouken Glen Rd., Thorn.	61	R19
Roukenburn St. G46	61	R18
Roundhill Dr., John.	45	G14
Rowallan Gdns. G11	20	S10
Rowallan La. G11	20	S10
Churchill Dr.		
Rowallan La. E. G11	20	S10
Churchill Dr.		
Rowallan Rd., Thorn.	61	R19
Rowallan Ter. G33	24	BB10
Rowan Av., Renf.	17	M10
Rowan Cres., Lenz.	13	CC5
Rowan Dr., Dalm.	4	K6
Rowan Gdns. G41	50	S14
Rowan Gdns. G71	69	HH18
Rowan Gate, Pais.	46	K15
Rowan Pl. G72	67	CC17
Caledonian Circuit		
Rowan Rd. G41	50	S14
Rowan Rd., Cumb.	71	QQ2
Rowan Rd., Linw.	28	E12
Rowan St., Pais.	46	K15
Rowand Av., Giff.	62	T19
Rowandale Av., Bail.	56	EE14
Rowanlea Av. G78	45	G16
Rowanlea Dr., Giff.	62	T18
Rowanpark Dr., Barr.	59	L17
Rowans, The, Bish.	10	X7
Rowans Gdns., Both.	69	HH18
Rowantree Av. G73	65	Y17
Rowantree Gdns. G73	65	Y17
Rowantree Rd., John.	43	D15
Rowchester St. G40	37	Y13
Rowena Av. G13	7	Q7
Roxburgh La. G12	20	T10
Saltoun St.		
Roxburgh Rd., Pais.	44	F16
Roxburgh St. G12	20	T10
Roy St. G21	22	W10
Royal Bk. Pl. G1	36	W12
Buchanan St.		
Royal Cres. G3	35	U11
Royal Cres. G42	51	V15
Royal Ex. Bldgs. G1	36	W12
Royal Ex. Sq.		
Royal Ex. Ct. G1	36	W12
Queen St.		
Royal Ex. Sq. G1	36	W12
Royal Inch Cres., Renf.	17	M9
Campbell St.		
Royal Inch Ter., Renf.	17	M9
Royal Ter. G3	35	U11
Royal Ter. G42	51	V15
Queens Dr.		
Royal Ter. La. G3	35	U11
North Claremont St.		
Royston Rd. G21	36	X11
Royston Sq. G21	36	X11
Roystonhill G21	36	X11
Rozelle Av. G15	6	P6
Rubislaw Dr., Bear.	7	R6
Ruby St. G40	53	Y14
Ruchazie Pl. G33	38	AA12
Ruchazie Rd. G32	38	AA13
Ruchill Pl. G20	21	U9
Ruchill St. G20	21	U9
Ruel St. G44	51	V16
Rufflees Av., Barr.	59	M18
Rugby Av. G13	18	P8
Rullion Pl. G33	38	AA12
Rumford St. G40	52	X14
Rupert St. G4	35	U11
Rushyhill St. G21	23	Y10
Cockmuir St.		
Ruskin La. G12	21	U10
Ruskin Pl. G12	20	T10
Great Western Rd.		
Ruskin Sq., Bish.	11	Y7
Ruskin Ter. G12	21	U10
Ruskin Ter. G73	53	Y15
Russel Pl., Linw.	28	E13
Gilmerton Rd.		
Russell Cres., Bail.	56	FF14
Russell Dr., Bear.	7	R5
Russell St. G11	34	S11
Vine St.		
Russell St., John.	44	E14
Russell St., Pais.	30	J12
Rutherford Av., Chr.	14	EE5
Chryston Rd.		
Rutherford La. G2	35	V12
Hope St.		
Rutherglen Rd. G5	36	W13
Ruthven Av., Giff.	62	T19
Ruthven La. G12	20	T10
Byres Rd.		
Ruthven Pl., Bish.	23	Z8
Ruthven St. G12	20	T10
Rutland Cres. G51	35	U13
Rutland La. G51	35	U13
Govan Rd.		
Rutland Pl. G51	35	U13
Ryan Rd., Bish.	11	Y7
Ryan Way G73	65	Z18
Rye Cres. G21	23	Z9
Rye Rd. G21	23	Z9
Rye Way, Pais.	45	G15
Ryebank Rd. G21	23	Z9
Ryecroft Dr., Bail.	40	EE13
Ryedale Pl. G15	6	P6
Ryefield Av., John.	43	C15
Ryefield Pl., John.	43	C15
Ryefield Rd. G21	23	Y9
Ryehill Gdns. G21	23	Z9
Ryehill Pl. G21	23	Z9
Ryehill Rd. G21	23	Z9
Ryemount Rd. G21	23	Z9
Ryeside Rd. G21	23	Y9
Rylands Dr. G32	55	DD14
Rylands Gdns. G32	55	DD14
Rylees Cres. G52	32	N12
Rylees Pl. G52	32	N13
Rylees Rd. G52	32	N13
Ryvra Rd. G13	19	Q9
Sackville Av. G13	19	R9
Sackville La. G13	19	R9
Sackville Av.		
Saddell Rd. G15	6	P6
St. Abbs Dr., Pais.	45	H15
St. Andrews Av., Bish.	10	X7
St. Andrews Av., Both.	69	HH19
St. Andrews Cres. G41	51	U14
St. Andrews Cres., Pais.	30	J11
St. Andrews Cross G41	51	V14
St. Andrews Dr. G41	50	T15
St. Andrews Dr., Pais.	30	K11
St. Andrews Dr. W., Pais.	30	J11
St. Andrews La. G1	36	W13
Gallowgate		
St. Andrews Rd. G41	51	U14
St. Andrews Rd., Renf.	31	M11
St. Andrews Sq. G1	36	W13
St. Andrews St. G1	36	W13
St. Anns Dr., Giff.	62	T19
St. Blanes Dr. G73	64	X17
St. Boswells Cres., Pais.	45	H15
St. Brides Rd. G43	50	T16
St. Bride's Way, Udd.	69	HH18
St. Catherines Rd., Giff.	62	T19
St. Clair Av., Giff.	62	T18
St. Clair St. G20	35	U11
Woodside Rd.		
St. Conval Pl. G43	50	S16
Shawbridge St.		
St. Cyrus Gdns., Bish.	11	Z7
St. Cyrus Rd., Bish.	11	Y7
St. Enoch Sq. G1	35	V13
St. Enoch Wynd G2	35	V12
Argyle St.		
St. Fillans Rd. G33	25	CC9
St. Georges Cross G3	35	V11
St. Georges Pl. G20	35	V11
St. Georges Rd.		
St. Georges Rd. G3	35	V11
St. Germains, Bear.	7	R6
St. Helena Cres., Clyde.	5	M5
St. Ives Rd., Chr.	15	GG6
St. James Av., Pais.	29	H12
St. James Pl., Pais.	30	K13
Love St.		
St. James Rd. G4	36	W12
St. James St., Pais.	30	K13
St. Johns Ct. G41	51	U14
St. Johns Quad. G41	51	U14
St. Johns Rd. G41	51	U14
St. Johns Ter. G12	35	U11
Southpark Av.		
St. Josephs Pl. G40	36	X13
Abercromby St.		
St. Kenneth Dr. G51	33	R12
St. Kilda Dr. G14	19	R10
St. Leonards Dr., Giff.	62	T18
St. Margarets Pl. G1	36	W13
Bridgegate		
St. Mark Gdns. G32	38	AA13
St. Mark St.		
St. Mark St. G32	38	AA13
St. Marnock St. G40	37	Y13
St. Marys La. G2	35	V12
West Nile St.		
St. Marys Rd., Bish.	10	X7
St. Mirren St., Pais.	46	K14
St. Monance St. G21	22	X9
St. Mungo Av. G4	36	W12
St. Mungo Pl. G4	36	W12
St. Mungo St., Bish.	22	X8
St. Mungos Rd. G67	70	NN3
St. Ninian St. G5	36	W13
St. Ninians Cres., Pais.	46	K15
Rowan St.		
St. Ninians Rd., Pais.	46	K15
St. Peters La. G2	35	V12
Blythswood St.		
St. Peters St. G4	35	V11
St. Ronans Dr. G41	50	T15
St. Ronans Dr. G73	65	Z17
St. Stephens Av. G73	65	Z18
St. Stephens Cres. G73	66	AA18
St. Valleyfield St. G21	22	X10
Ayr St.		
St. Vincent Cres. G3	34	T12
St. Vincent Cres. La. G3	35	U12
Corunna St.		
St. Vincent La. G2	35	V12
Hope St.		
St. Vincent Pl. G1	36	W12
St. Vincent St. G2	35	U12
St. Vincent Ter. G3	35	U12
Salamanca St. G31	37	Z13
Salen St. G52	33	R13
Salisbury Pl. G12	20	T10
Great Western Rd.		
Salisbury Pl., Dalm.	4	K5
Salisbury St. G5	51	V14
Salkeld St. G5	51	V14
Salmona St. G22	21	V10
Saltaire Av., Udd.	69	HH17
Salterland Rd. G53	60	N17
Saltmarket G1	36	W13
Saltmarket Pl. G1	36	W13
King St.		
Saltoun Gdns. G12	20	T10
Roxburgh St.		
Saltoun La. G12	20	T10
Ruthven St.		
Saltoun St. G12	20	T10
Salvia St. G72	66	AA17
Sanda St. G20	21	U10
Sandaig Rd. G33	39	DD13
Sandbank Av. G20	20	T9
Sandbank St. G20	20	T9
Sandbank Ter. G20	20	T8

Name	Grid	Ref
Shuttle St. G1	36	W12
Shuttle St., Kilb.	42	B14
Shuttle St., Pais.	46	K14
Sidelaw Av., Barr.	59	M19
Ochil Dr.		
Sidland Rd. G21	23	Z9
Sidlaw Av., Bear.	6	P5
Sielga Pl. G34	40	EE12
Siemens Pl. G21	37	Y11
Siemens St. G21	37	Y11
Sievewright St. G73	53	Z15
Hunter Rd.		
Silk St., Pais.	30	K13
Silkin Av., Clyde.	5	M7
Silverburn St. G33	38	AA12
Silverdale St. G31	53	Z14
Silverfir St. G5	52	W14
Silvergrove St. G40	36	X13
Silverwells, Both.	69	HH19
Silverwells Cres., Both.	69	HH19
Simons Cres., Renf.	17	M9
Simpson Ct., Udd.	69	GG17
Simpson St. G20	21	U10
Simshill Rd. G44	63	V18
Sinclair Av., Bear.	7	R5
Sinclair Dr. G42	51	U16
Sinclair St., Clyde.	17	M8
Singer Rd., Dalm.	4	K6
Singer St., Clyde.	5	L6
Sir Michael Pl., Pais.	46	J14
Sixth Av., Renf.	31	M11
Sixth St., Udd.	57	GG15
Skaethorn Rd. G20	20	S8
Skaterig La. G13	19	R9
Skaterigg Rd. G13	19	R9
Crow Rd.		
Skelbo Path G34	40	FF11
Auchengill Rd.		
Skelbo Pl. G34	40	FF11
Skene Rd. G51	34	S13
Skerray Quad. G22	22	W8
Skerray St. G22	22	W8
Skerryvore Pl. G33	38	BB12
Skerryvore Rd. G33	38	BB12
Skibo Dr. G46	61	R18
Skibo La. G46	61	R18
Skipness Dr. G51	33	R12
Skirsa Ct. G23	21	V8
Skirsa Pl. G23	21	U8
Skirsa Sq. G23	21	U8
Skirsa St. G23	21	U8
Skirving St. G41	51	U16
Skye Av. G67	31	M11
Skye Ct., Cumb.	70	MM4
Skye Cres., Old K.	4	J5
Skye Cres., Pais.	46	J16
Skye Dr., Cumb.	70	MM4
Skye Dr., Old K.	4	J5
Skye Gdns., Bear.	6	P5
Skye Pl., Cumb.	70	MM4
Skye Rd. G73	65	Z18
Skye Rd., Cumb.	70	MM4
Skye St. G20	20	T8
Bantaskin St.		
Slakiewood Av., Gart.	27	GG8
Slatefield St. G31	37	Y13
Sleads St. G41	35	U13
Sloy St. G22	22	W10
Smeaton St. G20	21	U9
Smith Cres., Clyde.	5	L5
Smith St. G14	33	R11
Smith Ter. G73	53	Y15
Smithhills St., Pais.	30	K13
Smiths La., Pais.	30	K13
Smithy Ends, Cumb.	71	PP1
Smithycroft Rd. G33	38	AA11
Snaefell Av. G73	65	Z18
Snaefell Cres. G73	65	Z17
Society St. G31	37	Y13
Soho St. G40	37	Y13
Sollas Pl. G13	18	N8
Solway Pl., Chr.	14	FF7
Solway Rd., Bish.	11	Z7
Solway St. G40	52	X15
Somerford Rd., Bear.	7	R7
Somerled Av., Renf.	31	L11
Somerset Pl. G3	35	U11
Somerset Pl. Meuse G3	35	U11
Elderslie St.		
Somervell St. G72	66	AA17
Somerville Dr. G42	51	V16
Somerville St., Clyde.	5	L7
Sorby St. G31	37	Z13
Sorn St. G40	53	Y14
Souter La., Clyde.	5	M6
South Annandale St. G42	51	V15
South Av., Clyde.	5	L7
South Av., Pais.	46	K16
South Av., Renf.	17	M10
South Bk. St., Clyde.	17	M8
South Brook St., Clyde.	4	K6
South Campbell St., Pais.	46	K14
South Carbrain Rd., Cumb.	71	PP4
South Chester St. G32	38	BB13
South Cotts. G14	33	R11
Curle St.		
South Cft. St., Pais.	30	K13
Lawn St.		
South Crosshill Rd., Bish.	11	Y7
South Deanpark Av., Udd.	69	HH19
South Douglas St., Clyde.	17	M8
South Dr., Linw.	28	E13
South Elgin Pl., Clyde.	17	M8
South Elgin St.		
South Elgin St., Clyde.	17	M8
South Erskine Pk., Bear.	7	Q5
South Ex. Ct. G1	36	W12
Queen St.		
South Frederick St. G1	36	W12
South Hill Av. G73	65	Z17
South Moraine La. G15	7	Q7
Moraine Av.		
South Muirhead Rd., Cumb.	71	PP3
South Pk. Dr., Pais.	46	K15
South Portland St. G5	35	V13
South Scott St., Bail.	56	EE14
South Spiers Wf. G4	35	V11
South St. G14	18	P10
South Vesalius St. G32	38	BB13
South Vw., Blan.	68	FF19
South Vw., Dalm.	4	K6
South Vw., Lenz.	13	CC7
Gadloch Av.		
South Wardpark Ct., Cumb.	71	QQ1
Wardpark Rd.		
South Wardpark Pl., Cumb.	71	QQ1
South William St., John.	43	D15
South Woodside Rd. G4	35	U11
Southampton Dr. G12	20	S9
Southbank St. G31	37	Z13
Sorby St.		
Southbar Av. G13	18	P8
Southbrae Dr. G13	19	Q9
Southbrae La. G13	19	R9
Milner St.		
Southcroft Rd. G73	52	X15
Southcroft St. G51	34	S12
Southdeen Av. G15	6	P6
Southdeen Rd. G15	6	P6
Southend Rd., Clyde.	5	L5
Southern Av. G73	65	Y17
Southerness Dr., Cumb.	71	PP1
Dornoch Way		
Southesk Av., Bish.	10	X7
Southesk Gdns., Bish.	10	X6
Southfield Av., Pais.	46	K16
Southfield Cres. G53	49	Q16
Southfield Rd., Cumb.	70	MM3
Southinch Av. G14	18	N9
Southinch La. G14	18	N9
Tweedvale Av.		
Southlea Av. G46	62	S18
Southlock St. G21	22	X10
Southmuir Pl. G20	20	T9
Southpark Av. G12	34	T11
Southpark La. G12	21	U10
Glasgow St.		
Southpark Ter. G12	35	U11
Southpark Av.		
Southview Ct. G64	22	X8
Southview Dr., Bear.	7	Q5
Southview Pl., Gart.	27	GG9
Southview Ter. G21	22	X8
Southwold Rd., Pais.	32	N13
Southwood Dr. G44	64	W17
Spateston Rd., John.	43	C16
Spean St. G44	51	V16
Speirs Pl., Linw.	28	E12
Speirs Rd., John.	44	E14
Speirshall Clo. G14	18	N9
Speirshall Ter. G14	18	N9
Spence St. G20	20	T8
Spencer Dr. G78	44	F16
Spencer St. G13	19	R8
Spencer St., Clyde.	5	L6
Spey Av., Pais.	45	G15
Spey Dr., Renf.	32	N11
Almond Av.		
Spey Pl., John.	43	C16
Spey Rd., Bear.	7	Q7
Spey St. G33	38	AA12
Spiers Rd., Bear.	8	S6
Spiersbridge Av., Thorn.	61	R18
Spiersbridge La. G46	61	R18
Spiersbridge Rd., Thorn.	61	R19
Spiersbridge Ter. G46	61	R18
Spindlehowe Rd., Udd.	69	GG17
Spingburn Way G21	22	X10
Spinner Gdns., Pais.	45	H14
Spinners Row, John.	43	C15
Spittal Rd. G73	64	X18
Spittal Ter. G72	68	EE19
Spoutmouth G1	36	W13
Spring La. G5	52	W14
Lawmoor St.		
Springbank Rd., Pais.	30	J12
Springbank St. G20	21	U10
Springbank Ter., Pais.	30	J12
Springboig Av. G32	39	CC13
Springboig Rd. G32	39	CC12
Springburn Rd. G21	22	X9
Springburn Way G21	22	X10
Springcroft Av., Bail.	40	EE13
Springcroft Dr., Bail.	40	EE13
Springcroft Rd., Bail.	40	EE13
Springfield Av., Bish.	23	Y8
Springfield Av., Pais.	47	M14
Springfield Av., Udd.	69	GG17
Springfield Ct. G1	36	W12
Springfield Cres., Bish.	23	Y8
Springfield Cres., Udd.	69	GG17
Springfield Dr., Barr.	60	N19
Springfield Pk., John.	44	E15
Springfield Pk. Rd. G73	65	Z17
Springfield Quay G51	35	U13
Springfield Rd. G40	53	Y14
Springfield Rd., Bish.	11	Y7
Springfield Rd., Cumb.	71	PP2
Springfield Sq., Bish.	23	Y8
Springhill Gdns. G41	51	U15
Springhill Rd., Bail.	39	DD13
Springhill Rd., Barr.	59	L19
Springkell Av. G41	50	T14
Springkell Dr. G41	50	S14
Springkell Gdns. G41	50	T15
Springkell Gate G41	50	T15
Springside Pl. G15	6	P6
Springvale Ter. G21	22	X10
Hillkirk Pl.		
Spruce Av., John.	44	E15
Spruce Dr., Lenz.	12	BB5
Spruce Rd., Cumb.	71	QQ2
Spruce St. G22	22	W9
Spynie Pl., Bish.	11	Z7
Squire St. G14	33	R11
Staffa Av., Renf.	31	M11

Staffa Dr., Pais.	46	K16
Staffa Rd. G72	66	AA18
Staffa St. G31	37	Y12
Staffa Ter. G72	66	AA18
Staffin Dr. G23	8	T7
Staffin St. G23	9	U7
Stafford St. G4	36	W11
Stag St. G51	34	T12
Stair St. G20	21	U10
Stamford St. G40	37	Y13
Stamperland Gdns.,	63	U19
Clark.		
Stanalane St. G46	61	R18
Standburn Rd. G21	23	Z8
Stanely Av., Pais.	45	H15
Stanely Ct., Pais.	45	H15
Stanely Cres., Pais.	45	H16
Stanely Dr., Pais.	46	J15
Stanely Rd., Pais.	46	J15
Stanford St., Clyde.	5	M7
Stanhope Dr. G73	65	Z17
Stanley Dr., Bish.	11	Y6
Stanley Pl., Blan.	68	FF19
Stanley St. G41	35	U13
Stanley St. La. G41	35	U13
Milnpark St.		
Stanmore Rd. G42	51	V16
Stark Av., Clyde.	4	K5
Startpoint St. G33	38	BB12
Station Rd. G20	20	T8
Station Rd. G33	24	BB9
Station Rd., Bail.	56	FF14
Station Rd., Bear.	7	Q6
Station Rd., Blan.	69	GG19
Station Rd., Both.	69	HH19
Station Rd., Chr.	26	FF9
Station Rd., Giff.	62	T18
Fenwick Rd.		
Station Rd., Kilb.	42	B15
Station Rd., Pais.	45	H14
Station Rd., Renf.	17	M10
Station Rd., Step.	25	CC9
Station Rd., Udd.	69	GG17
Station Way, Udd.	69	HH17
Mansefield Dr.		
Station Wynd G78	42	B15
Steel St. G1	36	W13
Steeple St., Kilb.	42	B14
Stenton St. G32	38	AA12
Stepford Path G33	40	EE12
Stepford Rd.		
Stepford Pl. G33	39	DD12
Stepford Rd. G33	39	DD12
Stephen Cres., Bail.	39	DD13
Stephenson St. G52	32	N12
Stepps Rd. G33	39	CC11
Stepps Rd., Lenz.	13	DD7
Steppshill Ter. G33	25	CC9
Stevbrae, Lenz.	13	DD5
Stevenson St. G40	36	X13
Stevenson St., Dalm.	4	K6
Stevenson St., Pais.	46	K14
Stewart Av., Renf.	31	L11
Stewart Ct., Barr.	59	M18
Stewart St.		
Stewart Dr., Bail.	41	HH13
Coatbridge Rd.		
Stewart Dr., Clyde.	5	L5
Stewart Rd., Pais.	46	K16
Stewart St. G4	35	V11
Stewart St., Barr.	59	M18
Stewart St., Dalm.	4	K6
Stewarton Dr. G72	66	AA17
Stewarton Rd., Thorn.	61	R19
Stewartville St. G11	34	S11
Stirling Av., Bear.	7	R7
Stirling Dr. G73	65	Y17
Stirling Dr., Bear.	7	Q5
Stirling Dr., Bish.	10	X6
Stirling Dr., John.	43	C15
Stirling Dr., Linw.	28	E13
Stirling Fauld Pl. G5	35	V13
Stirling Gdns., Bish.	10	X6
Stirling Rd. G4	36	W12
Stirling St., Cumb.	71	PP2
Stirling Way, Renf.	31	M11
York Way		
Stirrat St. G20	20	T9
Stirrat St., Pais.	29	H12
Stobcross Rd. G3	35	U12
Stobhill Rd. G21	22	X8
Stobs Dr., Barr.	59	L17
Stobs Pl. G34	40	FF11
Stock Av., Pais.	46	K15
Stock St., Pais.	46	K15
Stockholm Cres., Pais.	46	K14
Stockwell Pl. G1	36	W13
Stockwell St. G1	36	W13
Stoddard Sq., John.	44	F14
Glenpatrick Rd.		
Stonefield Av. G12	20	T9
Stonefield Av., Pais.	46	K15
Stonefield Cres., Pais.	46	K15
Stonefield Dr., Pais.	46	K15
Stonelaw Dr. G73	53	Y16
Stonelaw Rd. G73	53	Y16
Stoneside Dr. G43	62	S17
Stoneside Sq. G43	62	S17
Stoney Brae, Pais.	30	K13
Stoneyetts Cotts., Chr.	15	GG6
Stoneyetts Rd., Chr.	15	GG7
Stony Brae, Pais.	46	K16
Stonyhurst St. G22	21	V10
Stonylee Rd., Cumb.	71	PP3
Storie St., Pais.	46	K14
Stormyland Way, Barr.	59	M19
Stornoway St. G22	22	W8
Stow Brae, Pais.	46	K14
Stow St., Pais.	46	K14
Strachur St. G22	21	V8
Straiton St. G32	38	AA12
Stranka Av., Pais.	46	J14
Stranraer Dr. G15	7	Q7
Moraine Av.		
Stratford St. G20	21	U9
Strathallan La. G12	34	T11
Highburgh Rd.		
Strathallan Ter. G12	34	T11
Caledon St.		
Strathallon Pl. G73	65	Z18
Ranald Gdns.		
Strathbran St. G31	53	Z14
Strathcarron Pl. G20	20	T9
Glenfinnan Rd.		
Strathcarron Rd., Pais.	47	L15
Strathclyde Dr. G73	53	Y16
Strathclyde Path, Udd.	69	GG17
Strathclyde St. G40	53	Y15
Strathclyde Vw. G71	69	HH19
Strathcona Dr. G13	19	R8
Strathcona Gdns. G13	20	S8
Strathcona Pl. G73	65	Z18
Strathcona St. G13	19	R9
Strathdee Av., Clyde.	5	L5
Strathdee Rd. G44	63	U19
Strathdon Av. G44	63	U19
Strathdon Av., Pais.	46	J15
Strathdon Dr. G44	63	U19
Strathendrick Dr. G44	63	U18
Strathmore Av., Blan.	68	FF19
Strathmore Av., Pais.	47	M14
Strathmore Gdns. G12	35	U11
Gibson St.		
Strathmore Gdns. G73	65	Z18
Strathmore Rd. G22	21	V8
Strathord Pl., Chr.	15	HH6
Strathord St. G32	54	BB14
Strathtay Av. G44	63	U19
Strathview Gdns., Bear.	7	Q6
Strathview Gro. G44	63	U19
Strathview Pk. G44	63	U19
Strathy Pl. G20	20	T9
Glenfinnan Rd.		
Strathyre Gdns., Bear.	8	S5
Strathyre Gdns., Chr.	15	HH7
Heathfield Av.		
Strathyre St. G41	51	U16
Stratton Dr., Giff.	62	S19
Strauss Av., Clyde.	6	N7
Stravanan Av. G45	64	W19
Stravanan Rd. G45	64	W19
Stravanan St. G45	64	W19
Strenabey Av. G73	65	Z18
Striven Gdns. G20	21	U10
Stroma St. G21	37	Y11
Stromness St. G5	51	V14
Strone Rd. G33	38	BB12
Stronend St. G22	21	V9
Stronsay Pl., Bish.	11	Z7
Stronsay St. G21	37	Y11
Stronvar Dr. G14	18	P10
Stronvar La. G14	18	P10
Larchfield Av.		
Strowan Cres. G32	54	BB14
Strowan St. G32	54	BB14
Struan Av., Giff.	62	S18
Struan Gdns. G44	63	V17
Struan Rd. G44	63	V17
Struie St. G34	40	EE12
Stuart Av. G73	65	Y17
Stuart Dr., Bish.	22	X8
Succoth St. G13	19	R8
Suffolk St. G40	36	X13
Kent St.		
Sugworth Av., Bail.	40	EE13
Sumburgh St. G33	38	AA12
Summer St. G40	36	X13
Summerfield Cotts. G14	33	R11
Smith St.		
Summerfield Pl. G40	53	Y14
Ardenlea St.		
Summerfield St. G40	53	Y15
Summerhill Rd. G15	6	P6
Summerlee Rd., Thorn.	61	R18
Summerlee St. G33	39	CC12
Summertown Rd. G51	34	S12
Sunart Av., Renf.	17	L10
Sunart Gdns., Bish.	11	Y7
Sunart Rd. G52	33	R13
Sunart Rd., Bish.	11	Y7
Sunningdale Rd. G23	20	T8
Sunningdale Wynd, Both.	69	GG18
Sunnybank St. G40	53	Y14
Sunnylaw Dr. G78	45	H15
Sunnylaw St. G22	21	V10
Sunnyside Av., Udd.	69	GG17
Sunnyside Dr. G15	6	P7
Sunnyside Dr., Bail.	41	GG13
Sunnyside Pl. G15	6	P7
Sunnyside Dr.		
Sunnyside Pl., Barr.	59	L19
Sunnyside Rd., Pais.	46	J15
Surrey La. G5	51	V14
Pollokshaws Rd.		
Sussex St. G41	35	U13
Sutcliffe Rd. G13	19	R8
Sutherland Av. G41	50	T14
Sutherland Dr., Giff.	62	T19
Sutherland Rd., Clyde.	5	L7
Sutherland St., Pais.	30	J13
Swan La. G4	36	W11
Swan Pl., John.	43	C16
Swan St. G4	36	W11
Swan St., Clyde.	4	K6
Swanston St. G40	53	Y15
Sween Dr. G44	63	V18
Sweethope Pl., Both.	69	HH18
Swift Pl., John.	43	C16
Swindon St., Dalm.	4	K6
Swinton Av., Bail.	40	FF13
Swinton Cres., Bail.	40	FF13
Swinton Cres., Coat.	57	HH14
Swinton Dr. G52	32	P13
Swinton Gdns., Bail.	40	FF13
Swinton Av.		
Swinton Pl. G52	32	P13
Swinton Rd., Bail.	40	EE13
Swinton Vw., Bail.	40	FF13
Swinton Av.		
Switchback Rd., Bear.	7	R7
Sword St. G31	36	X13
Swordale Path G34	40	EE12
Swordale Pl.		
Swordale Pl. G34	40	EE12
Sycamore Av., John.	44	E15

Street	No.	Grid	Street	No.	Grid	Street	No.	Grid
Sycamore Av., Lenz.	13	CC5	Tay Cres., Bish.	11	Y7	Thornden Cotts. G14	18	N9
Sycamore Dr., Dalm.	5	L6	Tay Pl., John.	43	C16	*Dumbarton Rd.*		
Sydenham La. G12	20	S10	Tay Rd., Bear.	7	Q7	Thornden La. G14	18	N9
Crown Rd. S.			Tay Rd., Bish.	11	Y7	*Dumbarton Rd.*		
Sydenham Rd. G12	20	T10	Taylor Av. G78	42	A14	Thorndene, John.	44	E14
Sydney Ct. G2	35	V12	Taylor Pl. G4	36	W12	Thornhill, John.	44	E15
Argyle St.			Taylor St. G4	36	W12	Thornhill Av., John.	44	E15
Sydney St. G31	36	X13	Taylor St., Clyde.	17	M8	Thornhill Dr. G78	44	E15
Sydney St., Dalm.	4	J6	Taymouth St. G32	54	BB14	Thornhill Path G31	37	Z13
Sylvania Way, Clyde.	5	L7	Taynish Dr. G44	64	W18	*Beattock St.*		
Sylvania Way S., Clyde.	5	L7	Tealing Av. G52	49	Q14	Thornhill Path G31	37	Z13
Symington Dr., Clyde.	5	L7	Tealing Cres. G52	49	Q14	*Grier Path*		
Syriam Pl. G21	22	X10	Teasel Av. G53	60	P18	Thorniewood Gdns.,	57	HH16
Syriam St.			Teith Av., Renf.	32	N11	Udd.		
Syriam St. G21	22	X10	Teith Dr., Bear.	7	Q6	Thorniewood Rd., Udd.	57	GG16
			Teith Pl. G72	67	CC17	Thornlea Dr., Giff.	62	T18
			Teith St. G33	38	AA11	Thornley Av. G13	18	P9
Tabard Pl. G13	19	Q8	Telford Pl. G67	71	PP4	Thornliebank Rd. G46	62	S18
Tabard Pl. N. G13	19	Q8	Telford Rd., Cumb.	71	PP4	Thornliebank Rd., Thorn.	61	Q19
Tabard Rd.			Templar Av. G13	7	Q7	Thornly Pk. Av., Pais.	46	K16
Tabard Pl. S. G13	19	Q8	Temple Gdns. G13	19	R8	Thornly Pk. Dr., Pais.	46	K16
Tabard Rd.			Temple Pl. G13	19	R8	Thornly Pk. Rd., Pais.	46	K16
Tabard Rd. G13	19	Q8	Temple Rd. G13	20	S8	Thornside Rd., John.	44	E14
Tabernacle La. G72	66	BB17	Templeland Av. G53	49	Q15	Thornton La. G20	21	U8
Tabernacle St. G72	66	BB17	Templeland Rd. G53	49	Q15	Thornton St. G20	21	U8
Tain Pl. G34	40	FF12	Templeton St. G40	36	X13	Thorntree Way, Udd.	69	HH18
Tait Av., Barr.	59	M18	Tennant Rd., Pais.	29	H13	Thornwood Av. G11	34	S11
Talbot Dr. G13	18	P9	Tennant St., Renf.	17	M10	Thornwood Av., Lenz.	12	BB5
Talbot Pl. G13	18	P9	Tennyson Dr. G31	54	AA14	Thornwood Cres. G11	19	Q10
Talbot Ter. G13	18	P9	Tern Pl., John.	43	C16	*Thornwood Dr.*		
Talbot Ter., Udd.	57	GG16	Terrace Pl. G72	67	DD17	Thornwood Dr. G11	33	R11
Talisman Rd. G13	19	Q9	Terregles Av. G41	50	T15	Thornwood Dr., Pais.	45	H15
Talisman Rd., Pais.	45	G16	Terregles Cres. G41	50	T15	Thornwood Gdns. G11	34	S11
Talla Rd. G52	32	P13	Terregles Dr. G41	50	T15	Thornwood Pl. G11	20	S10
Tallant Rd. G15	6	P6	Teviot Av., Bish.	11	Y6	Thornwood Quad. G11	19	Q10
Tallant Ter. G15	7	Q6	Teviot Av., Pais.	45	G16	*Thornwood Dr.*		
Tallisman, Clyde.	5	M7	Teviot Cres., Bear.	7	Q7	Thornwood Rd. G11	33	R11
Onslow Rd.			Teviot St. G3	34	T12	Thornwood Ter. G11	33	R11
Tambowie St. G13	19	R8	Teviot Ter. G20	21	U10	Thornyburn Dr., Bail.	56	FF14
Tamshill St. G20	21	U9	*Sanda St.*			Thornyburn Pl., Bail.	56	FF14
Tamworth St. G40	37	Y13	Teviot Ter., John.	43	C16	Three Ell Rd. G51	34	T12
Rimsdale St.			Thane Rd. G13	19	Q9	*Govan Rd.*		
Tanar Av., Renf.	32	N11	Thanes Gate, Both.	69	GG17	Threestonehill Av. G32	38	BB13
Tanar Way, Renf.	32	N11	*Castle Gate*			Thrums Av., Bish.	11	Z7
Tandlehill Rd., Kilb.	42	B15	Tharsis St. G21	36	X11	Thrums Gdns., Bish.	11	Z7
Tanera Av. G44	64	W18	Third Av. G33	24	BB9	Thrush Pl., John.	43	C16
Tanfield Av. G32	39	CC12	Third Av. G44	51	V16	Thrushcraig Cres., Pais.	46	K15
Tanfield Pl. G32	39	CC12	Third Av., Lenz.	13	CC7	Thurso St. G11	34	T11
Tanfield Av.			Third Av., Renf.	31	M11	*Dumbarton Rd.*		
Tankerland Rd. G44	63	V17	Third Gdns. G41	50	S14	Thurston Rd. G52	32	P13
Tanna Dr. G52	49	R14	Third St., Udd.	57	GG16	Tibbermore Rd. G11	20	S10
Tannadice Av. G52	49	Q14	Thirdpart Cres. G13	18	N8	Tillet Oval, Pais.	30	J12
Tannahall Rd., Pais.	29	H13	Thistle Bk., Lenz.	13	CC6	Tillie St. G20	21	U10
Tannahall Ter., Pais.	29	H13	Thistle Cotts. G13	19	R9	Tillycairn Dr. G33	39	CC11
Tannahill Cres., John.	43	D15	*Crow Rd.*			Tilt St. G33	38	AA11
Tannahill Rd. G43	63	U17	Thistle St. G5	36	W13	Tintagel Gdns., Chr.	15	GG6
Tannoch Dr. G67	71	PP4	Thistle St., Pais.	46	J15	Tinto Dr., Barr.	59	L19
Tannoch Pl. G67	71	PP4	Thomas Muir Av., Bish.	23	Y8	Tinto Rd. G43	62	T17
Tannock St. G22	21	V10	Thomas St., Pais.	45	H14	Tinto Rd., Bear.	6	P5
Tantallon Dr., Pais.	45	H15	Thompson Pl., Clyde.	5	M5	Tinto Rd., Bish.	11	Z7
Tantallon Rd. G41	51	U16	Thomson Av., John.	43	D14	*Fintry Cres.*		
Tantallon Rd., Bail.	56	EE14	Thomson Dr., Bear.	7	R5	Tinto Sq., Renf.	31	L11
Tanzieknowe Av. G72	66	BB18	Thomson Gro. G72	54	BB16	*Ochil Rd.*		
Tanzieknowe Dr. G72	66	BB18	Thomson St. G31	37	Y13	Tinwald Av. G52	32	N13
Tanzieknowe Pl. G72	66	BB18	Thomson St., John.	43	D15	Tinwald Path G52	32	P13
Tanzieknowe Rd. G72	66	BB18	Thomson St., Renf.	31	M11	Tiree Av., Pais.	46	J16
Taransay St. G51	34	S12	Thorn Brae, John.	44	E14	Tiree Av., Renf.	31	M11
Tarbert Av., Blan.	68	FF19	Thorn Dr. G73	65	Z18	Tiree Ct., Cumb.	70	MM4
Tarbolton Dr., Clyde.	5	M6	Thorn Dr., Bear.	7	Q5	Tiree Dr., Cumb.	70	MM4
Tarbolton Rd. G43	62	T17	Thorn Rd. G46	62	S17	Tiree Gdns., Bear.	6	P5
Tarbolton Rd., Cumb.	71	PP3	Thorn Rd., Bear.	7	Q5	Tiree Rd., Cumb.	70	MM4
Tarbolton Sq., Clyde.	5	M6	Thorn St. G11	34	S11	Tiree St. G21	37	Z11
Tarbolton Dr.			*Dumbarton Rd.*			Tirry Way, Renf.	32	N11
Tarfside Av. G52	49	Q14	Thornbank St. G3	34	T11	*Morriston Cres.*		
Tarfside Gdns. G52	49	Q14	*Yorkhill Par.*			Titwood Rd. G41	50	T15
Tarfside Oval G52	49	Q14	Thornbridge Av. G12	20	T9	Tiverton Av. G32	55	CC14
Tarland St. G51	33	R13	*Balcarres Av.*			Tobago Pl. G40	36	X13
Tarras Dr., Renf.	32	N11	Thornbridge Av., Bail.	40	EE13	Tobago St. G40	36	X13
Tarras Pl. G72	67	CC17	*Bannercross Dr.*			Tobermory Rd. G73	65	Z18
Tassie St. G41	50	T16	Thornbridge Gdns.,	40	EE13	Todburn Dr., Pais.	46	K16
Tattershall Rd. G33	39	CC11	Bail.			Todd St. G31	37	Z12
Tavistock Dr. G43	62	T17	Thornbridge Rd., Bail.	40	EE13	Todholm Rd., Pais.	47	L15
Tay Av., Pais.	45	G15	Thorncliffe Gdns. G41	51	U15	Todholm Ter., Pais.	47	L15
Tay Av., Renf.	18	N10	Thorncliffe La. G41	51	U14	Toll La. G51	34	T13
Tay Cres. G33	38	AA11	Thorncroft Dr. G44	64	W18	*Paisley Rd. W.*		

Street	Page	Grid
Tollcross Rd. G31	37	Z13
Tolsta St. G23	9	U7
Tontine La. G1	36	W13
Bell St.		
Tontine Pl. G73	66	AA18
Toppersfield, John.	43	C16
Torbreck St. G52	33	R13
Torbrex Rd., Cumb.	71	PP3
Torburn Av., Giff.	62	S18
Tordene Path, Cumb.	70	MM2
Torgyle St. G23	8	T7
Tormore St. G51	33	Q13
Tormusk Dr. G45	65	Y18
Tormusk Rd. G45	65	Y18
Torness St. G11	34	T11
Torogay Pl. G22	22	X8
Torogay St. G22	22	W8
Torogay Ter. G22	22	W8
Toronto Wk. G32	55	CC16
Torphin Cres. G32	38	BB13
Torphin Wk. G32	38	BB13
Torr Rd., Bish.	11	Z7
Torr St. G22	22	W10
Torran Rd. G33	39	DD12
Torrance Rd., Bish.	11	Z5
Torrance St. G21	22	X10
Torridon Av. G41	50	S14
Torrin Rd. G23	8	T7
Torrington Av., Giff.	62	S19
Torrington Cres. G32	55	CC14
Torrisdale St. G42	51	U15
Torryburn Rd. G21	23	Z10
Torwood La., Chr.	15	HH7
Burnbrae Av.		
Toryglen Rd. G73	52	X16
Toryglen St. G5	52	W15
Toward Ct., Both.	69	GG19
Toward Rd. G33	39	CC12
Tower Av., Barr.	59	M18
Tower Cres., Renf.	31	L11
Tower Dr., Renf.	31	L11
Tower Pl. G20	20	T9
Glenfinnan Dr.		
Tower Pl., John.	44	E15
Tower Rd., John.	43	D15
Tower St. G41	35	U13
Tower Ter., Pais.	46	J14
Towerhill Rd. G13	7	Q7
Towerhill Ter. G21	23	Y10
Broomfield Rd.		
Towerside Cres. G53	48	P15
Towerside Rd. G53	48	P15
Towie Pl., Udd.	69	GG17
Townhead Rd., Gart.	41	HH11
Townhead Ter., Pais.	46	J14
Townmill Rd. G31	36	X12
Townsend St. G4	36	W11
Tradeston St. G5	35	V13
Trafalgar St. G40	52	X14
Trafalgar St., Dalm.	4	K6
Trainard Av. G32	54	AA14
Tranent Pl. G33	38	AA12
Traquair Av. G78	45	G16
Traquair Dr. G52	48	P14
Treeburn Av., Giff.	62	S18
Trees Pk. Av., Barr.	59	L18
Trefoil Av. G41	50	T16
Tresta Rd. G23	21	V8
Trident Way, Renf.	31	M11
Newmains Rd.		
Trinity Av. G52	49	Q14
Trinity Dr. G72	67	CC18
Trinley Brae G13	7	Q7
Trinley Rd. G13	7	Q7
Tronda Pl. G33	39	DD12
Tronda Rd. G33	39	DD12
Trondra Path G33	39	DD12
Trongate G1	36	W13
Troon St. G40	53	Y14
Trossachs Ct. G20	21	V10
Trossachs St.		
Trossachs Rd. G73	65	Z19
Trossachs St. G20	21	V10
Troubridge Av., John.	42	B16
Troubridge Cres. G78	42	B15
Troubridge Cres., John.	42	B16
Truce Rd. G13	18	P8
Truro Rd., Chr.	15	GG6
Tryst Rd. G67	70	NN3
Tudor La. S. G14	19	Q10
Orleans Av.		
Tudor Rd. G14	19	R10
Tudor St., Bail.	55	DD14
Tufthill Av., Bish.	10	X7
Tufthill Gdns., Bish.	10	X7
Tullis Ct. G40	52	X14
Tullis St. G40	52	X14
Tulloch St. G44	63	V17
Tullochard Pl. G73	65	Z18
Tummel St. G33	38	AA11
Tummel Way, Pais.	45	G15
Tunnel St. G3	35	U12
Turnberry Av. G11	20	S10
Turnberry Dr. G72	64	X17
Turnberry Gdns., Cumb.	70	NN1
Turnberry Pl. G73	64	X17
Turnberry Rd. G11	20	S10
Turnberry Wynd, Both.	69	GG18
Turnbull St. G1	36	W13
Turnlaw Rd. G72	66	BB19
Turnlaw St. G5	52	W14
Turret Cres. G13	19	Q8
Turret Rd. G13	19	Q8
Turriff St. G5	51	V14
Tweed Av., Pais.	45	G15
Tweed Cres. G33	38	AA11
Tweed Cres., Renf.	18	N10
Tweed Dr., Bear.	7	Q6
Tweed Pl., John.	43	C16
Tweedsmuir, Bish.	11	Z7
Tweedsmuir Rd. G52	48	P14
Tweedvale Av. G14	18	N9
Tweedvale Pl. G14	18	N9
Twinlaw St. G34	40	FF11
Tylnley Rd., Pais.	31	M13
Tyndrum Rd., Bear.	8	S5
Tyndrum St. G4	36	W11
Tyne St. G14	33	Q11
Tynecastle Cres. G32	38	BB12
Tynecastle Pl. G32	38	BB12
Tynecastle St. G32	38	BB12
Tynwald Av. G73	65	Z18
Uddingston Rd., Both.	69	HH18
Uig Pl. G33	39	DD13
Uist Cres. G33	25	DD10
Uist St. G51	33	R12
Ulundi Rd., John.	43	D15
Ulva St. G52	33	R13
Unden Pl. G13	19	R8
Underwood La., Pais.	30	J13
Underwood Rd. G73	65	Z17
Underwood Rd., Pais.	30	J13
Underwood St. G41	51	U16
Tantallon Rd.		
Union Pl. G1	35	V12
Gordon St.		
Union St. G1	35	V12
Union St., Clyde.	17	M8
Union St., Pais.	46	K15
Unity Pl. G4	35	V11
St. Peters St.		
University Av. G12	34	T11
University Gdns. G12	34	T11
University Pl. G12	34	T11
Unsted Pl., Pais.	47	L14
Uphall Pl. G33	38	AA12
Upland Rd. G14	19	Q10
Upper Bourtree Ct. G73	65	Z18
Upper Bourtree Dr.		
Upper Bourtree Dr. G73	65	Y18
Upper Glenburn Rd., Bear.	7	Q5
Ure Pl. G4	36	W12
Montrose St.		
Urquhart Cres., Renf.	31	M11
Urrdale Rd. G41	34	S13
Usmore Pl. G33	39	DD13
Vaila Pl. G23	21	U8
Vaila St.		
Vaila St. G23	21	U8
Vale Wk., Bish.	23	Z8
Valeta Pl., Dalm.	4	J6
Valeview Ter. G42	51	V16
Vallay St. G22	22	W8
Valley Vw. G72	67	CC17
Caledonian Circuit		
Valleyfield St. G21	22	X10
Ayr St.		
Van St. G31	37	Z13
Vancouver Pl., Dalm.	4	J6
Vancouver Rd. G14	19	Q10
Vanguard St., Clyde.	5	M7
Vanguard Way, Renf.	31	M11
Varna La. G14	19	R10
Varna Rd. G14	19	R10
Vasart Pl. G20	21	U10
Caithness St.		
Veitchs Ct., Clyde.	4	K5
Dumbarton Rd.		
Vennacher Rd., Renf.	17	L10
Vennard Gdns. G41	51	U15
Vere St. G22	22	W10
Vermont Av. G73	53	Y16
Vermont St. G41	35	U13
Vernon Dr., Linw.	28	E13
Verona Av. G14	19	Q10
Vesalius St. G32	38	BB13
Vicarfield Pl. G51	34	S12
Vicarfield St.		
Vicarfield St. G51	34	S12
Vicarland Pl. G72	66	BB18
Vicarland Rd. G72	66	BB17
Vicars Wk. G72	66	BB17
Victoria Circ. G12	20	T10
Dowanside Rd.		
Victoria Cres. G12	20	T10
Victoria Cres. La. G12	20	T10
Victoria Cres. Rd.		
Victoria Cres. Rd. G12	20	T10
Victoria Cross G42	51	V15
Victoria Rd.		
Victoria Dr., Renf.	17	L10
Victoria Dr. E., Renf.	31	M11
Victoria Pk. Cor. G14	19	Q10
Victoria Pk. Dr. N. G14	19	R10
Victoria Pk. Dr. S. G14	19	Q10
Victoria Pk. Gdns. N. G11	19	R10
Victoria Pk. Gdns. S. G11	19	R10
Victoria Pk. La. N. G14	19	Q10
Victoria Pk. La. S. G14	19	Q10
Westland Dr.		
Victoria Pk. St. G14	19	Q10
Victoria Pl. G73	53	Y16
Greenbank St.		
Victoria Rd. G33	25	CC9
Victoria Rd. G42	51	V15
Victoria Rd. G73	65	Y17
Victoria Rd., Barr.	59	L18
Victoria Rd., Lenz.	13	CC6
Victoria Rd., Pais.	46	J15
Victoria St. G73	53	Y16
Victoria St., Clyde.	5	M7
Victory Dr., Kilb.	42	B14
Glentyan Av.		
Viewbank, Thorn.	62	S18
Viewfield Av., Bail.	39	DD13
Viewfield Av., Bish.	22	X8
Viewfield Av., Blan.	69	GG19
Viewfield Av., Lenz.	13	CC5
Viewfield Dr., Bail.	39	DD13
Viewfield Dr., Bish.	22	X8
Viewfield La. G12	35	U11
Gibson St.		
Viewfield Rd., Bish.	22	X8
Viewfield Rd., Coat.	57	HH14
Viewfield Ter. G12	35	U11
Southpark Av.		
Viewmount Dr. G20	20	T8
Viewpark Av. G31	37	Y12
Viewpark Dr. G73	65	Y17
Viewpoint Pl. G21	22	X9
Viewpoint Rd. G21	22	X9

Street	Page	Grid
Viking Way, Renf.	31	M11
Vanguard Way		
Villafield Av., Bish.	11	Y6
Villafield Dr., Bish.	11	Y6
Villafield Ln., Bish.	11	Y6
Village Gdns., Both.	69	GG19
Village Rd. G72	67	DD17
Villiers Ct. G31	36	X13
Sword St.		
Vine St. G11	34	S11
Vinegarhill St. G31	37	Y13
Vinicombe La. G12	20	T10
Vinicombe St.		
Vinicombe St. G12	20	T10
Vintner St. G4	36	W11
Violet St., Pais.	47	L14
Virginia Bldgs. G1	36	W12
Virginia St.		
Virginia Ct. G1	36	W12
Virginia St.		
Virginia Pl. G1	36	W12
Virginia St. G1	36	W12
Viscount Av., Renf.	31	M11
Voil Dr. G44	63	V18
Vorlich Ct., Barr.	59	M19
Vulcan St. G21	22	X10
Ayr St.		
Waddel Ct. G5	36	W13
Waddel St. G5	52	W14
Waldemar Rd. G13	19	Q8
Waldo St. G13	19	R8
Walker Ct. G11	34	S11
Walker St.		
Walker Dr., John.	44	E15
Walker Sq. G20	20	T8
Bantaskin St.		
Walker St. G11	34	S11
Walker St., Pais.	46	J14
Walkerburn Rd. G52	48	P14
Walkinshaw Cres., Pais.	29	H13
Ferguslie Pk. Av.		
Walkinshaw Rd., Renf.	16	J10
Walkinshaw St. G40	53	Y14
Walkinshaw St., John.	43	D14
Walkinshaw Way, Pais.	30	J12
Broomdyke Way		
Wallace Av., John.	44	F15
Wallace Pl., Blan.	69	GG19
Wallace Rd., Renf.	31	L11
Wallace St. G5	35	V13
Wallace St. G73	53	Y16
Wallace St., Clyde.	17	L8
Wallace St., Pais.	30	K13
Wallacewell Cres. G21	23	Y9
Wallacewell Pl. G21	23	Y9
Wallacewell Quad. G21	23	Z9
Wallacewell Rd. G21	23	Y9
Wallbrae Rd., Cumb.	71	PP4
Wallneuk, Pais.	30	K13
Incle St.		
Wallneuk Rd., Pais.	30	K13
Walls St. G1	36	W12
Walmer Cres. G51	34	T13
Walmer Ter. G51	34	T13
Paisley Rd. W.		
Walnut Cres. G22	22	W9
Walnut Cres., John.	44	E15
Walnut Dr., Lenz.	12	BB5
Walnut Pl. G22	22	W9
Walnut Rd. G22	22	W9
Walter St. G31	37	Z12
Walton St. G41	51	U16
Walton St., Barr.	59	M18
Wamba Av. G13	19	R8
Wamba Pl. G13	19	R8
Wandilla Av., Clyde.	5	M7
Wanlock St. G51	34	S12
Warden Rd. G13	19	Q8
Wardhill Rd. G21	23	Y9
Wardhouse Rd., Pais.	46	J16
Wardie Path G33	39	DD12
Wardie Pl. G33	40	EE12
Wardie Rd. G33	40	EE12
Wardlaw Av. G73	53	Y16
Wardlaw Dr. G73	53	Y16
Wardlaw Rd., Bear.	7	R7
Wardpark Rd., Cumb.	71	QQ1
Wardrop St. G51	34	S12
Wardrop St., Pais.	46	K14
Ware Path G33	40	EE12
Ware Rd. G33	39	DD12
Warilda Av., Clyde.	5	M7
Warp La. G3	35	U12
Argyle St.		
Warren St. G42	51	V15
Warriston Cres. G33	37	Z12
Warriston Pl. G32	38	BB12
Warriston St. G33	37	Z12
Warroch St. G3	35	U12
Washington Rd., Renf.	30	K12
Washington St. G3	35	V12
Water Brae, Pais.	30	K13
Smithhills St.		
Water Brae, Pais.	46	K14
Forbes Pl.		
Water Rd., Barr.	59	M18
Waterfoot Av. G53	49	Q16
Waterford Rd., Giff.	62	S18
Waterloo La. G2	35	V12
Waterloo St.		
Waterloo St. G2	35	V12
Watermill Av., Lenz.	13	CC6
Waterside La., Kilb.	43	C15
Kilbarchan Rd.		
Waterside St. G5	52	W14
Waterside Ter., Kilb.	43	C15
Kilbarchan Rd.		
Watling St., Udd.	57	GG16
Watson Av. G73	52	X16
Watson Av., Linw.	28	E13
Watson St. G1	36	W13
Watson St., Udd.	69	GG17
Watt Low Av. G73	64	X17
Watt Rd. G52	32	N12
Watt St. G5	35	U13
Waukglen Av. G53	60	P19
Waukglen Cres. G53	61	Q18
Waukglen Dr. G53	60	P18
Waukglen Gdns. G53	60	P19
Waukglen Path G53	60	P18
Waukglen Rd. G53	60	P18
Waulkmill Av., Barr.	59	M18
Waulkmill St., Thorn.	61	R18
Waverley, Clyde.	5	M7
Onslow Rd.		
Waverley Ct., Udd.	69	HH19
Waverley Cres., Cumb.	70	MM4
Waverley Dr. G73	53	Z16
Waverley Gdns. G41	51	U15
Waverley Gdns., John.	44	F15
Waverley Rd., Pais.	45	G16
Waverley St. G41	51	U15
Waverley Ter. G31	37	Y13
Whitevale St.		
Waverley Way, Pais.	45	G16
Waverley Rd.		
Weardale La. G33	39	CC12
Weardale St. G33	39	CC12
Weaver La., Kilb.	42	B14
Glentyan Av.		
Weaver St. G4	36	W12
Weaver Ter., Pais.	47	L14
Weavers Av., Pais.	45	H14
Weavers Rd., Pais.	45	H14
Webster St. G40	53	Y14
Webster St., Clyde.	18	N8
Wedderlea Dr. G52	32	P13
Weensmoor Pl. G53	60	P18
Weensmoor Rd. G53	60	P17
Weeple Dr., Linw.	28	E13
Weighhouse Clo., Pais.	46	J14
Weir Av., Barr.	59	M19
Weir Rd., Linw.	28	E12
Weir St. G5	35	V13
Weir St., Pais.	30	K13
Weirwood Av., Bail.	55	DD14
Weirwood Gdns., Bail.	55	DD14
Welbeck Rd. G53	60	P17
Welfare Av. G72	67	CC18
Well Grn. G43	50	T16
Well Rd., Kilb.	42	B14
Well St. G40	36	X13
Well St., Pais.	30	J13
Wellbank Pl., Udd.	69	GG17
Church St.		
Wellbrae Ter., Chr.	15	GG7
Wellcroft Pl. G5	51	V14
Wellfield Av., Giff.	62	S18
Wellfield St. G21	22	X10
Wellhouse Cres. G33	39	DD12
Wellhouse Path G33	39	DD12
Wellhouse Rd. G33	39	DD12
Wellington La. G2	35	V12
West Campbell St.		
Wellington Pl., Dalm.	4	J6
Wellington Rd., Bish.	11	Z6
Wellington St. G2	35	V12
Wellington St., Pais.	30	J13
Caledonia St.		
Wellington St. E. G31	37	Z13
Wellington Way, Renf.	31	M11
Tiree Av.		
Wellmeadow Rd. G43	62	S17
Wellmeadow St., Pais.	46	J14
Wellpark St. G31	36	X12
Wells St., Clyde.	4	K6
Wellshot Dr. G72	66	AA17
Wellshot Rd. G32	54	AA14
Wellside Dr. G72	67	CC18
Wemyss Gdns., Bail.	56	EE14
Wendur Way, Pais.	30	J12
Abbotsburn Way		
Wenloch Rd., Pais.	46	K15
Wentworth Dr. G23	9	U7
West Av. G33	25	CC9
West Av., Renf.	17	M10
West Av., Udd.	69	HH17
West Brae, Pais.	46	J14
West Campbell St. G2	35	V12
West Campbell St., Pais.	45	H14
West Chapelton Av., Bear.	7	R6
West Chapelton Cres., Bear.	7	R6
West Chapelton Dr., Bear.	7	R6
West Chapelton La., Bear.	7	R6
West Chapelton Av.		
West Coats Rd. G72	66	AA18
West Cotts., Gart.	26	EE10
West Ct., Dalm.	4	K6
Little Holm		
West George La. G2	35	V12
West Campbell St.		
West George St. G2	35	V12
West Graham St. G4	35	V11
West Greenhill Pl. G3	35	U12
West La., Pais.	45	H14
West Lo. Rd., Renf.	17	L10
West Nile St. G2	35	V12
West Princes St. G4	35	U11
West Regent La. G2	35	V12
Renfield St.		
West Regent St. G2	35	V12
West St. G5	51	V14
West St., Clyde.	18	N8
West St., Kilb.	42	B14
West St., Pais.	46	J14
West Thomson St., Clyde.	5	L6
West Whitby St. G31	53	Z14
Westbank La. G12	35	U11
Gibson St.		
Westbank Quad. G12	35	U11
Gibson St.		
Westbank Ter. G12	35	U11
Gibson St.		
Westbourne Cres., Bear.	7	Q5
Westbourne Dr., Bear.	7	Q5
Westbourne Gdns. La. G12	20	T10
Lorraine Rd.		
Westbourne Gdns. N. G12	20	T10
Westbourne Gdns. S. G12	20	T10

Name	No.	Grid	Name	No.	Grid	Name	No.	Grid
Westbourne Gdns. W. G12	20	T10	Whins Rd. G41	50	T15	Willowbank St. G3	35	U11
Westbourne Rd. G12	20	S10	Whirlow Gdns., Bail.	40	EE13	Willowdale Cres., Bail.	56	EE14
Westbourne Ter. La. G12	20	S10	Whirlow Rd., Bail.	40	EE13	Willowdale Gdns., Bail.	56	EE14
Westbourne Rd.			Whistlefield, Bear.	7	R6	Willowford Rd. G53	60	N18
Westbrae Dr. G14	19	R10	Whitacres Path G53	60	P18	Wilmot Rd. G13	19	Q9
Westburn G72	67	DD17	Whitacres Pl. G53	60	P18	Wilson Av., Linw.	28	E13
Westburn Av. G72	67	CC17	Whitacres Rd. G53	60	P18	Wilson St. G1	36	W12
Westburn Av., Pais.	29	H13	Whitburn St. G32	38	AA12	Wilson St., Pais.	46	J14
Westburn Cres. G73	52	X16	White St. G11	34	S11	*William St.*		
Westburn Dr. G72	66	BB17	White St., Clyde.	17	M8	Wilson St., Renf.	17	M10
Westburn Fm. Rd. G72	66	BB17	Whitecraigs Pl. G23	21	U8	Wilsons Pl., Pais.	46	K14
Westburn Rd. G72	68	EE17	Whitefield Av. G72	66	BB18	*Seedhill*		
Westclyffe St. G41	51	U15	Whitefield Rd. G51	34	T13	Wilton Ct. G20	21	U10
Westend, Bear.	8	S7	Whiteford Rd., Pais.	47	L15	Wilton Cres. G20	21	U10
Maryhill Rd.			Whitehall Ct. G3	35	U12	Wilton Cres. La. G20	21	U10
Westend Pk. St. G3	35	U11	Whitehall St. G3	35	U12	*Wilton Cres.*		
Wester Cleddens Rd., Bish.	11	Y7	Whitehaugh Av., Pais.	31	L13	Wilton Dr. G20	21	U10
Wester Common Dr. G22	21	V10	Whitehaugh Cres. G53	60	P18	Wilton Gdns. G20	21	U10
Wester Common Rd. G22	21	V10	Whitehaugh Dr., Pais.	31	L13	Wilton Mans. G20	21	U10
Wester Common Ter. G22	21	V10	Whitehaugh Path G53	60	P18	*Wilton St.*		
Wester Rd. G32	55	CC14	Whitehaugh Rd. G53	60	P18	Wilton St. G20	21	U10
Westerburn St. G32	38	AA12	Whitehill Av. G33	25	CC9	Wiltonburn Path G53	60	P18
Westercraigs G31	36	X12	Whitehill Av., Cumb.	70	MM3	Wiltonburn Rd. G53	60	P18
Westergreens Av., Lenz.	13	CC5	Whitehill Fm. Rd. G33	25	CC9	Wilverton Rd. G13	19	R8
Parkburn Av.			Whitehill Gdns. G31	37	Y12	Winchester Dr. G12	20	S9
Westerhill Rd., Bish.	11	Y6	*Garthland Dr.*			Windhill Pl. G43	62	T17
Westerhill St. G22	22	W10	Whitehill La., Bear.	7	Q6	*Windhill Rd.*		
Westerhouse Rd. G34	40	EE11	*Whitehill Rd.*			Windhill Rd. G43	62	S17
Westerkirk Dr. G23	9	U7	Whitehill Rd. G33	25	CC8	Windlaw Ct. G45	64	W19
Western Av. G73	52	X16	Whitehill Rd., Bear.	7	Q5	Windlaw Gdns. G44	63	U18
Western Isles Rd., Old K.	4	J5	Whitehill St. G31	37	Y12	Windlaw Pk. Gdns. G44	63	U18
Western Rd. G72	66	AA18	Whitehurst, Bear.	7	Q5	Windmill Cres. G43	62	S17
Westerton Av., Bear.	19	R8	Whitekirk Pl. G15	6	P7	*Windmill Rd.*		
Westfield Av. G73	52	X16	Whitelaw St. G20	20	T8	Windmill Pl. G43	62	T17
Westfield Cres., Bear.	7	R7	Whitelawburn Av. G72	66	AA18	*Windmill Rd.*		
Westfield Dr. G52	32	P13	Whitelawburn Rd. G72	66	AA18	Windmillcroft Quay G5	35	V13
Westfield Dr., Bear.	7	R7	Whitelawburn Ter. G72	66	AA18	Windsor Cres., Clyde.	5	L6
Westfield Rd., Thorn.	61	R19	Whitelaws Ln., Both.	69	HH18	Windsor Cres., John.	44	E15
Westfield Vills. G73	52	X16	Whiteloans, Udd.	69	HH18	Windsor Cres., Pais.	31	L13
Westfields, Bish.	10	X6	*Wordsworth Way*			Windsor Rd., Renf.	31	M11
Westhouse Av. G73	52	X16	Whitemoss Av. G44	63	U18	Windsor St. G20	35	V11
Westhouse Gdns. G73	52	X16	Whitestone Av., Cumb.	70	MM2	Windsor St. G32	39	CC13
Westknowe Gdns. G73	65	Y17	*Dungoil Av.*			Windsor Ter. G20	35	V11
Westland Dr. G14	19	Q10	Whitevale St. G31	37	Y13	Windsor Wk., Udd.	57	HH16
Westland Dr. La. G14	19	Q10	Whithope Rd. G53	60	N18	Windyedge Cres. G13	19	Q9
Westland Dr.			Whithope Ter. G53	60	N18	Windyedge Pl. G13	19	Q9
Westlands, Bish.	10	X6	Whitrigs Rd. G53	60	N17	Wingfield Gdns., Both.	69	HH19
Westlands Gdns., Pais.	46	J15	Whitslade St. G34	40	EE11	*Blairston Av.*		
Westminster Gdns. G12	20	T10	Whittingehame Dr. G12	19	R9	Winifred St. G33	23	Z10
Kersland St.			Whittingehame Gdns. G12	20	S9	Winning Ct., Blan.	69	GG19
Westminster Ter. G3	35	U12	Whittliemuir Av. G44	63	U18	*Ness Dr.*		
Claremont St.			Whitton Dr., Giff.	62	T18	Winning Row G31	38	AA13
Westmoreland St. G42	51	V15	Whitton St. G20	20	T8	Winton Av., Giff.	62	T19
Westmuir Pl. G73	52	X16	Whitworth Dr., Clyde.	5	L7	Winton Dr. G12	20	T9
Westmuir St. G31	37	Z13	Whitworth St. G20	21	V9	Winton Gdns., Udd.	57	GG16
Westpark Dr., Pais.	29	H13	Whyte Av. G72	66	AA17	Winton La. G12	20	T9
Westray Circ. G22	22	W9	Wick St. G51	34	S12	Wirran Pl. G13	18	N8
Westray Ct., Cumb.	70	NN4	Wickets, The, Pais.	47	L14	Wishart St. G4	36	X12
Westray Pl. G22	22	W8	Wigton St. G4	21	V10	Wisner Ct., Thorn.	61	R18
Westray Pl., Bish.	11	Z7	Wigtoun Pl., Cumb.	71	PP2	Wiston St. G72	67	DD17
Ronaldsay Dr.			Wilderness Brae, Cumb.	71	PP2	Woddrop St. G40	53	Y15
Westray Rd., Cumb.	70	NN4	Wilfred Av. G13	19	Q8	Wolseley St. G5	52	W14
Westray Sq. G22	22	W8	Wilkie Rd., Udd.	69	HH17	Wood Fm. Rd., Giff.	62	S19
Westray St. G22	22	W8	Wilkie St. G31	37	Y13	Wood La., Bish.	23	Y8
Westwood Av., Giff.	62	S18	William St. G2	35	V12	Wood Quad., Clyde.	18	N8
Westwood Quad., Clyde.	5	M7	William St. G3	35	U12	Wood St. G31	37	Y12
Westwood Rd. G43	62	S17	William St., Clyde.	5	L5	Wood St., Pais.	47	L14
Weymouth Dr. G12	20	S9	William St., John.	43	D14	Woodbank Cres., John.	43	D15
Whamflet Av., Bail.	40	FF12	William St., Pais.	46	J14	Woodbank Ter., Gart.	27	GG9
Wheatfield Rd., Bear.	7	Q7	Williamson Pk. W. G44	63	U19	Woodburn Rd. G43	62	T17
Wheatlands Dr., Kilb.	42	B14	Williamson Pl., John.	44	E15	Woodburn Rd., Cumb.	70	MM3
Wheatlands Fm. Rd., Kilb.	42	B14	Williamson St. G31	53	Z14	Woodcroft Av. G11	19	R10
Whin Dr., Barr.	59	L18	Williamson St., Clyde.	5	L6	Woodcroft Ter. G11	19	R10
Whin St., Clyde.	5	L6	Williamwood Dr. G44	63	U19	*Crow Rd.*		
Whinfield Path G53	60	P18	Williamwood Pk. G44	63	U19	Woodend, Giff.	62	S19
Whinfield Rd. G53	60	P18	Willoughby Dr. G13	19	R9	*Milverton Rd.*		
Whinfold Av. G72	54	AA16	Willow Av., Bish.	23	Y8	Woodend Ct. G32	55	DD15
Whinhill Rd. G53	48	P14	Willow Av., John.	44	F15	Woodend Dr. G13	19	R9
Whinhill Rd., Pais.	47	L15	*Hillview Rd.*			Woodend Dr., Pais.	47	M14
			Willow Av., Lenz.	13	CC5	Woodend Gdns. G32	55	DD15
			Willow Dr., John.	43	D15	Woodend Pl., John.	44	E15
			Willow La. G32	54	BB15	*Malloch Cres.*		
			Willow St. G13	19	R8	Woodend Rd. G32	55	CC15
			Willowbank Cres. G3	35	U11	Woodend Rd. G73	65	Y18
						Woodfield Av., Bish.	11	Y7

Woodfoot Path G53	60	P18	Woodrow Circ. G41	50	T14	Wyvil Av. G13	7	R7
Woodfoot Pl. G53	60	P18	Woodrow Pl. G41	50	T14	Wyvis Av. G13	18	N8
Woodfoot Quad. G53	60	P18	*Maxwell Dr.*			Wyvis Pl. G13	18	N8
Woodfoot Rd. G53	60	P18	Woodrow Rd. G41	50	T14	Wyvis Quad. G13	18	N8
Woodford Pl., Linw.	28	E13	Woods La., Renf.	17	M10			
Woodford St. G41	51	U16	Woodside Av. G73	53	Z16			
Woodgreen Av. G44	64	W17	Woodside Av., Lenz.	13	CC5	Yair Dr. G52	32	P13
Woodhall St. G40	53	Y15	Woodside Av., Thorn.	62	S18	Yarrow Ct., Cumb.	67	CC17
Woodhead Av. G71	69	HH19	Woodside Cres. G3	35	U11	Yarrow Gdns. G20	21	U10
Old Bothwell Rd.			Woodside Cres., Barr.	59	M19	Yarrow Gdns. La. G20	21	U10
Woodhead Cres., Udd.	57	GG16	Woodside Cres., Pais.	46	J14	*Yarrow Gdns.*		
Woodhead Path G53	60	P17	*William St.*			Yarrow Rd., Bish.	11	Y6
Woodhead Rd. G53	60	N17	Woodside Pl. G3	35	U11	Yate St. G31	37	Y13
Woodhead Rd., Chr.	26	EE9	Woodside Pl. La. G3	35	U11	Yetholm St. G14	18	N9
Woodhead Ter., Chr.	26	EE8	*Elderslie St.*			Yew Dr. G21	23	Y10
Woodhill Rd. G21	23	Y9	Woodside Rd. G20	21	U10	*Foresthall Dr.*		
Woodhill Rd., Bish.	11	Y7	Woodside Ter. G3	35	U11	Yew Pl., John.	44	E15
Woodholm Av. G44	64	W17	Woodside Ter., Bish.	10	W6	Yoker Ferry Rd. G14	18	N9
Woodhouse St. G13	19	R8	Woodside Ter. La. G3	35	U11	Yoker Mill Gdns. G13	18	N8
Woodilee Cotts., Lenz.	13	DD5	*Woodlands Rd.*			Yoker Mill Rd. G13	18	N8
Woodilee Rd., Lenz.	13	DD5	Woodstock Av. G41	50	T15	Yokerburn Ter., Clyde.	17	M8
Woodland Av., Gart.	27	GG8	Woodstock Av., Pais.	45	G16	York Dr. G73	65	Z17
Woodland Av., Pais.	46	K16	Woodvale Av., Bear.	8	S7	York La. G2	35	V12
Woodland Cres. G72	66	BB18	Woodvale Dr., Pais.	29	H13	*York St.*		
Woodland Vw., Cumb.	71	PP2	Woodville St. G51	34	S13	York St. G2	35	V13
Braehead Rd.			Wordsworth Way, Udd.	69	HH18	York St., Clyde.	5	M7
Woodland Way, Cumb.	71	PP2	Works Av. G72	67	DD17	York Way, Renf.	31	M11
Woodlands Av., Both.	69	HH18	Wraes Av., Barr.	59	M18	Yorkhill La. G3	34	T12
Woodlands Cres., Both.	69	HH18	Wren Pl., John.	43	C16	*Yorkhill St.*		
Woodlands Cres., Thorn.	61	R18	Wright Av., Barr.	59	L19	Yorkhill Par. G3	34	T11
Woodlands Dr. G4	35	U11	Wright St., Renf.	31	L11	Yorkhill St. G3	34	T12
Woodlands Gdns., Udd.	69	GG18	Wrightlands Cres., Renf.	16	K8	Young St., Clyde.	5	L6
Woodlands Gate G3	35	U11	Wykeham Pl. G13	19	Q9	Young Ter. G21	23	Y10
Woodlands Gate, Thorn.	61	R18	Wykeham Rd. G13	19	Q9			
Woodlands Pk., Thorn.	61	R19	Wynd, The, Cumb.	71	PP1			
Woodlands Rd. G3	35	U11	Wyndford Dr. G20	20	T9			
Woodlands Rd., Thorn.	61	R19	Wyndford Pl. G20	20	T9	Zambesi Dr., Blan.	68	FF19
Woodlands Ter. G3	35	U11	*Wyndford Rd.*			Zena Cres. G33	23	Z10
Woodlands Ter., Both.	69	HH18	Wyndford Rd. G20	20	T9	Zena Pl. G33	23	Z10
Woodlea Dr., Giff.	62	T18	Wyndham St. G12	20	T10	Zena St. G33	23	Z10
Woodlinn Av. G44	63	V17	Wynford Ter., Udd.	57	HH16	Zetland Rd. G52	32	N12
Woodneuk Av., Gart.	27	HH9	*Dalry Rd.*					
Woodneuk Rd. G53	60	P17	Wyper Pl. G40	37	Y13			
Woodneuk Rd., Gart.	27	GG9	*Gallowgate*					